Helping English Language Learners Succeed in Pre-K–Elementary Schools

by Jan Lacina, Linda New Levine, and Patience Sowa

Collaborative Partnerships Between ESL and Classroom Teachers

Debra Suarez, Series Editor

TESOL Teachers of English to Speakers of Other Languages, Inc.

Typeset in Chaparral Pro and Avenir
by Capitol Communication Systems, Inc., Crofton, Maryland USA
Printed by United Graphics, Inc., Mattoon, Illinois USA
Indexed by Indexing by the Book, Tucson, Arizona USA

Teachers of English to Speakers of Other Languages, Inc.
700 South Washington Street, Suite 200
Alexandria, Virginia 22314 USA
Tel 703-836-0774 • Fax 703-836-6447 • E-mail tesol@tesol.org • http://www.tesol.org/

Publishing Manager: Carol Edwards
Copy Editor: Tomiko M. Chapman
Additional Reader: Sarah Duffy
Cover Design: Tomiko M. Chapman

ISBN 978-1-931185394
Library of Congress Control No. 2007900077

Contents

Series Editor's Preface

Debra Suarez

Cultural and linguistic diversity in the U.S. student population represents a challenge for all educators. The number of school-aged speakers of a language other than English continues to grow. In the early 1980s one in ten school-aged children was from a non-English-speaking background. By the early 1990s, the number increased to one in seven (Macías, 2000). During the 1993–1994 school year, the total reported number of limited English proficient (LEP) students in U.S. public schools was just over three million. A decade later, during the 2003–2004 school year, there were over five million identified LEP students, representing about 10% of the total public school enrollment and a 65% increase from the 1993–1994 LEP enrollment (NCELA, 2005). The nation's LEP enrollment is principally concentrated in the elementary school grades, and the highest numbers are in kindergarten through third grade (NCBE, 2000). These enrollment patterns in the early grades further ensure that this challenge will continue for the coming years.

The student population increasingly comprises ethnic minorities of color, immigrants, non-Europeans, and speakers of languages other than English. The teaching force, however, continues to be predominantly Caucasian, European-American, middle-class, female, U.S. born, and monolingual English speakers (Banks, 2001; NCATE, 2002; Sleeter, 2001; Taylor & Sobel, 2001). It is most probable that teachers will inevitably teach in classrooms where the cultural and linguistic backgrounds of their students differ from their own (Zeichner, 1993). And it is most probable that classroom teachers, of every subject matter and at each grade level, will teach LEP students.

There is a nationwide call to better provide schools with a teaching force equipped with knowledge, skills, and abilities to effectively teach this diversifying U.S. student population and to foster the academic achievement of all students, including the achievement of English language learners (ELLs).

This series aims to contribute to the field's responses to this nationwide call. This series is designed for both classroom teachers and ESL teachers, for both subject matter specialists and language education specialists—for all educators who are responsible for the academic achievement of students.

Traditionally, teacher preparation for ELLs has taken the approach of talking about *mainstreaming*—conversations directed toward classroom teachers about how they might integrate ESL students into the mainstream classroom. The mainstreaming conversations have also involved talking to ESL teachers about how they might prepare ELLs for the mainstream classroom. However effective these mainstreaming approaches have been, there is a gap in the professional development literature. There is a paucity of information or literature that offers specific, detailed direction about how ESL, subject matter, and grade-level educators can work together, and why they should. This series recognizes that each educator is a specialist in his or her own field and that, in order to promote academic achievement for ELLs, educators must know elements of one another's disciplines and develop techniques for working together, building on the particular strengths, knowledge, abilities, and dispositions that each partner brings to the collaborative effort.

This volume of the Collaborative Partnerships Between ESL and Classroom Teachers Series gives emphasis to collaborative partnerships for elementary school students. Each chapter is directed at ESL, subject matter, and grade-level specialists. The volume is organized around knowledge that is required of all educators, such as knowledge of curriculum, standards, assessment, and community. This volume is further organized around knowledge that is required of all educators if they are to be effective in teaching ELLs, such as knowledge of language, culture, and advocacy. Each chapter discusses pedagogical dilemmas and challenges from the perspective of teachers and administrators. After a focused literature review, each chapter offers examples of classroom-based and school-based collaborative partnerships from elementary schools in three U.S. states: Florida, Missouri, and Texas. Each chapter concludes with a case study that readers may analyze and apply to their own settings. By so doing, this volume builds a knowledge base for teachers and educators. By describing real-life examples of effective collaboration for school success, this volume underscores the value, and the reality, of creating a school that is a learning community in which expertise and knowledge are shared. In this volume, Jan Lacina, Linda New Levine, and Patience Sowa offer new ways of thinking about collaborative dialogue and its role in transforming pedagogy and redefining notions of school success.

Dedication

How we teach is ultimately a reflection of why we teach.
—Elliot Eisner, 2006

To all the teachers who helped us with this project—
Thank you.

Acknowledgments

The vignettes and examples of collaboration collected herein reflect research we conducted over a 2-year period in three U.S. states and several school districts. During that time, we interviewed many teachers and observed their lessons. The vignettes in this volume reflect the whole of that experience. At times, the vignettes are described as intact lessons that we observed. At other times, they reflect a variety of educational techniques observed and discussed with teachers within a school; on these occasions, we collapsed those practices into one vignette for brevity and to illustrate exemplary techniques more fully.

The names of teachers and some of the schools in this book are pseudonyms. However, we must acknowledge the exemplary teachers and other school personnel we met throughout the course of this research. Without their generous offerings of time and talent, this book would not have been possible.

INDIAN RIVER SCHOOL DISTRICT
Vero Beach, Florida

Fellsmere Elementary School
Jose Bianco; Migrant Parent Specialist
Kyle Creedon; Migrant Student Advocate
Catherine Crinegan; Teacher, Grade 4
Dominick Ferello; Principal
Amy Jacobs; Bilingual Tutor
Jennifer Lanam; ESL Specialist
Laurie Langer; Teacher, Grade 4
Paige Newsinski; Teacher, Special Education
Teri Pennington; Title I Writing Strategies Specialist
Carolyn Sanders; Science Coordinator and Grade 5 Teacher
Laurie Young; Team Leader, Grade 4

LUFKIN INDEPENDENT SCHOOL DISTRICT

Lufkin, Texas

Silvia Eubanks; Bilingual/ESL Coordinator
Donna Hart; Teacher, Slack Elementary
Suzanne Miller; Teacher, Slack Elementary
Laura Morado; Teacher, Slack Elementary
Daniel Spikes; Teacher, Lufkin Middle School

NACOGDOCHES INDEPENDENT SCHOOL DISTRICT

Nacogdoches, Texas

Dan Stanley; Bilingual/ESL Coordinator
Tara Newman; Teacher, Brooks Quinn Kindergarten and Raguet Elementary, Grade 4

FORT WORTH INDEPENDENT SCHOOL DISTRICT

Fort Worth, Texas

Charlita Smith; Teacher, Diamond Hill Elementary
Lynnette Mayo; Teacher, Rosemont, Grade 6

KANSAS CITY SCHOOL DISTRICT

Kansas City, Missouri

Alicia Miguel; Bilingual/ESL Coordinator

Gladstone Elementary School

Anne David; Principal
Julie Lykens; ESL Pull-out Teacher
Sharon Brown; ESL Pull-out Teacher
"The Red Family": Lucy Landes, Kindergarten Teacher; Peggy Todd, Grade 1 Teacher;
Amy Brock, Grade 2 Teacher; Glenda Cummins, Grade 3 Teacher; Barbara Sader,
Grade 4 Teacher; Tricia Taylor-Mulbaney, Grade 5 Teacher; Julie Lykens, ESL
Pull-out Teacher; Marcia Mack, Counselor and Grade 3 Teacher; Debbie Walker,
Science Teacher

East Elementary School

Wendy McNitt; Principal
Amy Teeple; Kindergarten and Sheltered ESL Teacher, Grade-Level Chair
Bethany Zaiser; ESL Pull-out Teacher

McCoy Elementary School

Jo Lynn Nemeth; ESL Pull-out Teacher
Anne Sewell; ESL Pull-out Teacher
Sherry Fetzer; ESL Pull-out Teacher

I would like to thank my family for helping me care for my twin daughters so I could write. Thank you also to, Caroline and Grace, my precious daughters who were born during the development of this project.

Jan Lacina

Thank you to my husband, Mike, for your helpful support and great patience.

Linda New Levine

I would like to thank my mother, Mercy, and late father, Theo, for instilling in me a love of education. I am grateful also to my family in the United States and United Kingdom for their patience, unconditional love, and support. Finally, I would like to thank the members of my writing group, who helped me enormously with this project.

Patience Sowa

CHAPTER 1

Introduction

How can collaboration among teachers and other school staff affect teaching and learning for English language learners? This book aims to describe the experiences of exemplary ESL and classroom teachers who regularly collaborate for the educational achievement of English language learners (ELLs).

Our research led us into classrooms, staff lounges, cafeterias, hallways, and parking lots where we observed the discussions and partnerships of many dedicated teachers. The teachers we chronicle in this book are stretching the mold of what it means to be a classroom teacher in a U.S. public school. They open their classroom doors, ask for help from their colleagues, observe one another in classrooms, team teach, and turn teach in an effort to improve professionally and to increase the academic achievement of the diverse learners in their classrooms.

In three states, Texas, Missouri, and Florida, we found teachers who engaged in critical assessment of practice within a forum of trust, collaboration, and experimentation. These conditions did not arise overnight. Indeed, many teachers worked in lonely isolation for years before they began to collaborate with others. For some, the collaborations arose because of outside pressures from administration or state and federal testing requirements. For others, collaboration began as a grade-level friendship that led to a wider arena of trust for coteaching and coplanning.

The types of programs we observed were also diverse. We observed early-exit bilingual programs, dual-language programs, sheltered ESL, transitional ESL programs, and English-only classrooms. Additionally, the school districts we spent time in were located in urban as well as rural communities. We found that teachers collaborate in both settings, and through such collaboration they find ways to meet the needs of individual students.

In this book, we attempt to show the many different factors that lead to collaborative partnerships as well as to identify the characteristics of effective collaborations. Through the use of vignettes and discussions, we record excellent instructional practices for a variety of content disciplines: writing, math, social studies, literacy, and science.

We examine collaboration using a sociocultural framework. We believe that "social relationships and political realities are at the heart of teaching and learning" (Nieto, 2001, p. 5). Indeed, in order to flourish, collaboration requires a school culture of rich social and personal relationships. Social skill development often occurs hand-in-hand with other forms of professional development. In addition, we advocate a learner-centered educational process in which children actively construct meaning, question, and dialogue with teachers.

Our methodology included teacher interviews and classroom observations. The teachers we interviewed were nominated by their school districts' ESL/bilingual coordinators, principals, and peers in their schools. They are exemplary professionals who encourage critical thinking, promote active learning, focus on collaborative decision making, and connect their teaching to their students' life experiences or cultures.

Each chapter treats a separate topic: curriculum, standards, language, culture, assessment, community, and advocacy. Chapters consist of three parts. The first part presents prereading questions and a narrative or vignette. Through observations of team planning meetings, individual planning sessions, and classroom lessons, we created vignettes illustrative of the professional practices that arose from the collaborative teams in Texas, Florida, and Missouri. The second part of each chapter links theory to practice by expanding upon the theoretical background of the chapter topic. We examine research pertaining to the topic, collaboration, a content area, and English language learning. Each chapter closes with an authentic case study illustrating problematic and challenging situations that occur when teachers collaborate. The case studies require in-depth reflection and discussion and will help graduate and undergraduate students in teacher education classes develop their own approaches to solving the problems inherent in the case study. A set of guiding questions following each case study highlights areas for analysis. Each chapter also includes a rich resource list with print and/or electronic sources.

Helping English Language Learners Succeed in Pre-K–Elementary Schools provides a snapshot of professional collaborative practice. As such, it illustrates the diversity of school structure and the variety of ways in which teachers work to raise student academic achievement. We hope that this snapshot is a preview of many more collaborative partnerships in the future.

CHAPTER 2

Curriculum

---◄ CASE STUDY ►---

Collaborating for Science Learning

Shelly is a fifth grade teacher with 10 years' experience in a migrant elementary school in Florida. She has a special interest in science education and is the science coordinator for her school. Patty is a special education teacher assigned to work with Shelly to promote achievement gains for the special education students in the class. Shelly's class has 19 students but only 3 of them are monolingual in English. The others have varying degrees of bilingual ability in English and Mexican Spanish. Neither Shelly nor Patty has taken course work in teaching linguistically diverse students nor do they speak Spanish, but they are working toward their English speakers of other languages (ESOL) credentials through self-study in an attempt to pass the district test qualifying them to teach ESOL students.

Shelly and Patty confer daily on ways to instruct the students in the class so that all can achieve at a high level. Both teachers have a special interest in science because they know that hands-on lessons work with ESOL as well as special education students. Currently, they are planning a unit on the differentiation of plant and animal cells. Patty asks Shelly about the focus of the unit: "What do the students really need to learn from this unit?" After prioritizing the most important objectives, they set to work deciding on how to assess student learning. "I can create a unit test," says Shelly, "but how will we assess Alon and Victor? They don't have enough English to read the test." Eventually, Shelley and Patty decide to assess the non-English-speaking students by using enlarged pictures of cells. In addition, they decide to create multiple assessments for all the students, including Venn diagrams, science journal entries, a lab experience, and a unit test.

- What is a curriculum?

- What are the components of a curriculum?

- How is a curriculum organized?

- What is an effective curriculum for English language learners?

- What are effective instructional strategies for classrooms of linguistically diverse learners?

- How do teachers collaborate for the improvement of a curriculum?

What Is a Curriculum?

Student achievement is highly correlated to the student's opportunity to learn from a "guaranteed and viable curriculum" (Marzano, 2003, p. 22). Common sense dictates that a student will not be able to learn that which has not been taught, and yet, for many students, the curriculum determined by a school district may not actually be implemented in a teacher's classroom or may not be learned by all students in that classroom. For this reason, Marzano distinguishes between the intended, implemented, and attained curricula. The *intended curriculum* is that which is specified in district or state curriculum guides. It may be altered by instructional choices made by classroom teachers. If a teacher ascertains that students lack the background knowledge or the language skills to learn the intended curriculum, then choices are made to amend the content that is taught to students. Thus, the *implemented curriculum* becomes the content actually taught by a teacher, and the *attained curriculum* is the content that is actually learned by students. English language learners in particular face discrepancies between the implemented and the attained curriculum. Although these students are physically present in the classroom while instruction is delivered, they may not have sufficient comprehension of English to be able to learn the material presented. Even for those learners who have attained an elementary level of oral English, the academic vocabulary and grammatical structures of the instructional input may leave them unable to learn the content.

The curriculum, therefore, is much more than the textbook or the district-prepared guide. The attained curriculum rests squarely on the shoulders of teacher choice and begins at the level at which the students are ready to learn. Teachers must be diagnosticians to determine the amount of prior knowledge acquired by students, their learning styles, their language abilities, and their preferred modes of learning. Teachers must also be designers. Wiggins and McTighe (1998) describe the teacher's task as one of designing a combination of curriculum and learning experiences necessary to reach a desired goal. They recommend *backward design*, whereby teachers have a desired curricular goal in mind and then design backward to determine the appropriate learning experiences necessary to reach that goal.

What Are the Components of a Curriculum?

We have discussed a view of teachers as diagnosticians, designers, and creators of the attained curriculum. This viewpoint implies that teachers constantly evaluate their students and the content to be taught, and make choices that enable the learning process to occur for all students. Teacher choice revolves around the major components of curriculum: the content, the process, the products, the learning environment and learning affect surrounding instruction (Tomlinson, 1999).

CONTENT

The content of a curriculum is the accumulation of the knowledge and skills, facts, principles, and concepts that students are expected to learn at a particular grade level. The content of the curriculum answers this question: What is it that students should know or be able to do? Content is often spelled out for teachers in textbooks or curriculum guides, and all teachers are expected to teach the content required at each grade level. Unfortunately, as we have indicated, the content intended for instruction is not always the content attained by students.

Content learning is problematic for students learning a language because content knowledge itself is demanding in the diversity of the core structures that comprise various subjects (August & Hakuta, 1998). Math, science, social studies, and the arts differ from one another in their patterns of reasoning, their systems of notation, and their arrangement of facts. In addition, the terminology required for achievement in the sciences, for example, is different from that required for social studies. Indeed, the grammatical patterns and language structures used for each are unique to the discipline.

Another complexity regarding curriculum content lies in the different kinds of knowledge required for mastery. Content learning requires *procedural knowledge* (skills such as reading, writing, and questioning) and *declarative knowledge* (facts and principles unique to the particular content). Although knowledge in certain skill areas, such as reading, will carry over from the first language to the second, these skills will not be useful to learners until their comprehension and use of the second language increases. The facts and principles composing declarative knowledge also endure from the first to the second language but students must learn the terminology needed to comprehend and discuss specific concepts before they can exhibit their prior knowledge in a classroom.

A third form of knowledge, *metacognition*, refers to a student's awareness of his or her own knowledge: knowing what is known, knowing how well it is known, knowing what needs to be learned, and knowing how to enhance learning through interventions such as note taking, summarizing, self-questioning, and other study skills. Learners who have acquired metacognitive knowledge are better able to utilize the knowledge they have already learned and to more efficiently acquire more content knowledge. Metacognition, therefore, is another important component of the content of the curriculum.

PROCESS

If curricular content dictates what should be taught, the curriculum process shows how it should be taught. The instructional process, designed by the teacher and pursued by the students, is a component of the curriculum not always included in curriculum guides. It includes the activities that enable students to use and develop their skills while understanding and learning essential knowledge. Process does not mean a teacher telling students information; students must actively work with the new concepts in order to understand them and make them their own. Activities are chosen by the teacher based on the students' prior knowledge, learning styles, language levels, and interests. The activities are also chosen because of the nature of the content to be learned. For example, science content lends itself to hands-on exploration, and writing development is enhanced by activities that include brainstorming, peer editing, redrafting, and sharing with an audience.

Language learning students respond to processing activities that

- have a clearly defined instructional purpose, including a focus on language

- identify a critical understanding for students

- cause students to use a critical skill and target language structures while working with new concepts

- ensure that students will understand (not just repeat) an idea

- help students relate the new learning to previous learning

- match each student's level of language and readiness (Tomlinson, 1999, p. 43)

Teachers can sequence instructional activities to enable ELLs to achieve success. Teachers first model the activity with clear instructions, then they publicly share the objectives with students in a comprehensible manner. Students then engage in the activity, using the target language structures with teacher or peer support. During this time, it is helpful to give feedback so that learners are aware of their performance levels. Finally, students reach a level of independence in the learning task, a level that requires limited support for success. As tasks range from including more to less teacher support, they also change from simple to complex.

PRODUCTS

Throughout the instructional process, teachers need to be aware of the products produced during instruction. They should ask themselves this question: How will I know what my students understand and can do with the instructional content? Culminating products are used as assessment instruments to measure the quality and quantity of student learning over an extended period of time. There is a wide range of products available for assessment: tests, science projects, visual displays, research reports, oral presentations, and many others. As curriculum designers, teachers decide on the product of instruction first and then begin to design the instructional activities that will lead to that successful product. For example, if the objective of instruction is to teach students to write a cohesive paragraph with a main idea and three supporting details, the product is the completion of a paragraph by each student. The instructional process required to achieve that goal depends on the students' level, current writing skills, language skills, previous instruction in writing, and the amount of support required to enable them to be successful.

Language learning students can achieve success with product assignments when teachers plan assignments that

- clearly display what students can do as a result of instruction
- provide for one or more modes of expression (e.g., reports, illustrations)
- exhibit clear, specific expectations for high-quality content (e.g., in a rubric)
- provide support for students as they pursue their work
- provide for variation and differentiation in student work due to readiness levels, interests, language levels, and learning styles (Tomlinson, 1999, p. 44)

LEARNING ENVIRONMENT AND LEARNING AFFECT

Language learning students come from homes in which the culture and language may not match that of the school and are therefore at a disadvantage in the learning process. By creating a culturally responsive learning environment in the classroom, a *positive learning affect*, teachers address fundamental differences in thinking and learning in an attempt to ensure that all students achieve at a high level. Culturally responsive teaching recognizes the importance of planning for children's cultural styles in all aspects of learning (Ladson-Billings, 1994).

Teachers who are *cultural mediators* for their students conduct research on their students' culturally different ways of learning. They speak with educators who are familiar with the students' cultures, interview parents and students about their preferences, and visit the students' communities. They develop various ways for students to succeed in their classrooms by allowing the use of the first language when appropriate, implementing familiar management systems, and encouraging learners to share their cultural knowledge with others.

Culturally responsive teaching employs varied teaching strategies, including both cooperative and independent learning, the use of role play, and the provision of a range of options for assessment. Cultural mediators create classroom environments that are collaborative and provide meaningful, student-centered learning experiences. The curriculum is integrated so that students' strengths in one subject area support new learning in another. Students' personal experiences provide a meaningful link to the development of new skills and knowledge. Resources are not limited to textbooks, but include the community, family members, and information from varying viewpoints.

Educators who are cultural mediators convey high expectations for their students and set specific, rigorous, yet realistic goals for them. By valuing students' differences, and supporting them in their learning, teachers can empower culturally different students to become independent learners.

How Is a Curriculum Organized?

Most state and district curricula are written in the form of a scope and sequence. Instruction is developed through a linear listing of topics developing, ideally, from the simple to the complex in any one content area. But curriculum can be structured in a variety of ways, and teacher choice plays a large role in the organization of a curriculum and its many components. Some of the more prominent organizational methods and their implications for ELLs are discussed next.

SPIRAL CURRICULUM

Dewey (1938) used the image of a spiral to describe how curriculum can be organized based on student inquiry, moving from problem to problem while continuously expanding the realm of student knowledge both in depth and breadth. Learning is prompted by problematic inquiry that results in the development of new questions and new ideas. The teacher grounds instruction in an authentic context and orders activities in ways to allow for a student's ever-developing skills, ever-widening knowledge, and ever-increasing ability to apply knowledge, comprehend issues, analyze, and evaluate. Learning adheres to an organizational structure, developing from the less complex particular instance to the more complex broader principle. What creates the spiral is the notion that learning is the starting point for the questioning and problem solving that leads to the production of new ideas.

The advantages of a spiral curriculum for language learning students include the necessity for teacher analysis of a student's current level of understanding and skill development, the grounding in authentic context, development of concepts and language that shift from simple to complex, and, finally, the ability to reintroduce past learning in new contexts for more in-depth understanding. All of these attributes promote long-term retention of concepts and language.

DESIGN-DOWN APPROACH

Wiggins (1998) advocates for a design-down approach that views curriculum development backwards. Teachers begin curriculum design by identifying the desired results of the teaching and learning experience. These results or outcomes are the overarching understandings to be learned, the essential questions to be answered, or the essential skills to be mastered in the learning unit (Wiggins & McTighe, 1998). Following identification of desired results, Wiggins advocates determining the acceptable evidence showing that students understand the overarching concepts. Evidence can consist of performance tasks, projects, tests, quizzes, work samples, teacher observations, and other assessment methods. The final step in design-down curriculum development is planning the learning experiences to accomplish the desired results. In this step, teachers ask themselves the following questions: What will students need to know or be able to do to achieve the goals of this unit? What teaching and learning experiences will help students achieve and demonstrate understanding of the unit goals?

Language learners benefit when teachers are clearly aware of the kinds of learning they want students to achieve in the classroom. Determining those desired results for both content and language helps to ensure that ELLs are accommodated by specially adapted assessments and learning activities.

CURRICULUM MAPPING

Promoted by H. H. Jacobs (2002), curriculum mapping encourages teachers and school districts to refine their curricula in order to identify gaps in instruction, redundancies, and misalignments between curriculum and assessment. It aims to improve student performance through ongoing review of both curriculum and assessment by a wide range of school district personnel. Mapping begins with essential questions that focus on the overarching principles and outcomes of instruction. These big ideas are then divided into content topics such as word problems, insects, or weather. Next, the skills needed to master the big-idea concepts are identified and the assessments providing evidence of learning are determined. At this point, teachers develop activities for the students to practice their skills and the resources needed to complete the teaching unit. In all areas, educators aim for curriculum consensus both to maintain consistency and to allow for flexibility in each content discipline.

Curriculum mapping also benefits ELLs because of its emphasis on the final learning product and the assessments that determine success. Emphasis on skill development readily leads to accommodations for students at a variety of language levels.

THEMATIC INSTRUCTION

Thematic and interdisciplinary curricula are created by organizing essential knowledge and skills in various areas of study around categories, concepts, points of view, and governing principles. Thematic organization is in contrast to a linear scope and sequence that isolates the content areas. The underlying principle of a thematic curriculum is the brain's search for meaningful patterns. These hierarchical patterns create the context for new information that otherwise would be meaningless (Jensen, 1998). In addition to providing meaningful context, patterns enable new learning to be *chunked* with prior knowledge, a more efficient method of retaining information than merely memorizing isolated pieces of information (Tomlinson, 1999). Thematic instruction aims to increase skills and knowledge through the exploration of core concepts, such as interdependency. Teachers create activities that help students approach the topic from a variety of content areas and through an array of learning experiences that range from the concrete to the abstract. Content elements (e.g., concepts, principles, facts, skills) are organized through a unifying structure. Examples of organizing structures might include Bloom's (1956) hierarchy of thinking skills and Mohan's (1986) knowledge framework.

Theme-based instruction is particularly relevant for teachers of language learning students as a beneficial way of organizing academic language and concepts into a unifying and efficient structure for long-term retention of content material. Theme-based instruction promotes collaboration among ESL and content teachers as they plan for the integration of topics and concepts under a broad but relevant theme. This approach encourages teachers to focus first on the essential elements that students need to learn in each of the subject areas. It promotes a progression of teaching activities from the concrete to the abstract that are scaffolded with context such as visuals and realia and that relate as much as possible to students' prior experiences and cultures.

SUMMARY

No matter how teachers decide to organize their curriculum, certain elements are necessary to achieve the best learning experiences for ELLs. Current outstanding curricula incorporate the following features:

- Curriculum design begins with the content of assessment.
- Goals are clearly articulated.
- Simple ideas and skills precede complex ones.
- Topics are either coordinated or integrated across disciplines.
- Learning is rigorous and requires a high level of cognitive engagement from all students.
- Topics and language are spiraled, revisited year after year in increasingly complex ways.
- Students relate personally and culturally to the topics studied.

What is An Effective Curriculum for English Language Learners?

The same curriculum is not effective for all learners. Students with special needs, language learning students, and gifted students have certain requirements for learning that can be addressed in the types of curricula that are used for their instruction. In particular, language learners need a curriculum that includes the following five attributes (August & Pease-Alvarez, 1996):

1. Alignment with standards
2. Rigorousness
3. Accessibility
4. Diverse content
5. Relevance

ALIGNMENT WITH STANDARDS

An effective curriculum is standards based. For ELLs, these should include the *ESL Standards for Pre-K–12 Students* (TESOL, 1997) as well as state and district content standards that are aligned to national content standards. An effective curriculum is sequenced with detailed goals and objectives that clearly indicate grade-level expectations. Language learning students should be challenged to work on grade-level concepts and skills. Instruction is most effective when organized thematically so as to promote more efficient instruction and provide multiple opportunities for developing the academic vocabulary and language structures required of the discipline. Because the topic of standards alignment is so important, we devote the next chapter to it.

RIGOROUSNESS

An effective curriculum provides students with rich academic programming that goes beyond instruction in basic skills. ELLs need to be engaged and challenged by rigorous instructional content that enables them to strengthen thinking skills, develop learning strategies, and participate in problem solving. Although we suggest that the instructional content be the same as that taught to language majority students, it must be adapted to suit the language levels and prior learning of the language learning students.

A rigorous curriculum is not necessarily one that is highly abstract—understanding can be better developed through in-depth investigations, problem solving, experimentation, and other highly contextualized activities. These adaptations lead learners to assimilate new learning into their existing knowledge structures and also to what Piaget (1971) calls *accommodation*—the modification of existing learning structures to ensure change and extend understanding. This kind of learning only results from complex and multiple interactions with new knowledge over time.

Rigorous curricula for language learners stress the importance of three types of knowledge: declarative, procedural, and metacognitive. *Declarative* knowledge, consisting of facts and propositions, and *procedural* knowledge, consisting of the skills required for learning facts and propositions, usually receive a good deal of attention from curriculum writers. But *metacognitive* knowledge is equally important for language learners; these students need to learn how to learn. Metacognition includes the skills required for assessing current knowledge and understanding and using affective and cognitive skills to acquire new learning.

ACCESSIBILITY

An effective curriculum is accessible to all learners. Students have the opportunity of access to high-quality content, materials, learning experiences, and teachers. Equality of educational opportunity, although desired for all learners, is often not available for ELLs (Reeves, 2005). Treating all students equally does not result in an accessible curriculum because English language learning students need accommodations to be able to comprehend and interact with complex content. However, differentiation of instruction "has a history of failing to achieve parity for linguistically and culturally diverse students" (Reeves, 2005, p. 46). A deficit view of learners may be one reason for this failure, as schools and teachers attempt to reshape learners whose languages and cultures do not match those of the more esteemed, dominant culture. Equal access to educational opportunity results from a shared community view of acceptance of diversity and learning opportunities for linguistically different students that are authentic and participatory. We discuss such experiences more fully later in this chapter.

DIVERSE CONTENT

An effective curriculum is diverse, accommodating various abilities, intelligences, knowledge, skills, cultures, languages, and learning styles. The most effective curricula are broad enough to apply to a wide range of languages, language proficiencies, knowledge, and skill levels. Specifically, variety in three areas produces achievement results: variety in knowledge arenas, level of difficulty, and approaches to teaching (August & Pease-Alvarez, 1996, p. 21).

RELEVANCE

An effective curriculum adapts to the students' cultures and interests. It is inclusive of their languages and based upon their prior experiences and knowledge bases. Teachers alter a curriculum to be more effective by creating instructional experiences that utilize parents' knowledge and languages, diverse household practices, and relevant cultural resources. When these personal and relevant sources are incorporated into the school's curricular and extracurricular activities, schools become more effective learning centers for linguistically diverse learners.

What Are Effective Instructional Strategies for Classrooms of Linguistically Diverse Learners?

Teachers who have access to curricula that are standards-based, rigorous, accessible, diverse, and relevant are ready to structure educational experiences that will provide academic success for all learners. Many choices of instructional strategies are available, and knowledgeable and skillful teachers are able to choose among these practices to match appropriate teaching experiences to a wide range of learners. Strategies that are particularly appropriate for linguistically diverse learners are discussed next.

1. Identify the specific focus of the instruction.

What is it that all students will know or be able to do at the end of the lesson? Objectives for language learning students include those related to declarative knowledge, procedural skills, metacognitive knowledge, and language learning skills and knowledge. Lesson objectives in all four areas maximize learning possibilities—not only for learning content but also for learning how to learn processes and the language needed to understand and express understanding.

For an early primary science lesson on the phases of the moon, for example, teachers would need to determine declarative and procedural content objectives such as the following:

- Students will understand that the moon has four phases.
- Students will illustrate the four phases of the moon.

The following is a language objective that relates to the application of those objectives:

- Students will use chronological signal words to report on the phases of the moon.

The following is a metacognitive skill objective that could be taught within this lesson context:

- Students will use a series of drawings to support their recall of the phases of the moon.

Of the many objectives possible for instruction, effective teachers determine which skills and processes must be mastered and which are not required for mastery. This distinction helps prioritize learning into a range of skills and knowledge—all of which are available to all learners but not required for successful learning of the basic concepts of the content area.

Specific objectives are more successful than general or vague ones. For example, students are not asked to *discuss*, when what is required is that they *report the results* of an experiment; students are not asked to *review* past learning when the teacher actually expects them to *restate the three causes* of an event.

Effective teachers communicate the day's objectives to learners in a public way that is understandable to all. Some teachers post objectives on the chalkboard as an easy referent that they can return to at the end of the lesson when conducting a final assessment. By alerting students to the lesson's specific objectives, teachers provide goals for themselves and the students, thereby increasing the chances of academic success.

2. Vary instruction to connect to students' cultures and learning styles.

Effective teachers connect instruction to students' lives by contextualizing the curriculum within the experiences of home and the community. Teachers talk to students, parents, and community members to learn about the local community and its diversity and then design learning activities in a meaningful way—a way that helps students make connections between new learning and their past experiences.

Some suggestions for connecting the novel to the familiar include planning community-based learning projects with students; including parent participation in classroom activities; incorporating student preference into instructional choice, such as competitive and cooperative activities; and varying styles of conversation to include those that appeal to a student's cultural norms—conarration (overlapping or simultaneous speech), call-and-response, and choral reading, among others (Dalton, 1998).

Within the structure of a well-organized classroom, it is helpful to use a wide range of strategies, materials, and instructional tools to provide variety and to match the age, achievement levels, interests, and learning styles of the students. Effective teachers match instruction to the students' needs by developing skill in delivering instruction in differing modalities, at various learning levels, and with a diverse group of instructional tools.

Teachers who are visual learners tend to teach through the visual modality. Teachers who are analytical learners favor independent, paper-and-pencil tasks. Extroverted, musical teachers turn lessons into songs. While using their strengths to enhance instruction, effective teachers keep in mind that children have varying modalities for learning.

A powerful teaching technique for connecting to students' lives and cultures is activation of prior knowledge. Before introducing a new topic of study, effective teachers attempt to prepare students for new learning by using activities that encourage students to attend to and recall what they already know about the topic. Cognitive psychologists agree; meaningful learning can only occur when "new information is linked with existing concepts, and integrated into what the learner already understands" (Edmondson & Novak, 1993, p. 548).

What the learner already understands about a topic is somewhat culturally based. Indeed, language conveys misconceptions that carry over into the ability to learn new information. In English, people talk about the sun coming up in the morning although the sun does not *come up* at all. Certain cultures teach that the moon has four distinct phases because mice nibble away at it nightly. Referring to oil as heavy leads one to believe that it should sink to the bottom of the rain puddle—not float on top of it. Prior cultural experiences and beliefs permeate classroom learning. By uncovering these metaphors that can become obstacles, teachers can help students to make better connections to new learning.

The outcomes resulting from activating prior knowledge provide the teacher with a wealth of information:

- Teachers gather data to use in adapting the lesson to student knowledge or interest.
- Teachers reveal student misconceptions.
- Relevant factual and conceptual knowledge arises from students' daily experiences and prior study.

And the benefits to language learners are many:

- Students become cognitively engaged and focused.
- Students feel empowered and more confident.
- Students begin to acquire the language of the topic content. (V. A. Jacobs, 2002)

Activities used to activate prior knowledge include the KWL chart (what I know, what I want to know, what I learned), the 5W chart (who, what, when, where, why), paired verbal interviews, and picture previewing of both fiction and nonfiction texts.

3. Challenge students cognitively.

Engage students in complex tasks that require them to address content in new ways. Rigorous standards can provide these challenges for students; however, instructional strategies that increase student understanding to more advanced levels are also necessary. It would be a mistake to require a high level of English knowledge before involving math students in problem solving. Basic skill-and-drill math lessons do not advance student understanding to a higher level of complexity either. But teacher support and meaningful context promote the understanding needed to solve complex problems.

Learning requires multiple exposures to and complex interactions with knowledge. The multiple exposures are most effective when a variety of input modalities are used.

For example, teachers can provide students with direct learning experiences that involve a real or simulated physical activity as well as indirect experiences that do not require students to be physically involved but are dependent upon demonstrations, films, readings, and observations (Marzano, 2003). Effective teachers create activities that move students to develop wider and greater understanding of the topic. Some of the strategies that are successful in supporting growing cognitive complexity include the following:

- activating prior knowledge
- generating and testing hypotheses
- relating instruction to real-life experiences
- advance organizers
- note taking
- nonlinguistic representations such as pictures and graphic organizers
- minimal cue questioning
- summarizing
- homework for practice, review, and application
- providing clear and direct feedback on student performance (Marzano, Pickering, & Pollock, 2001)

4. Emphasize language, reading, and writing across the curriculum.

Academic literacy instruction presupposes that teachers of linguistically diverse students assist language development while teaching content-area topics. Purposeful conversation engages students in the academic discourse required for the reading and writing of academic texts. Effective teachers connect student language with content knowledge through carefully designed listening, speaking, reading, and writing activities. Student language thus progressively advances to include academic language structures and vocabulary.

Teacher supports for academic language development include the use of modeling, eliciting, clarifying, probing, restating, questioning, wait time, eye contact, and praising in specific ways. Teachers can encourage students to use academic vocabulary while expressing their understanding during frequent opportunities to interact with classroom peers and teachers. Activities can be structured in such a way as to require students to use the academic language of the content lesson. These interactional interludes allow students to practice academic language usage in preparation for reading and writing activities. When possible, teachers should group students in order to clarify misconceptions and support understanding through the use of the native language.

5. Promote collaborative, interactive learning.

Collaborative learning encourages experts and novices to work together toward a common goal or product. Working and conversing together, students increase their academic achievement, motivation, self-esteem, and empathic development (August

& Hakuta, 1997). When teachers join students in a *joint productive activity* (JPA), they have opportunities to support student collaboration in positive ways (Dalton, 1998) as well as model the language required in the academic discipline. This type of teacher support helps students expand their *zone of proximal development* (Vygotsky, 1978), the learning arena wherein student skill is insufficient for individual performance but teacher support can lead students to success.

Effective teachers design instructional activities requiring some form of collaborative activity and arrange classroom furniture to promote communication and group work. Groupings can be structured in a variety of ways depending on the purpose of the activity. Occasionally students can be grouped by friendship or common native language; these groupings are desirable when the use of the native language can promote understanding of complex material. At other times, students can be grouped according to mixed academic ability or mixed interests to encourage more interaction in the target language. Buddy groups are helpful for providing students with a few minutes of processing time during a lesson.

Excellent classroom management skills are needed in classrooms where JPA is the norm. Students move from one activity to the next forming groups, working in pairs, and then working individually. Efficient movement eliminates downtime that detracts from instructional time.

6. Provide instructional clarity.

Students value the teacher who can explain things clearly so that they can understand. Clarity is a skill that all teachers can refine, but it is most essential when teaching young ELLs. Clarity involves presenting information and skills clearly and sequentially while providing context in the form of explanatory devices (e.g., charts, graphs, graphic organizers, pictures, demos) and simple or expanded language.

Effective teachers increase the clarity of their instruction when they use the blackboard to write new vocabulary, point to it as they talk about it, draw pictures that represent simple concepts, create graphs to show change and charts to display information, use synonyms and antonyms to clarify vocabulary, utilize their bodies and faces to express emotions, and simplify their language to eliminate hesitations and idioms.

7. Check student comprehension frequently.

Effective teachers know if students are understanding the content during instruction because they consistently check on student comprehension. With language learning children, it is not sufficient to check at the end of the lesson. That may be too late. These children do not often raise their hands to ask the teacher questions and, when asked if they understand, usually respond in the affirmative. To be sure that all children comprehend, effective teachers use a variety of techniques to determine the level of comprehension, including asking questions on the same topic to all students throughout the lesson, using wait time, asking for signal responses, and encouraging meaningful peer interactions, all of which require students to ask and answer questions and to clarify information. These activities take only a few minutes of class time, but they pay off in the long run with increased comprehension on the part of all students.

8. Provide feedback to students and reinforce effort.

Following the check for comprehension, effective teachers provide prompt, detailed, and personal feedback to students on how they are mastering the new skill or comprehending the new knowledge. Students need to know what they are doing well and what they need to improve. Teacher feedback can also be used to clarify misunderstandings that emerge during the lesson. It is important that feedback be timely, on-the-spot information that can be used during, not after, the learning experience.

For the most part, feedback relating to content is more critical than feedback relating to mispronunciations or grammatical errors. Language errors that do not impede comprehension can be resolved by teacher modeling of the correct structure or through instruction and practice at a later date.

Rubrics are an excellent method of improving student performance through specific feedback. The most effective rubrics describe student performance levels specifically. They provide a mirror allowing students to assess their learning by comparing themselves to the rubric. Self-assessment activities can also be developed to suit the learning. For example, teachers can ask students to monitor their comprehension while listening or reading and to rate their comprehension levels on a scale. Teachers can also use journals to encourage students to self-assess their understanding of the new concepts and ask questions of the teacher; a teacher's response in a communication journal is an excellent source of feedback.

Finally, effective teachers give feedback to students by recognizing the effort students expend and explicitly connecting their efforts and their achievements. Not all students believe that their efforts lead to academic success. Many think that bad luck, task difficulty, or lack of innate ability cause their failure (Weiner, 1974). This belief system is a self-fulfilling prophecy. If a student is not successful, the student has very little opportunity to improve when that student believes that he or she is untalented or unlucky. However, there is evidence that teacher input can affect change in students by demonstrating that added effort pays off in achievement gains (Craske, 1985). When students do poorly, effective teachers react in a highly energetic way, explaining to students what is wrong with the poor work and how to make it better. When students are successful, these teachers praise them and attribute their success to the result of the effort the students expended. Another technique for promoting effort is to use a rubric for student self-assessment. The mirror of the rubric allows students to effectively assess the amount of effort they have expended on their learning.

9. Present content concepts to illustrate critical similarities.

Elementary math teachers follow this precept when they teach multiplication by showing its similarity to addition. Social studies teachers compare events in history to show that wars have similar causes. Science teachers show the similarities among animal species or requirements of various ecosystems. All of these examples focus on the critical "overarching principles or concepts" (Marzano, 2003, p. 118) that underlie each of the content areas. They highlight the *sameness* that exists in the new information and promote more effective transfer of prior knowledge to the new learning situation.

Language learners benefit from instruction that is presented in a manner that promotes efficiency of learning. Explicit demonstration of critical features also highlights the similar language that is used to explain the sameness existing among a group of concepts. Attention to similar language and similar content links these categories in the learner's mind and results in a higher probability of academic achievement.

10. Manage classroom organization and routines efficiently.

Classroom management is most effective when outside observers are least aware that it is occurring. New teachers often struggle to maintain behavior standards for their students and even long-time teachers are challenged occasionally when confronted with a group of students different from ones they have worked with in the past. Classroom management is so important that experienced teachers may tell new members of the staff that they cannot start teaching until they have classroom behavior and organization under control.

Good management is similar to good teaching. Effective teachers clearly specify their behavior expectations; teach the expected behaviors; provide immediate feedback; and use techniques to prevent, redirect, or stop inappropriate behavior. These are four separate arenas of teaching, and each requires different techniques and activities. Specifying behavior expectations requires clarity and an unambiguous description of performance levels. Teaching the expected behaviors requires specificity of instruction, clarity, modeling and demonstration, and practice. Providing immediate feedback reinforces appropriate behavior and requires specific communication about where performance falls short. Techniques to prevent or redirect inappropriate behavior include wait time, proximity, *I* messages, pre-alerts, and eye contact.

Teachers of language learners are aware that different cultures have varying behavioral standards. The free-flowing nature of some U.S. classrooms may lead more disciplined students to believe that there are no rules. Teaching techniques such as saying "One two three, eyes on me" may result in a cultural clash with students who believe that direct eye contact with a teacher is disrespectful. Varying cultural norms can result in a mismatch between teacher expectation and student behavior. Knowing one's students and their cultures well can prevent these mismatches.

One of the major goals of classroom management is to promote time on task—keeping all students involved in a learning task throughout the lesson. Teachers know how challenging this can be, but when it occurs, students are on the road to achievement. Maximizing time on task requires that teachers know their students well, have excellent behavior management in place, deliver challenging yet engaging lessons, and assure that all students can be successful in the learning experience. Teachers who are said to have eyes in the back of their head have developed skill in keeping all students focused on instruction.

How Do Teachers Collaborate for the Improvement of Curriculum?

Shelly and Patty teach together twice a week during the 45-minute science block. Today, they are in the middle of a unit on microbes and cells. During planning sessions that take place almost daily after school, they have isolated the objectives for the day's lesson on cell cookies:

- **Content objective:** Students will describe the components and their functions for both plant and animal cells.
- **Thinking/study skill objective:** Students will match the components with the functions on a chart.
- **Language objective:** Students will use the target vocabulary to describe the differences between plant and animal cells and to describe the functions of parts of the cell.

These objectives are based on the state objectives and expectations for fifth-grade science:

- **Sunshine State standard:** Standard 1 Processes of Life SC.F.1.2. The student describes patterns of structure and function in living things.
- **Expectations:** Students will know the parts of plant and animal cells

In addition to the district scope and sequence and the state standards and expectations, Shelly and Patty have access to the Houghton Mifflin Science program *Discovery Works* (2000). This resource has excellent full-color pictures of plant and animal cells with annotated vocabulary.

The students' science books are full of sticky note tabs. Shelly and Patty have been teaching the use of sticky notes as a study skill. They use them to teach the children how to isolate the most important information in their texts. Dayelle has written the following on the tabs in her book:

- A plant cell is the only one with a cell wall.
- All cells have things in common.
- Cells are basic units of structure and function of all living things.

But Shelly and Patty often use other resources to augment the basic text. They try to find science activities that their students will relate to, personally and culturally. They have done a search on their topic in the Beacon lesson plan library (Beacon Learning Center, n.d.), an online educational resource funded through the Technology Innovation Challenge Grant from the U.S. Department of Education. There they found several lessons related to cellular structure and chose the one called Cell Cookies as the most appropriate for their students.

Shelly starts the lesson by reminding the students of the learning they have already accomplished in this unit: "You wrote the differences between plant cells and animal cells in your science notebooks. Who can remind me by telling me something you wrote?" The students refer to their notebooks and also to the Venn diagram hanging in the classroom, with the critical vocabulary structure words clearly written on it.

Next, Shelly surveys the five groups of students and assigns translator roles for the two non-English speakers in the class: "Maggie, will you translate for Alon? Dayelle, will you translate for Victor? Today you'll be working in cooperative groups to learn about the differences in plant and animal cells. You'll be using cookies and different kinds of candy to make your cells. Remember, the plant cell is rectangular, so you'll have to change the shape of your cookie. The animal cell is *ovoid*, almost the same shape as the cookie." Patty draws appropriate shapes on the blackboard for the two different types of cells while Shelly itemizes the learning objectives for the students.

"Your job is to find out the function of the parts of the cell. What is the job of each part? We talked about the nucleus—what is it? That's right; it's like the brain of the cell. That is its function, its job."

All of the students have been assigned to create either a plant or animal cell. They have been provided with vocabulary cards listing the components of a cell and function cards listing the job of each component.

"Look at the chart on your handout. Let's list the parts of the cell. Write *cytoplasm* in the first column. We're going to use vanilla frosting *[holds up]* to be the cytoplasm of our cell cookies. Write *vanilla frosting* on your chart. Where should you put the vanilla frosting? Yes, you'll put the cytoplasm inside your cell first."

While Shelly shows the students the different types of candy that they will use to create each part of the cell, Patty lists the same information on a similar chart in the front of the class. Those students with limited English skills pay close attention to the chart Patty creates. Shelly continues to probe for review information as she mentions each cell component: "Some of you will not use the green-colored candy. Why? Yes, the green is for the *chloroplasts*. Those are only found in plant cells."

Finally, Patty checks for understanding: "Raise your hand if you are confused." Six or seven hands go up. Patty and Shelly begin to check the work of individual students. Shelly then checks again: "*Mitochondria*. Raise your hand if you have that."

Next, Shelly calls the names of the students who will work in lab groups and asks each group to choose a materials handler to help her distribute the materials. When students begin to talk noisily during this time, Shelly says, "I like the way Maggie is sitting quietly waiting for directions." The noise is immediately hushed.

As the students begin to work, they talk about the project using both English and Spanish. Dayelle's group includes Gustavo, Janet, Arielli, and Victor, a non-English-speaking student. Dayelle confers with Gustavo before translating for Victor.

Gustavo says, "The green one is chloroplasts. It goes close to the nucleus." He checks his science text and then says, "Your nucleus goes in the middle and ours goes on top." Dayelle and Arielli translate the information for Victor. Because the girls have never studied cell structure in Spanish, they don't know the scientific terms in that language. Instead, they use the English terms they are currently learning.

Patty and Shelly circulate around the room while the students work. They observe and listen to the group conversations, occasionally asking questions of each group: "If you have an animal cell, are you going to use chloroplasts? If you have a plant cell will you need *vacuoles*? Who needs mitochondria?"

When the cookies are completed, the students begin to search through their function cards to record the function of each cell component. Shelly reminds them, "It's your responsibility to complete the functions column by yourself."

Patty and Shelly continue to check comprehension: "What is the job of the *cytoplasm*?"

Janet reads from her function card, "The cytoplasm is the clear jelly-like material inside the cell."

When the charts are complete, Patty says, "If you have a plant cell, stand in front of the room with your cell." Eleven students come to the front. "Animal cell people, check their cells. Are they correct?" The students check each other and determine that the plant cells are all correct.

Patty continues, "Animal cell people come on up. Now check these. Some of these look different. Why are they different?"

Selene volunteers, "That one *[pointing]* shouldn't have a . . . *[Selene checks her chart]* a plant vacuole."

"That's right," says Shelly, "this cell shouldn't have a plant vacuole because it's a what? That's right; an animal cell. Animal cells don't have plant vacuoles." Elissa and Justin quickly remove the vacuoles from their cells.

To summarize the lesson, Patty asks the group questions such as "Who can tell me every part of their cell?" Maggie responds, using her chart for help. All of the students and teachers clap. Next Crystal tells the parts of the plant cell and all clap again. Patty says, "Gustavo, tell me one thing you learned today."

Gustavo consults his text and pauses. "Plant and animal cells are different," he says. "The nucleus is different." Other students volunteer to summarize their learning but Alon doesn't raise his hand.

Shelly asks Alon, "What's the green part of your plant cell called?" Alon grins and shrugs while two members of his group frantically translate the question.

Finally Alon responds, "Chloroplast." All of the students clap and Alon grins broadly.

After lunch, Patty won't be in the classroom but Shelly has planned to use the language arts block to teach the students to read a short nonfiction article about cellular composition and to write a summary paragraph of what they learned in the morning lab. Shelly and Patty often integrate science concepts into math instruction, but they have been struggling to relate these more closely to reading and writing instruction as well.

The assessment of the unit will be challenging because the students are diverse. In addition to the non-English-speaking students, some class members are classified as ESE (special education), and several are part of the gifted and talented program. Most of the students in the class are bilingual, but three students speak only English. Shelly and Patty have already decided to use multiple methods of assessment geared to the diverse members of the class.

Shelly and Patty together have created a learning environment that helps all of their diverse learners succeed. Through a successful collaborative effort, each has used her own strengths to add to the strengths of the other.

Shelly is an experienced science teacher. She tends to be a big-picture person who sees the curriculum as a whole rather than in incremental parts. She is capable of envisioning major projects and is energetic in carrying them out. She is in charge of the school's science club and directs the school garden, where students regularly work to grow vegetables. Shelly is very familiar with the science curriculum from kindergarten to fifth grade. She is aware not only of what the students should have learned before fifth grade but also that there may be large gaps in their learning because of their migrant status and because the focus on reading and math in this school does not leave much time for science instruction. Because of this, she is able to determine where problems may occur in learning grade-level science concepts.

Patty has taught for fewer than 5 years and is primarily responsible for the special education students in fifth grade. She is analytical. She approaches planning in a methodical manner, analyzing the material and teaching it step by step. She focuses specifically on lesson objectives, sequencing them from the simple to the more complex. Patty asks "What is it they must really learn?" and helps Shelly identify the essential facts, vocabulary, and skills in every lesson. Patty generally uses visuals for concept development. She has helped Shelly use color coding and matching, especially for vocabulary development. For example, in teaching the unit on matter, Patty used pictures clearly representing each of the three states of matter. She also brought concrete objects such as foam balls, balloons, paper bags, and chocolate candies. The students worked to classify each of these objects on a graphic organizer according to the three states of matter.

The collaboration between Shelly and Patty has resulted in a great deal of professional development for each teacher. During the years of their collaboration, they have developed teaching strategies that are particularly successful with their language learning students. Patty has shown Shelly the importance of *creating predictable classroom environments*. Language learners and special-needs students alike thrive in a classroom of structured routines and predictable behaviors. Cooperative and group learning is used often in their classroom and students are familiar with the routines of group assignments, rotating roles, and shared decision making. They are comfortable with assisting each other, translating for each other, and sharing in the clean-up activities. Patty initiated the practice of creating smooth transitions in the classroom by giving advance warning of new activities, communicating clearly what is expected of each student and each group of students, and preparing materials well in advance so there is no down time during a lesson.

Both Shelly and Patty are aware that the traditional classroom configuration of frontal teaching is not appropriate for their learners. Their goal is to *maximize language usage* by the students during instruction. As a result, they use cooperative groupings frequently and intersperse their lessons with activities that allow for extended responses and sustained dialogue on the part of the learners.

The end of the cell lesson includes one of these opportunities as the students summarizes their learning for the day. The charts, textbook, and cell and function cards provide the scaffolding that the children need to accomplish their summaries. These supports are evidence of the focus on communication, which is primary in this classroom. Throughout the lesson, both teachers initiate multiple conversations with group members, asking questions that require extended responses. Rather than asking for one-word answers, they ask *why* questions, which enable them to assess students' understanding of the main concepts. They ask open-ended questions "Tell me something that . . . ," which require extended-discourse responses. These oral responses are then followed by reading and writing activities that echo the language patterns and vocabulary of the lab activity.

Because Shelly is an advocate for excellent science education at the elementary level, she has led Patty to see the benefit of *involving students as active participants* in classroom learning through group activities, lab experiments, and projects. These are now routine in their classroom. In these situations, all students are involved in creating a project in collaboration with other learners. Shelly initiates discovery learning at every opportunity in her science class as another way of involving students in active learning. For example, during the unit on force and motion, groups of students create ramps for rolling cars. They predict the effects of friction, object mass, and speed on the length of their runs and determine rules of momentum following their observations. Although students work in groups for many of these lab lessons, they are each responsible for their own learning. The assessments at the end of the unit require this responsibility, but Shelly and Patty are careful to build in individual responsibility for each lesson. During the cell lesson, for example, students are responsible for completing the function column on their individual charts without assistance from the group.

Shelly's experience in working with language learning students has led her to develop numerous techniques for *scaffolding content learning*. She and Patty have shared their techniques with each other and developed a variety of formats for scaffolding:

1. They guide students' efforts through extensive modeling. Work products, cooperative roles, and oral responses are modeled by a teacher to the degree that each student requires it. Shelly searches for resources to support students' independent learning efforts. For example, while working on science projects for the science fair, she sought outside sources to assist each project group. Questioning techniques are another way that Shelly and Patty support and guide the students. Open-ended questions are used for extended discourse, but pinpoint questioning is also used as a way of helping students think through their responses and reach a correct conclusion:

   "Jose, which part of your cell directs and controls the cell's activities?"
   "Um, I don't know."
   "What's that?"
   "Um, the nucleus."

"What does the nucleus do for the cell?"

"It's the brain." (consulting his chart)

"That's right. What's the job of the human brain?"

"Tell you what to do?"

"And what's the job of the cell nucleus?"

"The nucleus tells the cell what to do."

2. Shelly and Patty support their students by adapting their speech to the levels of the different learners in the classroom. They have acquired the skill of restating complete sentences as a series of simple sentences, sometimes at a slightly slower pace, and using pauses to stress target vocabulary. They avoid idioms but often use standard phrases of idiomatic language that the class has learned in selective situations:

"Jose, will you use a green chloroplast in your animal cell?"

"Yes." The class gasps and laughs as Jose grins. He's teasing the teacher.

"That's 20 slaps with a wet noodle for you." Everyone laughs.

Most important, Shelly and Patty use academic terms in their classroom language and provide visual support for the meaning of these terms through vocabulary cards, a word wall, and specific descriptions followed by frequent questioning.

3. Patty has helped Shelly think about additional supports to classroom instruction that are necessary for ELLs. Both teachers now routinely bring objects, photos, and other artifacts into the classroom to provide examples of basic concepts. Graphic organizers and graphics, charts, lab report forms, pictures, and sticky notes are used to emphasize important concepts. Textbook learning is taught through the graphics and bold print that emphasize the target vocabulary and key understandings. Students are also given time to discuss their learning in both English and Spanish.

4. Cooperative and group learning form the framework for most learning experiences in this classroom. Patty has learned to use these cooperative structures when dealing with class groupings rather than with her more familiar small-group instructional format. The students are familiar with these structures because all classrooms in the school use cooperative formats to some degree. Not only does cooperative learning relate to the communal structures of the students' culture, it also provides each learner with more support and the opportunity to process new learning in both English and Spanish.

5. Students are permitted to use their first language in the classroom, although neither Shelly nor Patty speaks any Spanish. Students translate for each other during group work through a mixture of Spanish with target English vocabulary. This occurs because most of the students do not know the Spanish words for the academic scientific terms. Spanish is also used for teasing and joking and for including the nonnative-English speakers in the community of learners. All lab reports and learning products are produced in English, so students

use their L1, or first language, for clarifying and processing new information. This understanding is then related in English.

Shelly is determined to *increase the relevancy of science instruction in her students' lives*. She and Patty are aware that their students have not had the same experiences as the monolingual middle-class students in the school. The two teachers speak about the restrictions these students might have in their daily lives. They may have had few opportunities to visit historical, scientific, or artistic sites. Books and newspapers may not be as common in these students' homes. Although the school is located near the beach, many of the students may never have learned how to swim. And yet these children travel yearly between the United States and Mexico, moving back and forth between cultures and languages. The teachers try to build upon these experiences. Shelly's class received a donation to finance a trip to the local electric company as part of their unit on energy and to enable the teachers to take the entire class on a camping trip.

Using the daily lives and experiences of their students, Shelly and Patty connect new science learning to what the children already know about the topics. Shelly's vegetable garden behind the school and her after-school science club are two ways in which children connect to science in their school. And in every lesson taught, the teachers encourage students to talk about their past learning and experience with the topic while using learning structures that are compatible with the way these students learn. Shelly frequently encourages learners to take their science projects home to share with their families and invites families to school to learn about class projects. In this way, learning extends beyond the classroom and science becomes more relevant to students and their families.

Shelly uses an excellent science text, but she is aware that one text will not meet the needs of all students. She must often *adapt the science materials* to the children she teaches. Her class is diverse in both language and educational background. Many of the children have not been in school consistently, and they have gaps in their skills and content knowledge. This is especially apparent in science class.

Shelly is aware, for example, that many of the migrant students in her class have no prior experience with microscopes. Although not a part of this learning unit, she and Patty prepare the students for the magnification work they will do in the unit on cells and microbes by including instruction first on the use of a microscope.

Lab reports are also adapted for language learners so that they can be used as advance organizers for lab experiments. Shelly outlines the steps of the experiment on one side of the lab report, providing space for the outcomes on the other side. When completed, the reports scaffold oral language summaries and provide the needed vocabulary and grammatical structures for written summaries in the science journal.

Further adaptations are made to allow students to get information from the science text. The reading levels of the text are much higher than what most of Shelly's students have achieved, so she first summarizes the major points in the reading material orally. She teaches skimming and scanning techniques to help students search for the most important facts, and she teaches reading skills through SQR3 (Robinson,

1970). This five-step quick study method aims to help students acquire the study skills necessary to learn from a printed text:

1. **Survey:** Before reading, preview the boldfaced headings and subheadings. Briefly scan the introductory and summary paragraphs, and try to identify some of the major ideas in the chapter.

2. **Question:** Ask questions such as the following: What is this chapter about? What questions have I or my teacher raised that this chapter can answer? It is particularly helpful to turn each heading into a question.

3. **Read:** As you read, look for the answer to the question proposed by the heading. This is active reading and requires concentration. Read slowly and carefully for meaning.

4. **Recite:** Write or say key phrases that summarize the major point of the reading section. Try not to copy a phrase from the text but to use your own words to express the idea.

5. **Review:** Repeat steps 2 to 4 as you read through the text. You will have a list of key phrases that create an outline for the major points of the chapter. Try to recall the ideas from each key phrase. Then cover them up and try to remember the key phrases. If you are unable to remember some of them, go back and reread that section of the text.

Shelly and Patty help each other create *multiple formats for assessment*. The plant and animal cell lesson lends itself to color coding the two kinds of cells and labeling the parts. This assessment, with a minimum of reading, adequately tests whether Alon and Victor have learned the major concepts of the lesson.

For the other students, the two teachers will also use a variety of additional assessments. All students write in a science journal and take a matching quiz as well as a unit test. Shelly and Patty also use graphic organizers as assessment instruments, as well as self-assessments and oral questioning. In the lesson on the cell, the cell cookies provide an assessment product that is quickly eaten at the end of the class.

SUMMARY

Shelly and Patty are two different people with different classroom styles. Their training has also been somewhat different in that Patty is an ESE specialist and a recent graduate of a teaching program, and Shelly is an elementary-certified teacher with years of classroom experience and an interest in science education.

The team-teaching, collaborative approach that these teachers have elected to use for science instruction has produced professional development rewards for both of them. Shelly has learned new teaching techniques and an analytical approach to formulating and assessing objectives. Patty has learned a great deal about classroom management, the instruction of language learning students, and the fifth-grade science curriculum.

Although not in a formal partnership, Shelly and Patty have developed a mutual trust that helps them extend themselves into new teaching and learning arenas, increases the excitement of teaching, and provides the impetus for experimentation with increasingly complex classroom practices.

Case Study: The Science Class

Margie Santos is a recent graduate from a 5-year teacher education program. She has a master's degree in elementary education with an ESOL endorsement. Margie has taught for 2 years at Pelican Bay Elementary, a school with a large migrant and bilingual population. This year, her fifth-grade class has four ESOL students, two of whom are recent arrivals and do not speak English. Margie is struggling to find ways to teach these children according to the state standards.

Ellen Ramirez is the ESL specialist at Pelican Bay. This is her first year on the job. She taught third and fourth grades for 10 years at the school before volunteering for this assignment. Ellen is responsible for the administrative tasks related to the ESOL population. She tests each student in the fall to determine if they qualify for bilingual ESOL assistance. She also monitors students' progress by conferring with classroom teachers four times within the first 2 years after the students exit the program. Ellen has seen that students who do not make adequate progress are frequently referred to the ESE committee to be tested for learning disabilities and possible classification as special education students. Ellen feels that her job is mostly administrative and is frustrated by time constraints that keep her from the classrooms where she could effect change in student outcomes.

Margie and Ellen frequently eat lunch together and their conversations tend to revolve around Margie's classroom experiences. This month, she is planning to begin the science unit on energy. Although she taught this unit last year, she is concerned that the concepts will be too difficult for the ESOL students in the class. She shows Ellen the grade-level expectations:

- The student knows how to trace the flow of energy in a system (e.g., electricity in a circuit to produce heat, light, sound, or magnetic fields).

- The student knows that energy can be described as stored energy (potential) or energy of motion (kinetic).

- The student knows that the sun provides energy for the Earth in the form of heat and light.

- The student knows ways that energy can be transformed (e.g., electricity to light, light to heat, mechanical to heat).

- The student knows that moving electric charges produce magnetic forces and moving magnets produce electric currents.

- The student extends and refines use of a variety of tools to measure the gain or loss of energy.

- The student knows that some materials conduct heat better than others.

- The student understands that convection, radiation, and conduction are methods of heat transfer.

Margie tells Ellen, "I'm concerned that the concepts and the vocabulary load are going to be too high for my ESOL students. Javier and Maria can't speak any English, and Ingris and Brian have only been here one year. This unit will be difficult for the rest of the class as well. Most of them are still acquiring academic English. I don't think I can do this without help, but the other fifth-grade teachers don't have ESOL students as language limited as mine are. Their lesson plans won't work for my kids."

Ellen understands the frustrations that Margie is feeling. She feels responsible for offering help because she is the ESL specialist in the school. She also enjoys collaborating with other teachers, something she did routinely when she taught third and fourth grade. Her job description does not include working in the classroom or collaborating with classroom teachers, though. She is unsure how to handle the situation and wonders if she should talk to Betty Bennett, the school principal, to discuss her concerns about her position. Betty is a new principal this year. She used to be the school's reading coordinator. Betty is facing a great deal of pressure from the school district to raise the school from its current grade of D back to the previous grade of C. Ellen is unsure of Betty's position on teacher collaboration.

QUESTIONS FOR DISCUSSION

Actors

1. How would you characterize Margie Santos, Ellen Ramirez, and Betty Bennett? (List descriptive phrases for each individual.)

2. How does Ellen view her role as ESL specialist? How does Margie view her role as teacher? How might Betty view her role as school principal?

3. How does Ellen feel about Margie's problem?

4. How might Betty feel about the situation?

Issues

1. What concerns does Margie express to Ellen? Are her concerns justified? Did her conversation with Ellen resolve her concerns? What are her expectations for Ellen?

2. What concerns might Ellen have about Margie's classroom situation? Are her concerns justified? What are her expectations for herself? For Margie?

3. When presented with the problem, how might Betty react? What concerns might she experience about the situation?

4. Does Pelican Bay Elementary have a culture of collaborative inquiry? Why or why not?

5. In your opinion, will collaboration with Ellen help Margie resolve her class problems? Will this collaboration occur? Why or why not?

Problems or Conflicts

1. List the problems or conflicts in this case.

2. Prioritize these problems according to their impact on the students in the fifth grade.

Solutions

1. Determine what Margie can do to improve her classroom science instruction for all learners.

2. How can Ellen contribute to resolve the problem presented in this case?

3. How can Betty contribute to resolve the problem?

4. What kind of instructional plan will ensure that all students in Margie's class are successful in the grade-level expectations for the energy unit?

5. Determine how Pelican Bay can develop a collaborative culture.

Summary of Main Ideas

1) Curriculum consists of
   a)   the intended curriculum, that which is specified in district or state curriculum guides
   b)   the implemented curriculum, that which is actually taught by the teacher
   c)   the attained curriculum, that which is actually learned by students

2) The components of curriculum consist of
   a)   content, the accumulation of knowledge and skills, facts, principles and concepts that students are expected to learn at each grade level
   b)   process, the instructional activities sequenced by the teacher
   c)   products, which are produced by students and used to assess learning
   d)   learning environment and affect, a classroom organization that responds to students' cultures and learning styles

3) Curriculum is organized in many ways, for example:
   a)   The spiral curriculum is based on student inquiry and moving from problem to problem while continuously expanding the realm of student knowledge in both depth and breadth
   b)   The design-down approach first identifies the desired results of the teaching/learning experience
   c)   Curriculum mapping encourages teachers and school districts to refine their curricula in order to identify gaps in instruction, redundancies and misalignments between curriculum and assessment
   d)   Thematic instruction organizes essential knowledge and skills in various areas of study around categories, concepts, points of view, and governing principles

4) Effective curriculum for language learning students is
   a)   standards based
   b)   rigorous
   c)   accessible
   d)   diverse
   e)   relevant

<table>
<tr><td>5)</td><td colspan="2">Effective instructional strategies for linguistically diverse learners include</td></tr>
<tr><td></td><td>a)</td><td>identification of specific instructional objectives</td></tr>
<tr><td></td><td>b)</td><td>varied instruction that connects to students' cultures and learning styles</td></tr>
<tr><td></td><td>c)</td><td>cognitively challenging coursework</td></tr>
<tr><td></td><td>d)</td><td>emphasis on language, reading, and writing across the curriculum</td></tr>
<tr><td></td><td>e)</td><td>collaborative, interactive learning</td></tr>
<tr><td></td><td>f)</td><td>instructional clarity</td></tr>
<tr><td></td><td>g)</td><td>frequent comprehension checking</td></tr>
<tr><td></td><td>h)</td><td>prompt, detailed feedback and reinforced effort</td></tr>
<tr><td></td><td>i)</td><td>illustration of critical similarities</td></tr>
<tr><td></td><td>j)</td><td>efficient classroom organization and routines</td></tr>
<tr><td>6)</td><td colspan="2">Teachers collaborate effectively for the improvement of curriculum when they</td></tr>
<tr><td></td><td>a)</td><td>create predictable classrooms</td></tr>
<tr><td></td><td>b)</td><td>maximize language use in the classroom</td></tr>
<tr><td></td><td>c)</td><td>involve students as active participants</td></tr>
<tr><td></td><td>d)</td><td>scaffold learning and comprehension</td></tr>
<tr><td></td><td>e)</td><td>increase relevancy of science instruction to students' lives</td></tr>
<tr><td></td><td>f)</td><td>adapt science materials</td></tr>
<tr><td></td><td>g)</td><td>use multiple assessments</td></tr>
</table>

Print Resources

Dong, Y. R. (2005). Getting at the content. *Educational Leadership, 62*, 14–19.

Content teachers can further academic language learning by teaching content-specific language.

Educational Leadership. (2002). Reading and writing in the content areas [Theme Issue]. *60*(3).

An excellent issue with many teacher strategies for promoting language, reading, and writing across the curriculum.

Educational Leadership. (2004). Improving achievement in math and science [Theme Issue]. *61*(5).

A comprehensive issue that approaches the teaching of math and science from a variety of perspectives, including curricular design, lesson aids, and high-quality instruction.

Gibbons, P. (2003). Mediating language learning: Teacher interactions with ESL students in a content-based classroom. *TESOL Quarterly, 37*, 247–273.

This research illustrates how two teachers interact with language learning students to advance the students' language from their linguistic levels at the beginning of the interaction. The teachers build linguistic bridges to connect the students to the language of scientific academic discourse. "Both teachers and learners are active participants in the coconstruction of language and curriculum knowledge."

Jacob, E., Rottenberg, L., Patrick, S., & Wheeler, E. (1996). Cooperative learning: Context and opportunities for acquiring academic English. *TESOL Quarterly, 30*, 253–280.

This research looks at the results of cooperative learning for second language acquisition in a sixth-grade social studies classroom. Results indicate that teachers need to have an understanding of academic language, include this language in their instructional goals, structure classrooms for learning opportunities for second language students, and monitor groups closely.

Kaufman, D., & Brooks, J. G. (1996). Interdisciplinary collaboration in teacher education: A constructivist approach. *TESOL Quarterly, 30*, 231–251.
> Research in teacher education programs indicates that teacher collaboration is imperative. This collaboration integrates language pedagogy with science instruction with an aim to enhance classroom interdisciplinary environments that "better foster students' linguistic and academic growth."

Ko, J., Schallert, D. L., & Walters, K. (2003). Rethinking scaffolding: Examining negotiation of meaning in an ESL storytelling task. *TESOL Quarterly, 37*, 303–324.
> Four types of interactional structures improved student storytelling language. This research expands the view of scaffolding to include the roles of both the teacher and the student.

Marzano, R. J., Marzano, J. S., & Pickering, D. J. (2003). *Classroom management that works: Research-based strategies for every teacher*. Alexandria, VA: Association for Supervision and Curriculum Development.
> Research is presented from more than 100 studies that support types of classroom organization and management that lead to raised student achievement levels.

Short, D., & Echevarria, J. (2005). Teacher skills to support English language learners. *Educational Leadership, 62*(4), 8–13.
> This article discusses what mainstream teachers can do to scaffold instruction for English language learners.

Stoynoff, S. J. (Ed.). (2003). Promoting L2 literacy [Special Issue]. *TESOL Journal, 12*(3).
> Of special note in this issue is "Linking Our Worlds: A Collaborative Academic Literacy Project." by R. J. Vann and S. B. Fairbairn. Middle school students preparing multimedia presentations achieve higher literacy skills when teachers collaborate.

Verplaetse, L. S. (1998). How content teachers interact with English language learners. *TESOL Journal, 7*(5), 24–28.
> This article reports on a study investigating how middle to high school content teachers shaped the interactional opportunities of their mainstreamed ESL students.

Zwiers, J. (2005). The third language of academic English. *Educational Leadership, 62*(4), 60–63.
> Five strategies are included to help English language learners read academic texts.

Internet Resources

Beacon Learning Center. (n.d.). Retrieved August 15, 2006, from http://www.beaconlearningcenter.com
> This online educational resource is funded through the Technology Innovation Challenge Grant from the U.S. Department of Education.

Burkart, G. S., & Sheppard, K. (1995). *Content-ESL across the USA: A training packet, Vol. III. Training packet material*. Washington, DC: National Clearinghouse for English Language Acquisition & Language Instruction Educational Programs.

Retrieved September 15, 2006, from http://www.ncela.gwu.edu/pubs/cal
/contentesl/contente.htm

> The 15 guides in this training packet were compiled from data gathered in a 3-year study of content-
> ESL programs across the United States. They include information on curriculum development, material
> selection and adaptation, and lesson planning.

Dalton, S. S. (1998). *Pedagogy matters: Standards for effective teaching practice* (Research
Report No. 4). Retrieved August 15, 2006, from http://crede.berkeley.edu/pdf
/rr04.pdf

> This paper presents five standards for pedagogy that are applicable across grade levels and have proven
> successful with majority and minority at-risk students in a variety of teaching and learning settings.

Fathman, A. K., Quinn, M. E., & Kessler, C. (1992). Teaching science to English learners, grades 4–8. (Program Information Guide, No. 11). Retrieved August 15, 2006,
from http://www.ncela.gwu.edu/pubs/pigs/pig11.htm

> This paper describes how to integrate language and science instruction, basic learning, and teaching
> principles for science education of linguistically diverse students and methods of designing lesson
> plans.

Jacobs, H. H. (1989).The growing need for interdisciplinary curriculum content.
In H. H. Jacobs (Ed.), *Interdisciplinary curriculum: Design and implementation*. Retrieved September 15, 2006, from http://www.ascd.org/portal/site
/ascd/template.chapter/menuitem.5d91564f4fe4548cdeb3ffdb62108a0c
/?chapterMgmtId=0bcd8aec2ecaff00VgnVCM1000003d01a8c0RCRD

> This chapter argues for the need for curriculum integration.

Snow, D. (2003). *Noteworthy perspectives: Classroom strategies for helping at-risk students*
(Rev. ed.). Retrieved August 18, 2006, from http://www.mcrel.org/topics
/productDetail.asp?productID=152

> This publication includes seven chapters dedicated to research and strategies for improving instruction
> for language learning students. Instructional practices discussed include whole-class instruction,
> small-group instruction, peer tutoring, and computer-assisted instruction.

Zehler, A. (1994). *Working with English language learners: Strategies for elementary and
middle school teachers* (Program Information Guide, No. 17). Retrieved August 18,
2006, from http://www.ncela.gwu.edu/pubs/pigs/pig19.htm

> This paper provides many practical suggestions for teaching strategies. Of special note is the section
> describing scaffolding techniques and teacher mediation strategies.

CHAPTER 3

Standards

$$\boxed{\text{CASE STUDY}}$$

Collaborating for Standards-Based Writing Achievement

Pelican Bay Elementary School is located in the northwest corner of Indian River County in Florida. Most students live in the rural community surrounding the school. The economic base of the community is agricultural, with many families working in the citrus industry. A large segment of these workers are designated as migrant farm workers. More than 85% of the students in this school speak English as a second language.

The fourth-grade teachers have gathered all of their students into the school cafeteria this morning to write an essay. Keri is the school's Title I writing strategies specialist. Her position is federally funded under the 1965 Elementary and Secondary Education Act. Title I focuses on the academic achievement of the disadvantaged and ensures that they have a fair, equal, and significant opportunity for a high-quality education.

Keri is leading the group in expository essay writing—an evaluative task culminating the prior 9 weeks of instruction. Keri has taught at Pelican Bay for 20 years and is highly respected for her knowledge and leadership skills. She works closely with the four fourth-grade teachers in the area of writing. Although most fourth-graders in this school are bilingual, neither Keri nor any of their teachers speak Spanish.

Keri begins by introducing the writing web that students will use to organize their information. She places it on the overhead projector and indicates the important areas of the web to complete, pointing to each and giving a brief example from past lessons. Next, Keri directs the students to their writing resource books, where they can see a copy of the web. She reminds the class of the items to be included in their introductory paragraphs and urges them to use a grabber word, correct mechanics and punctuation, and restate wording from the essay prompt.

Keri says, "State the three main topic ideas and use a transition sentence to tell the writer what you will be writing about. The concluding paragraph is described on page five. Remember to restate the prompt, summarize the three main topic ideas, and use a zinger sentence to leave the reader with a smile."

Grabbers and zingers are supplied in the writing resource book. The children are aware of these and know how to find them. In addition, spicy-savory words hang on the cafeteria's word wall. Because most of the students come from Spanish-speaking families, they frequently consult the word wall and word lists. After Keri is finished, Lainie, a fourth-grade teacher, hangs the word *meanwhile* on the wall under the 'M' words.

Lainie says, "Remember the word meanwhile? We learned how to use this word yesterday."

Next, the teachers introduce the prompt for the essay: Halloween is a very exciting time of year. One of them says, "Think about all the different things you like to do at Halloween time. Now tell what you like to do and explain why you like to do them."

The children are very excited as they see this prompt. Halloween is 3 days away.

As the students begin work on their essays, the teachers circulate around the room, prompting students with questions to help them remember the kinds of activities they will describe in their essays.

At one end of the room, Sue, the bilingual tutor for this grade, is sitting with three girls. Ingris, Linda, and Sandra have been in the United States for 2 years. They will take the Florida Comprehensive Assessment Test (FCAT) in February, and their scores will be averaged into the school's scores for the first time. Sue speaks to the girls in English but occasionally slips into Spanish when she speaks to Sandra. She prompts Sandra to think about last Halloween and remember the things she did and enjoyed. Sandra is shy and hesitant to offer ideas, but she continues the conversation with Sue while Linda and Ingris complete their webs and begin to write their essays.

Keri checks in on Sue and the girls frequently. She hopes that most of the fourth-grade class will be able to pass the writing test this year, but she worries that not all of them will. She begins thinking about the meeting she will have with the fourth-grade teachers after class to plan for the next 9 weeks of writing instruction, and she thinks about the suggestions she will make for improvement.

PREREADING QUESTIONS

- What is the promise of the standards movement?
- What is the history of the standards movement?
- What are the characteristics of quality standards?
- Why are ESL standards necessary?
- How are ESL standards aligned with content standards?
- How do teachers collaborate for standards-based instruction?

What Is the Promise of the Standards Movement?

PROMOTE STUDENT ACHIEVEMENT FOR ALL

The standards movement has made clear the goal that all students in public schools must be taught to a high standard. Parents, students, and teachers are now aware of the essential knowledge that all children must learn during their K–12 education. Given the diversity of learners, variations in teaching styles, and differences in learning communities, this is a lofty goal. It presupposes that teachers make no mistakes. There is no room for error. Every student must achieve to a predetermined standard. A democratic society aims for no less than this.

U.S. society has long supported standards in other arenas of public life, such as aeronautical engineering, bridge construction, water quality, and medical care. Standards have brought about improvements in these areas, and it is logical to believe that standards will raise achievement levels for public school students as well.

ALLOW EQUITABLE ACCESS TO MEANINGFUL CONTENT

Standards ensure that all students have access to a challenging academic curriculum regardless of their racial, ethnic, linguistic, or learning characteristics. ELLs can acquire language skills within the context of a grade-appropriate social studies or science curriculum rather than wait years until their English is at the same level as the other students in the class. Special needs students can meet their individual goals while working with knowledgeable peers. The same high standards, articulated across a grade level or a school district, provide the invitation that diverse learners need to enter into the instructional conversation.

PROVIDE BENCHMARKS TO JUDGE THE PERFORMANCE OF PUBLIC SCHOOLS

Not all public schools are equal in terms of funding, teacher quality, class size, or achievement levels. The standards movement aims to provide a ruler with which to measure the outcomes of all schools and attain an equitable academic level for all children to reach, regardless of race or economic class.

Learning can be measured by defining the expected learning levels or benchmarks at various grade levels: primary, upper elementary, middle, and high school. Standardized testing can then be used to determine if all students have met the benchmarks. In this way, parents, lawmakers, school officials, and the public can be made aware of the success or failure of a school system.

What Is the History of the Standards Movement?

The publication of *A Nation at Risk* may have been the precipitating event for the modern standards movement. As the report stated,

> the educational foundations of our society are presently being eroded by a rising tide of mediocrity that threatens our very future as a nation and as a people. . . . We have, in effect, been committing an act of unthinking, unilateral educational disarmament. (National Commission on Excellence in Education, 1983, p. 5)

Growing concern following the publication of this report led to an education summit in 1989 that established six broad goals for education. The goals, which were to be achieved by 2000, were published as *The National Education Goals Report: Building a Nation of Learners* (National Education Goals Panel, 1991). Two of the six goals related to academic achievement. Goal 3 stated that by 2000, students in Grades 4, 8, and 12 would demonstrate competency in core subjects such as math, science, history, and geography. Goal 4 stated that by 2000, U.S. students would be the first in the world in science and math achievement. These goals have not yet been met, but they were instrumental in the development of the standards movement in the United States.

The National Council of Teachers of Mathematics (NCTM) didn't wait for the publication of *The National Education Goals Report*. NCTM became the first national subject-matter organization to establish national content standards when it published *Curriculum and Evaluation Standards for School Mathematics* in 1989. Following the lead of NCTM, standards in science, civics, dance, theater, music, art, English language arts, history, and social studies followed. Teachers of English to Speakers of Other Languages, Inc. (TESOL) published the *ESL Standards for Pre-K–12 Students* in 1997.

Following the publication of content standards by national subject-matter organizations, states began to write their own standards for each of the core content areas. But the quality of these state standards is not consistent. Some states have included too many concepts in their standards documents, and teachers cannot effectively teach all of them. Other states' standards are vague and unclear, leaving their meanings open for interpretation.

Standards-based testing is now utilized in most states to determine whether students have achieved the level demanded by the content standards. Unfortunately, wide-scale testing is more effective in sorting students than in supplying information about whether those students have become more skilled or knowledgeable. To determine whether standards have been met, more comprehensive and diverse assessment systems are necessary.

The most promising outcomes from the standards movement revolve around those school communities that are grappling with how to use standards to raise achievement levels. Current trends occurring in some school communities are good examples of what should be done for the improvement of national standards. These trends include the following:

- redefined school leadership in which principals are educational leaders rather than organizational managers
- redefined district offices that monitor student learning closely and provide opportunities for better teaching and better school organization
- strengthened professional development to help teachers define standards and increase their teaching repertoires
- alignment of district curriculum to state and national standards so that schools conform to teaching the most essential knowledge and skills to students
- united school communities focused on academic achievement

- increased time for academics
- standards-based instructional materials

What Are the Characteristics of Quality Standards?

CLARITY

Standards must be clear so that teachers, parents, and students understand what will be taught and learned. Content standards should be detailed and precise enough to guide a teacher's instructional program. Without clarity, teachers will fall back on other strategies, such as teaching the concepts that they enjoy or teaching to the tests, both of which negate the goal of providing a rigorous curriculum for every learner (Gandal & Vranek, 2001).

SPECIFICITY

One of the complaints about many state standards is that they lack specificity; they are written in a general manner that leaves many teachers struggling to interpret them. As a result, vague standards provide a barrier to student learning:

> How can we expect students to master a body of knowledge if we fail to define what that body of knowledge is—and then convey it to them in a meaningful and accessible way? How can we monitor their progress toward benchmarks if we refuse to state those benchmarks in clear, identifiable, and measurable ways? Vague standards set schools adrift without a map or compass—or even a destination. (Finn, Petrilli, & Vanourek, 1998, p. 6)

One example of a vague standard is the ubiquitous *enjoyment of reading* found in many standards documents. How can a teacher determine if students have achieved this standard? Asking if a standard can be measured is one test of determining specificity.

COMPREHENSIVENESS

Good standards must include the essential areas of the content subject and leave no gaps in the major concepts of a field (Izumi, 1999). They must have adequate breadth and depth to enable students to understand the content area and they must be inclusive at every grade level. Imagine a reading curriculum for the first grade that excludes phonics or a literature course for high school students that does not require students to actually read any major works of literature. These essential elements in the course of study are necessary to learn to read or to critically evaluate literature, and they cannot be omitted.

MANAGEABILITY

Comprehensive standards must not be so in-depth that they are overwhelming for the teacher or impossible to implement within the course of a school year. Manageable standards convey the essential but not trivial concepts of a content area. Unfortunately, some state standards are unmanageable because they contain more concepts than can reasonably be taught in the time allowed. At present, the NCTM (1989) math standards include many more topics than those in Japan, for example, where the entire standards document for 12 grades is only 47 pages long. NCTM's standards, on the other hand, exceed 250 pages. Perhaps because content standards are written by experts in that field, to them all concepts related to the subject are important. But we as educators need to ask whether they are all essential. Some critics (e.g., Scherer, 2001) have recommended cutting the numbers of standards and the content within them by two-thirds in order to implement them effectively.

RIGOR

Standards must be rigorous and set high expectations for all students. Some would argue that poor, minority, and at-risk students are not up to the challenge of a rigorous curriculum and are doomed to failure. Yet in cities and states where rigorous standards have been implemented, these students rise to the challenge. In New York City the numbers of Latino ninth graders passing the more demanding Regents science classes quadrupled by 1995, and Latino students in El Paso passing standardized math tests rose from 36.2% in 1992–1993 to 86.4% in 1997–1998 (Izumi, 1999, p. 5). Minority students, like all students, rise to the expectations set for them.

In addition to being rigorous, standards must be dedicated to academic concepts and avoid transforming into social and political issues, politically slanted views, moral dogma, behavioral change, or attempts to manipulate student feelings or thought.

PUBLICNESS

Standards are public when all stakeholders know about them and are able to understand them. Teachers, parents, and students must be aware of the target so that they all can have a part in hitting it squarely. It is critical that teachers share learning goals with students and give them timely feedback on their progress. Standards-directed learning permits all students to be more aware of what these learning goals are.

BALANCE

Standards must include a balance between skills and knowledge. Skills include the ability to perform tasks such as note taking, researching, reporting, analyzing, or reciting a poem. However, skills acquisition is not sufficient in itself. Students are taught to take notes within a content area where there is essential knowledge to be learned. Reciting a poem is meaningless unless there is a knowledge concept to be learned through the act of recitation. Doyle and Pimental (1997) support a balance between skills and knowledge, with an emphasis on knowledge:

> How is it possible to decide, analyze, investigate, compare, or classify without content? Skills can't be taught in the abstract. Neither can they be assessed. Knowledge is the scaffolding upon which critical thinking is built. (p. 39)

CUMULATIVENESS

Learning is cumulative in that the skills and knowledge learned at one grade level are used to build increasingly more complex and abstract levels of skill and knowledge at the next grade level. This continuum of learning is essential to enable students at more advanced grade levels to deal with rigorous academic content. If the standards don't reflect this complexity, and they simply repeat the same requirements from one grade level to another, teachers will have no indicators of how far to develop student skill and knowledge throughout the grades.

MEASURABILITY

Good standards can be easily assessed. They are written with action verbs that define the measurement task; these verbs are key to assessment. Specific verbs such as *compare*, *demonstrate*, *evaluate*, *analyze*, *identify*, *locate*, and *illustrate* lend themselves to measurability (Izumi, 1999). Vague verbs leave teachers uncertain. How can teachers assess a standard that requires children to *explore data* (Izumi, 1999, p. 14)? Better standards require children to *count*, *order*, or *sequence* objects. These verbs prescribe the manner of assessment.

Why Are ESL Standards Necessary?

The school population of the United States is one of increasing linguistic and cultural diversity. The limited-English-proficient (LEP) population grew by 95% from 1991 to 2002. Compare this to a 12% growth in the general K–12 population ("The Growing Numbers," 2003). Many U.S. cities now have minority populations greater than 50%. Future projections indicate that entire states will have minority populations of more than 50% by 2015 (U.S. Department of Education, 2002). These students must be accounted for within the standards movement.

ESOL students vary in proficiency levels and academic needs (TESOL, 1997). Language learning students make up one of the most diverse populations in U.S. public schools. They vary in their languages, ethnicities, religions, cultural backgrounds, ages, and prior schooling. Many come to this country for diverse reasons as well. Some are privileged and others are escaping hardship, but all are in need of an appropriate education.

TESOL's (1997) ESL standards describe the language skills necessary for social and academic purposes. Although the National Council of Teachers of English (NCTE) has developed English standards, these do not specifically describe the language skills needed to engage in grade-appropriate, rigorous academic instruction. These specific skills include the use of social language, academic language, and culturally appropriate language.

ESL standards provide a bridge to the content standards (TESOL, 1997). The goal for all learners is to achieve at a high level in core subject content standards, and language learners need to learn language skills in order to accomplish that goal. The

ESL standards are the bridge that permits these learners to participate in rigorous classroom learning. They are important because they

- articulate the English language development needs of ESOL learners
- provide directions to educators on how to meet the needs of ESOL learners
- emphasize the central role of language in the attainment of other standards (TESOL, 1997, p. 2)

How Are ESL Standards Aligned With Content Standards?

The alignment of state and national standards to district curricula is one promising outcome of the standards movement. Alignment aims to ensure that a district's curriculum supports content standards designed to raise instructional outcomes for all learners. The ESL standards need to be aligned with both content standards and district curriculum to ensure positive outcomes.

One model for that alignment process is called ASCRIBER (Short, 2000). The ASCRIBER model can be used by a district's curriculum development team comprising ESL teachers, content teachers, and, if applicable, bilingual educators. There are eight stages in the alignment process:

1. Alignment: Standards, curriculum objectives, and ESL standards are placed side by side in two columns so that the similarities and differences can be identified.

2. Standard setting: A new composite standard is created based on the comparisons.

3. Curriculum development: Courses, grades, and program levels are determined for each standard, perhaps through the use of a matrix that lists the standards in the left column and grade levels across the top horizontally. In this way, the ESL standards can be infused into the content standards at each grade level. The matrix allows for a clear presentation of the responsibilities of teachers at each grade level.

4. Retooling: An ongoing professional development plan, not a one-time workshop, must be developed to help teachers understand and eventually implement the standards. In addition to understanding what the standards look like in a classroom setting, retooling efforts are also necessary for assessment of the standards.

5. Implementation: After the curriculum is written, teachers need professional development opportunities and appropriate materials in order to implement the standards in classrooms. Field testing in selected classrooms might be one way to begin the implementation.

6. Benchmarking: Determining levels of progress or achievement is a task for district teachers. They need to reach a consensus on the quality of work that is good enough for determining that a student has achieved a standard.

7. Evaluation: An evaluation of the curriculum implementation must be planned for at the outset of the alignment process. In this way, relevant data can be collected throughout the implementation. Student work samples, teachers' lesson plans, anecdotal records, test scores, and interviews are some of the data that could be used for evaluation purposes.

8. Revision: Based on the evaluation, districts will need to revise the standards, objectives, and curriculum. This process should be accomplished yearly with a thorough examination of each of the eight stages. In this way, the ASCRIBER model is a cyclical process of examination, reflection, assessment, and revision.

If Keri and her colleagues at Pelican Bay Elementary had used the ASCRIBER model to align the Sunshine State Standards (Florida Department of Education, n.d.) with the *ESL Standards for Pre-K–12 Students* (TESOL, 1997), they might have begun by selecting the appropriate grade level and content standards in both documents, aligning those standards side by side, comparing them for similarities and differences, and then developing new composite standards that matched their ELLs' needs. Keri's goals for her students emerge clearly as a result of this process, as shown in Figure 1.

How Do Teachers Collaborate for Standards-Based Instruction?

Keri, the Title I writing strategies specialist, meets with the fourth-grade teachers at Pelican Bay Elementary four times a week. The 25-minute planning sessions provide opportunities for the teachers and Keri to plan for instruction in writing based on the FCAT standards.

Today, Jane and Kathy, who are new teachers at the school, meet with Lainie and Keri in the faculty room immediately following their large-group writing lesson in the school cafeteria. Lainie is the team leader for the fourth grade. She has been a teacher for 16 years, 8 of them at Pelican Bay. She is nationally board certified and holds the Florida ESOL endorsement as well as reading certification. The team plans to introduce narrative writing instruction to the students the following week.

Keri starts the conversation with a question, "How should we begin?"

The teachers then begin to tell Keri what the students already know about narrative writing: character, setting, and plot terminology. They have learned these elements from narrative reading.

The group decides to begin the unit by modeling narrative writing using the overhead projector. Jane suggests using macaroni at the learning centers for practice in writing with quotation marks. The teachers agree with this idea and Keri reinforces it by reminding the group that the Sunshine State Standards specifically require punctuation conventions and mention beginning and ending quotation marks. The teachers agree that the narrative web is intentionally different from the expository web they have just taught, and they plan to hang the new web on the walls of their classrooms prior to instruction.

All agree that the transitions between events in the narratives will be the hardest element for their students to learn. They realize that they need to teach transition phrases explicitly. Transitional devices are part of Sunshine State Standard 1 for writing in the fourth grade and will be on the FCAT in the spring. Many of the students in this group have limited knowledge of how to use transitional words in a narrative piece of writing. Keri suggests teaching similes at one point in the 9-week unit using a collection of colorful pictures she will bring to the classrooms. She also suggests that teachers make use of the list of dialogue tags she has compiled to provide students with alternatives for the word said.

As the meeting ends, the teachers indicate that they will teach sentence expansion, complex sentences, and clauses to prepare students for writing narratives. On Monday and Tuesday, Keri will come into each classroom to coteach the first writing lessons, which will be based on teacher modeling of a narrative.

COLLABORATIVE INQUIRY

The Pelican Bay fourth-grade writing team has created a culture of collaborative inquiry that supports and propels their instructional decisions and their standards implementation efforts. The dedication of the group is seen in their routine of meeting together four times a week for the purpose of improving the writing skills of their students, many of whom are from Mexican migrant families. The team has achieved a high level of collegial and collaborative workmanship. All members of the group offer suggestions; voice doubts; encourage each other; share teaching techniques; and examine, challenge, and create classroom practices. They seek to better understand children, teaching, and learning within the context of improved writing skills and higher standards. The trust that exists among them is apparent.

Teaching is a profession mired in norms of privacy. Teachers typically see themselves as autonomous decision makers, entrepreneurial individuals whose solitary classroom work is grounded in the very organization of schools. Creating collaborative cultures in schools is a difficult task requiring teachers to move from a comfortable position of independent autonomy to one of interdependent support. Interdependence is common in other professions; brain surgeons work in collaborative teams, and airline pilots and personnel in traffic control towers have strong bonds of interdependence. But true collaborative interdependencies are rare among teachers (Little, 1990). The collegial sharing of materials is not sufficient to produce the results that researchers have ascribed to true teacher collaboration: higher student achievement, increased teacher morale, creation of innovative practices, and support for new teachers. Weak forms of collaboration are a result of the voluntary acquiescence of individual teachers. For strong interdependent collaborative bonds to develop, internal and external forces are necessary. For Keri and the fourth-grade teachers at Pelican Bay, that pressure comes from the high standards required by the state and the nation, specifically through the FCAT writing test required of all fourth-grade students.

Teachers in interdependent collaborative teams operate under a different structure from traditional teachers. They have an increased frequency and intensity in their

Worksheet for aligning ESL standards, and Sunshine State Standards: Writing, grade 4

1. Select subject area and grade level: fourth-grade writing.
2. Consult TESOL's ESL standards (Goal 2, Standard 2) and the Sunshine State Language Arts standards for writing, fourth grade (LA.B.1.2).
3. Select relevant standards from each document.
4. Compare standards for similarities and differences.
5. Identify gaps that occur in the standards documents.
6. Create composite standards for fourth-grade writing at Pelican Bay Elementary School.

TESOL's ESL Progress Indicators Goal 2, Standard 2 Grades 4–8	Sunshine State Language Arts Standards Writing LA.B.1.2	Composite Standards for Pelican Bay Elementary Grade 4 Writing
A. Take a position and support it orally or in writing.	A. Focus on a central idea.	A. Tell or write the main idea in a sentence.
	B. Establish a purpose for writing.	
B. Record observations.	C. Use a variety of strategies to prepare for writing (e.g. making lists, mapping ideas, rehearsing ideas, grouping related ideas, creating story webs).	B. Brainstorm ideas orally and record them in writing journals.
C. Construct a graphic showing data.		C. Organize brainstormed information on a graphic organizer for expository writing.
D. Edit and revise written assignments.	D. Use the inscription process effectively.	D. Share the writing with a buddy, make corrections, and add ideas that make the writing clear.

Figure 1. Alignment worksheet

interactions, there is a higher probability for mutual influence, and collective judgments and decision making are the norm. Joint collaborative work requires shared responsibility for teaching. Teachers reach decisions in concert toward a single course of action or decide upon a set of priorities that govern the decision making of individual teachers (Little, 1990). As Little explains, the shift from personal autonomy to public collective involves both gains and losses:

> Personal prerogative is made subject to collectively developed values, standards, and agreements; but personal initiative is also accorded greater collective and institutional force. Independent action is both constrained and enabled. Teachers open their intentions and practices to public examination, but in turn are credited for their knowledge, skill, and judgment. Indeed, the close scrutiny of practice within

a group perhaps is sustained only where the competence and commitment of the members is not in doubt. (p. 521)

The benefits gained by strong collaborative teaching appear to outweigh the possibilities of conflict and loss of personal autonomy. These benefits include increased knowledge of subject matter, increased knowledge of instruction, increased ability to observe students, stronger collegial networks, stronger connection of daily practice to long-term goals, stronger motivation and sense of efficacy, and improved quality of available lesson plans. Keri and the fourth-grade team see collaboration as necessary for implementing higher writing standards in a school of migrant ELLs.

New teachers who find themselves in schools with cultures of collaborative inquiry have better teacher satisfaction, are better served by the professional development resonating from the collaborative experience, and ultimately remain in public school teaching longer than colleagues in schools without these cultures (Johnson & Kardos, 2002).

GROUP NORMS

Successful collaborative groups have commonalities that promote reflective inquiry. Teachers in these groups develop norms for group work and communication skills that help to "establish and maintain a safe and trusting environment and encourage group members to reexamine, clarify and transform their thinking so they can help students succeed" (Langer, Colton, & Goff, 2003, p. 14). The norms that exist in collaborative groups develop over time and are often not explicitly defined. Yet when new teachers arrive at a school, they become aware of how things are done and quickly follow suit. Kathy and Jane, although new to Pelican Bay, adapted quickly to the collaborative culture and expressed appreciation for the support they received from their colleagues.

Collaborative group norms vary from school to school but typically include agreement on practices such as starting and ending meetings on time, supporting each others' ideas; withholding criticism and judgment; focusing on teaching issues and student work; and engaging in open, honest communication (Langer, Colton, & Goff, 2003). Teachers tend to develop group norms based on a need to create a collaborative experience that is efficient and, most important, trusting. The best professional development opportunities are created within groups of teachers who work together in a collegial environment toward a common goal.

COMMUNICATION SKILLS FOR COLLABORATION
FOR STANDARDS IMPLEMENTATION

The communication skills acquired by teachers in collaborative groupings help move the work forward. Communication begins with effective listening in which the listener

- attends to the message
- interprets what has been heard
- responds in a manner that communicates interest and understanding

Attending to a message means listening to the words and paying attention to the gestures and intonation that surround the message. Pausing to interpret what has been heard gives the listener time to reflect on whether the message is understood. Responding enables the listener to match the verbal and nonverbal cues of the speaker (e.g., body orientation, eye contact, facial expression, gestures, tone, rate of speech) as a signal that the message is understood and the speaker is respected. This response mode opens up the lines of communication further, leading to more conversation and participation.

Specific communication skills often used in collaborative, collegial teams include the following:

- paraphrasing
- probing for more information
- probing for assumptions and beliefs

Examples of these communication skills are evident in the Pelican Bay team's dialogues. When Lainie indicated that the "narrative web is really different from the expository web," Keri responded, "Yes, the narrative web is intentionally different," a paraphrase with added information. Keri probed the teachers for further information by asking "What elements of this unit will be the most difficult for your students?" and "What do they already know?" She sought suggestions for activities by asking "What will we do first?" Even though Keri is the school expert in writing, her communication sends a message that the group is the expert. Teachers are thus empowered to contribute ideas and share their individual expertise.

ORGANIZATIONAL SUPPORT

Collaborative cultures rarely develop without organizational support. Elements of support structures vary from district office curriculum guidance to allotment of meeting and planning time. The school principal is an important element in a team's support structure, as is the facilitator.

The group facilitator is essential to the development of a collaborative culture. Keri facilitates the meetings at Pelican Bay, in part because her job title (Title I writing strategies specialist) makes her a natural for the part. She also exhibits the skills needed by collaborative facilitators, such as an aptitude for effective communication. It is helpful for the facilitator to be a trusted colleague who is able to quickly build rapport in the group. Indeed,

> leaders' styles of interaction and the nature of their relationships [are] often more important than their knowledge of particular issues, though knowledge remain(s) important as well. This suggests that, if we seek change in teachers' practices, leaders need to build positive relationships with teachers in order to facilitate the fruitful exchange of information. (Diamond, 2004, para. 10)

Good facilitators are active listeners. They communicate their open-mindedness and their willingness to learn from others in the group. They are honest about their limitations, and they model consensus building. Good facilitators are able to determine the kinds of materials and support that will be most helpful to the group's progress and find ways to provide the necessary information. At Pelican Bay, Keri often provides material support such as graphic organizers, lists of specific adjectives, or dialogue tags. She models lessons and coteaches writing lessons with the teachers. She helps the team analyze student writing samples to determine future writing instruction. She organizes large group lessons, such as the one in the cafeteria, and she schedules planning meetings. Her position in the school is determined by the need for continuing professional development in light of higher state and national standards.

Grade team leaders often provide the daily support needed by teachers. Lainie guides the new teachers at her grade level in their acclimation to the school and to the culture of collaborative inquiry. She leads study groups held once a month at the school, participates in district curriculum writing projects and text analyses, and teaches summer workshops to fellow teachers. She models the communication and listening skills needed for a collaborative leader. She helps new teachers on the team become familiar with and use state standards and ESOL strategies. Fourth grade is a crucial year for standardized testing in Florida, and Lainie works daily with Keri, the new teachers at her grade level, and the instructional assistants to ensure that standards are implemented in the classroom. In this way, Lainie has multiple roles to play in her school. She is a mentor, a model teacher, a team leader, and an in-class coach.

Effective principals are no less important than teacher facilitators and grade team leaders. They ensure that collaborative teams are respected, and they facilitate the team's work in many ways. Mr. Lubell, the principal of Pelican Bay Elementary, is in his third year at the school. He uses his background as a reading specialist to infuse literacy into every aspect of the school. Literacy and math are the two areas that have impacted his school as a result of standardized testing, and he must lead his teachers to teach to higher standards or suffer consequences such as reduced federal funding and professional transfers.

Mr. Lubell's leadership aims to help teachers focus on discourse about students and instructional practices—what is and is not working. He requires daily reporting of Sunshine State Standards in lesson plan books. He is visibly engaged in the daily life of the school and the professional life of the teachers. He begins each day with a book talk broadcast from the school TV station, where he and a student share a book discussion. Other innovations include the book buckets scattered around the school, the "Caught You Reading" coupons used for special prizes, and the monthly family reading nights. Mr. Lubell made the local paper recently when he dyed his black hair blond—he was honoring a promise made to the youngsters who had successfully attended a summer reading program at his school. The leadership focus in this school is on the implementation of higher standards for reading and writing.

Mr. Lubell's support for Keri, Lainie, and the fourth-grade writing team is based on practical necessities—the fourth-grade writing test requires an increasingly higher standard of writing from the students. For this reason, the fourth-grade team is guaranteed a common meeting time four times a week. Teachers are encouraged to observe each other's classes. Mr. Lubell visits classrooms frequently, offering feedback and celebrating successes with impromptu treats such as the chocolate cherries and soda he provided to teachers on Valentine's Day. In these ways, he leads the teachers toward long-term goals including improved writing scores on the FCAT, standards-based teaching, professional development, collegiality, and organizational health.

Principals can also support collaboration by providing resources. Pelican Bay, for example has a *Pelican Bay Plan* for both reading and writing to high state and national standards. These booklets offer teachers at various grade levels specific techniques for increasing student literacy and writing skills. They alert teachers to materials available for their use and set specific examples of the standards needed at each grade level. In the *Pelican Bay Plan* for fourth-grade writing, for example, expository and narrative webs are defined and graphics provided. Key words are listed that define an expository or narrative essay. There are an outline of a whole-class language experience, descriptions of various kinds of student conferencing formats, rubrics, lists of specific vocabulary, advice on grammar correction, and descriptions of various language skills required in the fourth grade. Specific to this grade level, the state standards expect students to learn to write using simile. A mature fourth-grade example is provided: My three-year-old sister looks as funny as a clown when she puts on mother's make-up. Lists of similes are also included for illustration. Higher-order critical thinking skills are required by state standards at the fourth-grade level. The *Pelican Bay Plan* outlines suggested questions to stimulate children's thought processes, and samples of student responses to critical thinking prompts are provided.

Students in the fourth grade are each given a student version of the *Pelican Bay Plan*, which supports them in their writing achievement goals. This booklet includes examples of various types of expository and narrative graphic organizers and lists of words for various purposes, such as for comparison and transition. There are signal words, *juicy* words, and descriptive words. Word maps illustrate methods for learning new vocabulary, and a character analysis framework structures character description from literature.

The importance of teaching to a high standard is made explicit in the lesson plan formats that Mr. Lubell asks all teachers to use at Pelican Bay. Teachers list the Sunshine State standards they are teaching, the objectives for each lesson, and the ESOL strategies (see Table 1) they use to help their students comprehend and engage in learning. The ESOL strategies are found in each teacher's lesson plan book and are specified daily in every lesson. In this way, teachers have become very familiar with all of them and incorporate them as part of their teaching practice.

DISTRICT, STATE, AND NATIONAL SUPPORT

Because Florida has the third largest population of ELLs in the United States, all teachers in the state are required to obtain an ESOL endorsement (*LULAC et al. v. SBE* Consent Decree, 1990) specifying the requirements for instructional and administrative personnel:

- 300 in-service hours (all elementary, English, and special education teachers teaching the language arts) or five 3-credit-hour university courses

Table 1. ESOL strategies for LEP students

1. Modified Curriculum	• Analyze textbook material from ESOL students' point of view. • Prioritize objectives to ensure that the most essential content is presented within the designated timeframe.
2. Language Experience Approach	• Provide background experience and personalize the lesson. • Draw examples from the students' experiences. • Provide background knowledge to facilitate the understanding of ideas and themes presented in the lesson.
3. Essential Vocabulary	• Identify and teach essential vocabulary. • Limit the vocabulary list to 12 words or less, and build on these.
4. Oral Strategies	• Speak at a slightly slower pace. • Read aloud. • Use facial expressions and gestures to add meaning. • Shorten sentences. • Elicit Total Physical Response (TPR) from spoken statements.
5. Visual Advance Organizers	• Use a variety of visual aids (e.g., pictures from textbooks, magazines, newspapers, overheads, maps, chalkboard). • Use collages. • Use picture charts, graphs, and math-word science puzzles.
6. Whole-Language Approach	• Simplify grammatical structures, and paraphrase to involve ESOL students. • Summarize sections for testing purposes—grouping. • Create audio recordings for listening stations. • Emphasize key words via highlight, underline, or upper case.
7. Word Pronunciation and Meaning	• Reinforce language while teaching content. • Model pronunciation of key or difficult words in lesson and during oral response. • Be aware that many English words have multiple meanings. • Identify idiomatic expressions when appropriate.
8. Study Habits Enforcement	• Teach study skills and use of textbook skills. • Use explicit definitions in texts, glossaries, pictures, graphs, and illustrations to assist students in understanding the technical vocabulary. • Teach skimming and scanning techniques.
9. Suggestopedia	• Use manipulative materials and hands-on activities. • Prepare activities that require students to be actively involved in solving problems through experimentation, measuring, cutting, weighing, and so forth. • Prepare learning centers that provide materials for exploration and discovery. • Use multimedia materials to support learning of content and processes.
10. Monitoring Student Progress	• Get feedback on a continual basis. • Use formal and informal types of evaluation during teaching. • Ask students to perform simple tasks and observe whether or not they are understanding—TPR. • Develop a code—thumbs up/thumbs down.

(Continued on p. 49)

Table 1 (continued). ESOL strategies for LEP students

11. Cooperative Learning	• Encourage peer tutoring. • Use cooperative small-group work. • Incorporate shared book experience.
12. Teaching to Two Objectives	• Teach two different groups and assess differently.
13. Provide Alternative Instruction	• Tap into other tutorial resources that are available. • Use computer assisted instruction. • Use same language tutorial assistance. • Create an ESOL pull-out class. • Assign independent projects. • Direct individual or small group library research. • Invite guest speakers.

- the in-service work must include 60 points in the following five specific areas: methods of teaching ESOL, curriculum in ESOL, testing and evaluation in ESOL, applied linguistics and TESOL, and cross-cultural understanding

The teachers at Pelican Bay are supported in this endeavor by taking in-service courses within their school district after school and during the summer. This requirement ensures that all teachers in the district have the skills and knowledge to teach ESOL students. Every teacher in the school has the responsibility of instructing ESOL students in an appropriate manner. This collective responsibility for student learning eliminates the divisions found in some schools between the ESOL and mainstream English population.

CRITICAL ASPECTS OF COLLABORATION FOR STATE AND NATIONAL STANDARDS

Pelican Bay has been successful in collaborating to a high standard for state, national, and ESL standards in student writing. The FCAT scores for fourth-grade writing in the 1996–1997 school year showed 25% of students writing at a level of 3.0 or above—the standard set by the state for grade-appropriate writing. In the 2003–2004 school year, 92% of the fourth grade scored at level 3.0 or higher. These results cannot be credited to any one change that the school made for improvement. Many changes in school organization and instructional practices helped students improve to this level, but most of these changes came about through collaborative efforts.

The following elements are seen to be central to standards collaboration at Pelican Bay:

- a school culture of collaborative inquiry

- leadership for improvement from the principal, the Title I facilitator, and the grade-level leader

- ongoing meetings among teachers and the facilitator geared to inward planning for instructional practices and focusing on how best to meet student needs for improved writing skills
- implementing state and national standards (Sunshine State Language Arts and ESOL) in daily lessons
- documenting standards and ESOL strategies in daily lesson plans
- demonstrating and sharing strategies—including cognitive and metacognitive strategies—for improvement in writing
- coteaching writing lessons among members of the fourth-grade writing team
- developing resources such as the *Pelican Bay Plan* for writing to guide teachers toward attainment of the standard
- sharing materials among members of the team
- analyzing student writing as a team effort

Case Study: The Writing Test

Marcella Garcia is a new teacher at Elmira Elementary, a school in Florida with a large migrant population. The school is 90% bilingual. Marcella was excited to be hired by Mr. Lopez, the principal, because she is a third-generation Mexican American and is eager to work with students struggling with many of the same problems her parents encountered in school. Marcella received her ESOL endorsement as part of her course work at Florida Atlantic University. She told Mr. Lopez that, although she is not fluent in Spanish, she feels well prepared to teach students who are still learning English. She has been assigned to teach a fourth-grade class consisting of 19 students, 15 of whom are bilingual Spanish/English speakers. Four students are still in the process of learning English; three of those students have been in the United States for 2 years and one is a new arrival this year.

Marcella is working with a fourth-grade team headed by Kathy Dawes. Kathy has 15 years of teaching experience, all of it at Elmira. Kathy is highly regarded by other teachers at the school who admire the fact that she has recently begun to work toward her doctorate in education. Mary Jane Luken is the third member of the team. She has worked at Elmira for 10 years and has 8 years of experience at another elementary school in the district. Mary Jane and Kathy are friends and often drive to work together.

Mr. Lopez has gathered the fourth-grade team together today with Pam Aston, the Title I specialist. The reason for the meeting is the upcoming FCAT writing test required of all students in the fourth grade in Florida. Mr. Lopez and Pam are concerned that some of the fourth graders will not be able to demonstrate sufficient writing skills to pass the FCAT. Ten students across the grade level are still in the process of learning English but have been in the United States for 2 years and are thus eligible to take the test and have their scores included with the general population of the school. Mr. Lopez wants the group to put together a plan for writing achievement in the fourth grade.

Kathy and Mary Jane look at each other and then begin to tell Mr. Lopez and Pam all the instructional strategies they have been using. Kathy produces a list of techniques she has collected that she and Mary Jane have been sharing throughout the year. Pam asks to see the list and is surprised at some of the innovative ideas the teachers have tried. "Well, it looks like you're on the right track," Mr. Lopez responds. Kathy and Mary Jane beam as Pam and Mr. Lopez pore over the list.

Marcella is silent during the meeting. She feels as if she has nothing to contribute to the discussion. She also is hurt that Kathy and Mary Jane have been working together toward the writing test but haven't included her in any of their discussions. She wonders if Pam would help her and she decides to approach Pam with the problem after the meeting is over.

QUESTIONS FOR DISCUSSION

Actors

1. How would you characterize Mr. Lopez, Pam Aston, Marcella Garcia, Kathy Dawes, and Mary Jane Luken? (List descriptive phrases for each individual.)

2. How did each of the people in this case feel before the meeting? After the meeting?

3. What kind of principal is Mr. Lopez?

4. How do Kathy and Mary Jane view their roles as teachers? How does their friendship influence that role?

5. How does Pam view her role?

Issues

1. What concerns caused Mr. Lopez to call the meeting? Were his concerns justified? Did the meeting resolve his concerns?

2. Why was Pam included in the meeting? What were the expectations of the principal and the teachers regarding her role in resolving the problem?

3. When presented with the problem, how did Mary Jane and Kathy react? Why did they react in this way? What are their concerns?

4. Why was Marcella silent? What are her concerns? Were they addressed?

5. Does Elmira Elementary have a culture of collaborative inquiry? Why or why not?

6. In your opinion, will Marcella's ESOL students have difficulty passing the writing exam to the required standard?

Problems or Conflicts

1. List the problems or conflicts in this case.

2. Prioritize these problems according to their impact on the students in the fourth grade.

Solutions

1. Determine what Mr. Lopez can do to provide organizational support for all of the fourth-grade teachers in his school.

2. Determine how Mr. Lopez can advance a collaborative culture in his school.

3. How can Pam contribute to resolve the problem presented in this case?

4. How can Kathy and Mary Jane contribute to resolve the problem?

5. What can Marcella do to develop professionally and become a functional member of the fourth-grade team?

6. How can the group as a whole ensure that the fourth-grade students receive appropriate writing instruction to enable them to write to a high standard by test time?

Summary of Main Ideas

1) The standards movement promises to
    a)   promote student achievement
    b)   allow equitable access to meaningful content for all students
    c)   provide benchmarks to judge the performance of public schools

2) The history of the standards movement includes the following events:
    a)   the publication of *A Nation at Risk* (National Commission on Excellence in Education, 1983)
    b)   the educational summit in 1989 and *The National Education Goals Report* (National Education Goals Panel, 1991)
    c)   the development of national content standards beginning with the standards for school mathematics (National Council of Teachers of Mathematics, 1989)
    d)   the development of wide-scale testing programs to determine the effectiveness of national standards
    e)   positive changes in school communities as a result of national, state, and local standards

3) Quality standards are
    a)   clear
    b)   specific
    c)   comprehensive
    d)   manageable
    e)   rigorous and academic
    f)   public
    g)   balanced
    h)   cumulative
    i)   measurable

4)	ESL standards are needed in addition to content standards to ensure that instruction	
	a)	attends to linguistic and cultural diversity
	b)	attends to varying proficiency levels and academic needs
	c)	attends to the language skills needed to achieve academically
	d)	bridges from ESL standards to the content standards
5)	ESL standards need to be aligned to content standards and district curriculum.	
6)	Teachers collaborate effectively for standards-based instruction	
	a)	within a school culture of collaborative inquiry
	b)	by developing group norms and communication skills that promote collegiality
	c)	when given strong organizational support from the state, district, principal, and group facilitators
	d)	by meeting routinely on an ongoing basis for the purpose of discussion and planning for student needs
	e)	by implementing and documenting content standards
	f)	by coteaching
	g)	by developing resources to meet common needs
	h)	by sharing materials and teaching strategies
	i)	by jointly analyzing student products

Print Resources

Bushman, J., Goodman, G., Brown-Welty, S., & Dorn, S. (2001). California testing: How principals choose priorities. *Educational Leadership, 59*(1), 33–36.

Principals react to standards by making changes that they believe will help students make achievement gains.

Educational Leadership. (1999). Using standards and assessment [Theme issue]. *56*(6).

This issue is a collection of key articles that, together, provide insight into standards-based education across grade levels and content areas.

Freedman, S. W. (1991). *Evaluating writing: Linking large-scale testing and classroom assessment* (JPRI Occasional Paper No. 27). Berkeley, CA: Japan Policy Research Institute.

This paper examines the testing of writing in both large-scale testing (national, state, district, or school level) and classroom assessment. It discusses the role of portfolio assessment for both.

George, P. S. (2001). A+ accountability in Florida? *Educational Leadership, 59*(1), 28–32.

Principals in Florida respond to the standards-based accountability programs imposed by the state.

Marzano, R. J., & Kendall, J. S. (1996). *A comprehensive guide to designing standards-based districts, schools, and classrooms.* Alexandria, VA: Association for Supervision and Curriculum Development.

This guide discusses standards-based education, history, rationale, sources, and formats.

McLaughlin, M. W., & Shepard, L. A. (1995). *Improving education through standards-based reform: A report by the National Academy of Education panel on standards-based reform*. Stanford, CA: The National Academy of Education, Stanford University.
> This report presents a comprehensive examination of the possibilities, implementation, and consequences of standards-based reform.

Scherer, M. (2001). How and why standards can improve student achievement: A conversation with Robert J. Marzano. *Educational Leadership, 59*(1), 14–18.
> This article is a concise discussion in response to some of the most common questions about standards.

Snow, M. A. (Ed.). (2000). *Implementing the ESL standards for pre-K–12 students through teacher education*. Alexandria, VA: TESOL.
> This book is a must-have for teacher educators. It is especially well suited for master's programs in ESL/TESOL, English language arts, and reading. Preservice and in-service teachers will find all eight chapters important for any work on standards implementation and curriculum development.

Internet Resources

Achinstein, B. (2002). Conflict amid community: The micropolitics of teacher collaboration. *Teachers College Record, 104*(3), 421–455. Retrieved October 26, 2006, from http://www.tcrecord.org/Content.asp?ContentID=10846
> While conflict is often considered a dysfunctional aspect of community, this article argues that it can also reflect a natural and potentially positive part of teacher professional communities. Using case studies, the author explores micropolitical processes among teachers.

Betty Lake's The Art Teacher Connection. (n.d.). *National standards for art education*. Retrieved October 26, 2006, from http://www.artteacherconnection.com/pages/standards.htm
> This site lists the standards for school art programs.

Grossman, P., Wineburg, S., & Woolworth, S. (2001). Toward a theory of teacher community. *Teachers College Record, 103*(6), 942–1012. Retrieved October 26, 2006, from http://www.tcrecord.org/Content.asp?ContentID=10833
> The authors use their experience with a professional development project to propose a model of teacher community in the workplace.

Hilliard, A. (1998). The standards movement: Quality control or decoy? *Rethinking Schools, 12*(3). Retrieved October 26, 2006, from http://www.rethinkingschools.org/archive/12_04/hill.shtml
> This article is condensed from a speech by Asa Hilliard, professor of urban education at Georgia State University in Atlanta. Hilliard gave the speech at a conference at Howard University called "Moving Beyond Standards To Provide Excellence and Equity in the African-American Community."

National Association for Sport and Physical Education (NASPE). (2004). *Newly revised national standards for physical education released*. Retrieved October 26, 2006, from http://www.aahperd.org/naspe/template.cfm?template=pr_032504.html
> This site lists the national standards for physical education.

National Council for Music Education (MENC). *National standards for music education.* Retrieved October 26, 2006, from http://www.menc.org/publication/books /standards.htm

    This site lists the standards for school music programs.

National Council for the Social Studies (NCSS). (1994). *Expectations of excellence: Curriculum standards for social studies.* Retrieved October 26, 2006, from http://www .socialstudies.org/standards/

    This site lists the national standards for social studies.

National Council for Teachers of English (NCTE). (2006). *Standards for the English language arts.* Retrieved October 26, 2006, from http://www.ncte.org/about/over /standards/110846.htm

    This site lists the national standards for the English language arts.

National Council for the Teaching of Mathematics (NCTM). (2004). *Number and operations standard.* Retrieved October 26, 2006, from http://standards.nctm .org/document/appendix/numb.htm

    This site lists the principles and standards for mathematics.

National Science Teachers Association (NSTA). (2006). *National science education standards.* Retrieved October 26, 2006, from http://www.nsta.org/standards

    This site lists the national standards for the sciences.

Teachers of English to Speakers of Other Languages (TESOL). 2006. *ESL standards for pre-K–12 students, online edition.* Retrieved October 26, 2006, from http://www .tesol.org/s_tesol/seccss.asp?CID=113&DID=1583

    A full-text copy of *ESL Standards for Pre-K–12 Students* is available at this Web site as well as two companion documents: *Managing the Assessment Process* and *Promising Futures.*

CHAPTER 4

Language

Integrating Language Instruction With Subject-Matter Learning

Debra and Maria are teaching partners in the fifth-grade dual-language program at Texas Elementary in east Texas. Debra is a native-English-speaking teacher who became a fluent Spanish speaker over the course of many years by extensively studying the Spanish language. Maria is a native Spanish speaker who grew up in rural east Texas. Both teachers explain that they enjoy teaching in a dual-language program because they love the children in this program; there is a genuine love for learning and language, which both teachers appreciate.

Dual-language programs are often referred to as the *50/50 model*, because they seek to maintain a balance between native English and native Spanish speakers. Students at Texas Elementary receive instruction in Spanish for half of the school day and in English the other half of the day. The dual language program at the school remains intact and well established as a result of its strong teacher, parent, and community support, unlike other dual-language programs in the area that were dissolved as the emphasis on high-stakes testing and student performance in English intensified. Although teachers at this school feel the intense pressure for accountability from the state, they maintain their focus on how to best prepare ELLs, while at the same time preparing them to be successful on the mandated test.

Debra and Maria explain that fifth grade is a very important grade in Texas public schools because of the high-stakes achievement test, the Texas Assessment of Knowledge and Skills (TAKS). Students are tested in the content areas of math, science, and reading. Because students only have minimal time to learn English before they are expected to take and pass the assessment test, Debra and Maria integrate language instruction throughout the content areas. They work together to not only plan content-area language instruction, but also to plan ways to prepare students for the difficult state-mandated assessment test. By planning together, Debra and Maria find that they can accomplish much more in the classroom and, even more important, they find ways to better meet the needs of the ELLs in their classroom.

Today, Debra plans to scaffold language instruction while teaching math, and at the same time she reviews and integrates language arts. Debra and Maria often coplan such lessons because Maria reinforces vocabulary learned in the content area when planning Spanish language lessons. In this way, students learn important content-area vocabulary in both Spanish and English. Debra first begins introducing the technical term *mean*. This lesson is taught as an introductory lesson, as she prepares students for more in-depth lessons on probability and statistics. Because routines are important while ESL students adapt to the mainstream classroom, Debra's lesson is intentionally predictable. She first writes the lesson's objective on the chalkboard:

- **Content objective:** Students will describe the process for calculating the mean.
- **Thinking/study skill objective:** Students will calculate the mean for a group of numbers.
- **Language objective:** Students will use the target vocabulary to describe the meaning of the mathematical term, mean.

These objectives are based on the state objectives and expectations for fifth-grade math:

- **Texas Essential Knowledge and Skills:** Standard 12 Probability and statistics. The student describes and predicts the results of a probability experiment.
- **Expectations:** The student is expected to use fractions to describe the result of an experiment and use experimental results to make predictions.

Debra begins the lesson by focusing on students' prior knowledge. Because a new mathematical concept is being introduced today, students immediately know to take their spiral notebooks from their desks. In these notebooks, they write new mathematical vocabulary and definitions. Debra thinks that vocabulary in a content area is challenging when students are learning a new language, and the spiral notebook is used to help students when they struggle with math vocabulary. Debra begins by discussing the vocabulary associated with the lesson. She connects homonyms to today's lesson because the word mean has multiple meanings, and she thinks that discussing the various meanings of the word will help students better understand the term. She says, "In language arts last week, we learned about homonyms. Jose, can you summarize what we learned about homonyms?" Jose explains that homonyms are words that may sound the same but have different meanings. Debra guides the students to brainstorm a few examples of homonyms (see Figure 1).

Once students recall the meaning of homonyms, Debra makes the connection between the language arts study of homonyms to today's lesson. She explains that mean is also an example of a homonym. She guides the students as they define the different meanings of the word:

mean = average
mean = malicious
mean = understanding

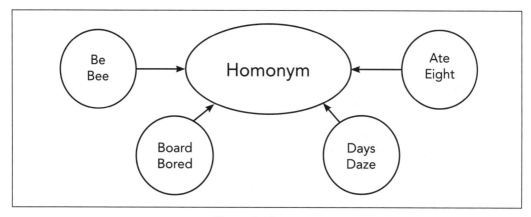

Figure 1. Homonyms

Lexical ambiguities are often confusing, so Debra clarifies those ambiguities. She finds that students remember the definitions better when she explicitly teaches vocabulary. After discussing the definition of mean, she demonstrates the steps for calculating mean. She posts a series of numbers on the chalkboard:

80   90   90   100   85   90

Then she models by thinking aloud the process to solve the mean. She says, "To solve the mean, I need to add the numbers and divide by how many there are":

$$(80 + 90 + 90 + 100 + 85 + 90) / 6 = 89 \ 1/6.$$

Debra posts the steps to calculate mean in her classroom, so students can refer to the steps on the class wall and to the notes in their spiral notebook while solving problems (See Figure 2).

After she models how to calculate the mean, Debra posts a series of numbers on the chalkboard, and the students work in small groups to solve the problems. As the students work, Debra walks through the class, observing which students seem to be struggling with today's lesson and which have a clear understanding of how to solve the problems. As she circulates through the room, she notices that Jose and Angelica are having difficulty completing their assigned group task.

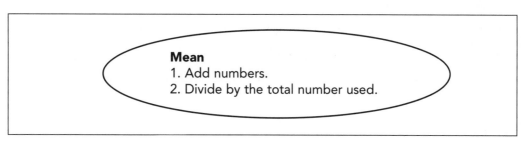

Figure 2. Steps to calculate mean

Angelica is staring intently at the blank white pages of her spiral notebook, while Jose is flipping through the math textbook. Jose is a fluent English speaker, but on a recent TAKS pretest, he barely passed the reading/language arts section. Typically, he does fairly well in math. Understanding the fifth-grade English mathematical vocabulary may be why Jose is struggling with the problems. Angelica emigrated from Mexico a little over a year ago. On a recent IDEA English Proficiency Test (IPT), she scored limited English proficient (LEP) and, because of this score, she will take the upcoming TAKS test in Spanish. The IPT measures oral proficiency and reading and writing ability for K–12 students. The test measures vocabulary, syntax, and reading for understanding. Because Debra believes that the students' difficulty in understanding today's math lesson is a language issue, she writes down a few notes. She is meeting today to plan with her dual-language partner, Maria. Debra and Maria understand that these two students are struggling with language issues in the content areas and know they must plan additional mini lessons to scaffold content-area instruction. Debra and Maria collaborate to plan lessons to meet the needs of such students. Many of their lessons focus on scaffolding the language of nonfiction texts.

Once the students solve the problems, Debra calls for student volunteers to summarize the process they went through to calculate the mean. Once it is clear that the class understands the process, she models and explains Bloom's word problem for today. She calls the word problems Bloom's Taxonomy Problems because the problems focus on using higher-level thinking skills, especially in the area of application (Arends, 2004). This is one way Debra prepares her students for the TAKS test, on which application is emphasized. Today, cooperative learning groups work on solving five word problems. The students know the routine for cooperative learning groups because this grouping is used regularly in Debra's class. Each group member has a role to play, and the group works together to solve the word problems.

While the class works on the new set of problems, Debra invites Jose and Angelica to the small table near the window. Debra uses numerous visuals that she has collected over the years to show students how to work problems. Because she is fluent in Spanish, Debra scaffolds the English reteaching of the math lesson while explaining the more difficult concepts in Spanish. By providing further modeling and practice in both Spanish and English, Debra helps Jose and Angelica understand how to work the math problems.

PREREADING QUESTIONS

- What types of program models meet the needs of English language learners?
- What is language?
- What are language learning strategies and why are they important?
- How do teachers teach language in the content areas?
- How can teachers collaborate to benefit English language learners?

What Types of Program Models Meet the Needs of English Language Learners?

Theories and models of language development and teaching are important not only for ESL or bilingual teachers, but for all teachers. All teachers must be familiar with such theories and models because high numbers of ELLs are often part of the mainstream classroom, which is why collaboration between mainstream and English language teachers is so important. Because of high immigration rates from Mexico and South America, and high birth rates from those immigrants, the numbers of ELLs continue to rise (Carrasquillo & Rodriguez, 2002; Macias, 1998; Waggoner, 1998). The U.S. Census Bureau predicts from the 2000 Census that the Hispanic population in the United States will surpass the African American population within the next few years. According to the 2000 Census, Mexican Americans represent the largest Hispanic group, with 58.5%, and the Hispanic population is the fastest-growing ethnic group in the United States.

The placement of ELLs in schools varies greatly. Several factors impact the types of programs school districts design. Such factors include the number of ELLs enrolled in the school district, the number of teachers certified to teach ESL or bilingual education, and the resources available to support a program. For example, many Texas school districts have a high teacher shortage in the area of bilingual education, and as a result districts often hire Spanish-speaking support staff to work with the monolingual classroom teacher when a bilingual teacher cannot be recruited.

A program's success depends on numerous factors, such as the number of experienced and certified teachers teaching at the school and the amount of money allocated for the program. Lindholm-Leary (2005) reviews research and best practices of effective features of dual-language education programs for the Center for Applied Linguistics and the National Clearinghouse of English Language Acquisition at The George Washington University. She explains that effective programs are typically defined as successfully promoting ELLs' academic achievement. She finds that successful dual-language programs have much in common with successful mainstream programs. Both types of programs have similar categorical features, but the terminology may differ. For example, at the campus level, both programs have a collegial and professional environment, and there is active parental involvement. At the staff level, teachers implement a variety of research-based instructional strategies and practices. Dual-language programs that are proven effective possess the following characteristics:

- a cohesive school-wide shared vision and set of goals

- equity at district, school, and classroom levels with respect to treatment of students, families, and teachers

- effective leadership in place

- a language education model in place that upholds second language development, bilingual and immersion theory and research, instructional methodologies and classroom practice, and belief in and commitment to a dual-language education model

- a program in place for ongoing, continuous planning. (Lindholm-Leary, 2005, p. 26)

Texas Elementary exemplifies an effective dual-language program, based on Lindholm-Leary's work. Debra teaches English and language arts (spelling, reading, grammar, and writing), and math in English, whereas Maria teaches science and social studies, and language arts in Spanish. Students are instructed half of the day in Spanish and the other half of the day in English. The dual-language class is composed of 60% native English speakers and 40% native Spanish speakers. The students in fifth grade receive reading and language arts instruction in both Spanish and English. This model has been a success at this school because both Debra and Maria find ways to encourage parents to participate in school activities. They give students their home and cell phone numbers. Students are first asked to call a classmate for homework help, but if there is still confusion, they are encouraged to call one of the teachers. This dual language program is a success because administrators recruit and retain qualified teachers. For example, because Maria is moving to a new school closer to her rural home, administrators encouraged a school bilingual paraprofessional to complete her college course work so she can serve as Maria's replacement next year. Recruiting individuals who are already a part of the teaching community is one successful strategy for retaining bilingual teachers. Bilingual and ESL teachers also receive a stipend each year, but it is not the money that attracts teachers to Texas Elementary; teachers want to stay because of the community. They like working with a teaching partner to plan instruction and procedures. Debra explains that despite the increased stress of state-mandated achievement tests, the collaborative partnership that she has with her dual-language partner is what keeps her in the teaching field.

In addition to the successful dual-language program model at Texas Elementary, there are numerous other types of successful program models. Table 1 outlines common programs designed for ELLs.

It is important to be familiar with a variety of program models to be able to understand why and how language curriculum is organized and delivered.

What Is Language?

Debra is an experienced ESL teacher, as is Maria. They both completed graduate coursework in ESL, and they think their academic background prepared them to better apply what they learned about language learning theory to classroom practice. They find that their basic understanding of how language develops and how children learn a language is directly applicable to teaching.

Defining language in a single, simple sentence is impossible. Language learning is a complex and complicated process. Language is typically defined as a complex system of symbols used in various modes as a way to communicate (Lessow-Hurley, 1996). There are also affective and cultural components to learning a language (Brice, 2002; Hadaway, Vardell, & Young, 2002). People communicate differently based on gender, socioeconomic status, and cultural background. For example, people may speak more formally in a school setting than with a group of friends, and men may speak in a

Table 1. Program models

Program	Characteristics
ESL Pull-Out	• This is the most common and also least effective approach to teaching ELLs. • It is used primarily at the elementary level. • Students spend most of the school day in a mainstream classroom, but they are pulled out for part of each day to receive specialized instruction by an ESL teacher.
ESL Self-Contained	• This is used primarily in middle school settings or in elementary schools that have high populations of ELLs. • Teachers use ESL strategies to scaffold content in all of the content areas. • Students may be grouped based on their level of English proficiency (Levels 1, 2, 3, 4, 5).
Early-Exit Bilingual	• This program provides initial instruction in the students' first language, primarily for the introduction of reading, but also for clarification. • Instruction in the first language is phased out over time.
Two-Way Bilingual (or Dual-Language)	• These programs group language minority students from a single language background in the same classroom with language majority (English-speaking) students. • Instruction is provided in both English and the minority language. • Programs typically seek a 50/50 balance in class population.
Sheltered English	• This type of program groups language minority students together in classes where teachers teach content-area instruction, using language teaching strategies to scaffold the instruction.
Structured Immersion	• Students are completely immersed into a mainstream program without receiving specialized ESL services. This type of program is often referred to as a sink or swim approach.

different way to other men than they would speak to a group of women. Over the years, researchers have made connections between learning language and the areas of literacy and culture (Nieto, 2002). Language learning in schools can be controversial and political, as policy makers and politicians assert their personal beliefs about groups of people and majority and minority languages. Researchers like Nieto (2002) and Griego Jones and Fuller (2003) state that there must be an intersection between language, literacy, and culture in teacher education in order to best prepare future teachers to address the distinct needs of today's students, who overwhelmingly come from diverse racial, language, and cultural backgrounds—very different backgrounds from their often Caucasian, middle-class teachers. Frequently, there is an assumption that students fail because of a language barrier; however, numerous other variables could cause students to drop out of school or fail academically, including alienation, discrimination, low expectations, and poverty (Griego Jones & Fuller). Educators must understand the relationship between language, literacy, and culture to better understand where children come from—and what their needs are, cognitively, culturally, and on a personal level.

Despite the complexity of defining language, the following structural elements are considered the basic components of language: phonology, morphology, syntax, semantics, and pragmatics. Learning the definitions of these components can be simple; however, applying the components to actual classroom practice is more challenging for the novice teacher. Table 2 offers definitions and examples of each language component.

Table 2. Language elements and examples

Language Component	Definition	Example
Phonology	This involves the sound system of language, including how sounds are produced. Phonology is important because each language uses a small number of various possible sounds that humans are able to utter (Lessow-Hurley, 1996).	In some languages *p* and *b* are heard as identical sounds. For languages that do not distinguish between voiced and voiceless sounds, words like *pan* and *bay* are heard alike (Lessow-Hurley, 1996).
Morphology	This involves basic units of meaning. Morphemes are the smallest units of meaning. Children learn to combine morphemes with prefixes and suffixes at a subconscious level (Hadaway et al., 2002). Most important, morphology is known as the system of how words are built, which is a systematic process.	*Thank(ful)* Thank = base morpheme Ful = suffix *Boys* has two morphemes *Boy* has one morpheme—when the *s* is added, it indicates the word is plural
Syntax	Syntax is the way sentences are structured. It is different from grammar, because it looks at whether sentences are structured a particular way. Syntax involves the rules on how language is governed.	"I ain't got no money." This sentence is viewed as incorrect—since grammatically it is incorrect; however, it conforms to English syntax (subject, verb, etc.).
Semantics	This is the study of meaning. One aspect of semantics is the study of words. For example, the word *fox* can have multiple meanings. It can mean a person who is very attractive; or, used in a different context, it refers to an animal. Semantics is also the study of phrases and sentences. For example, if sentences are phrased in a certain way, ambiguities may be present.	Jim is a *pig*. The word *pig* has more than one meaning. In this phrase, *pig* could mean either Jim is greedy or Jim is an animal. Ambiguous sentences: "Janice was climbing the wall, when the idea suddenly hit her." "Peter is his right hand."

(Continued on p. 65)

Table 2 (continued). Language elements and examples

Language Component	Definition	Example
Pragmatics	Pragmatics is how language is used in various social contexts. Language use is determined by how humans interact. For example, what might be considered polite in one language may not be considered polite in another language.	"Give me a call sometime." Americans often use this phrase when parting. The speaker does not literally mean to call him or her at that moment. It is an informal parting; however, for a nonnative speaker of English, such a parting could be confusing. The nonnative speaker may think he or she should call the speaker soon. A female teacher blurts out "Jose, I just love you!" when Jose answers a difficult mathematical problem correctly. For Jose, this is confusing. He thinks his older female teacher is in love with him.

Why is it important to be familiar with the definitions and applications of language components and the many aspects of learning a language? As Hadaway et al. (2002) mention, many professional organizations (e.g., TESOL, International Reading Association, NCTE) recommend that teachers have knowledge of linguistics and language in their professional training. More specifically, NCTE (2005) explains that teacher candidates must know and respect diversity in language use, patterns, and dialects and show ways to accommodate such diversity in their teaching. Applying knowledge of language and patterns in order to accommodate diverse learners can be difficult for novice teachers; however, with proper training, mentoring, and collaboration, all teachers can learn how to do so.

LANGUAGE VARIES

Teachers need to be familiar with a number of language issues. One such issue is the understanding of, and the respect for, language variety. Typically, the field of multicultural education has been slow to embrace linguistic diversity, and there remains a stigma regarding speaking a language other than English in public (Nieto, 2002). For that stigma to be removed, educators must begin to view language diversity as an asset. The responsibility for educating language minority students does not merely lie with the ESL or bilingual teacher any longer; educating language minority students is the responsibility of all teachers (Nieto, 2002).

Educators need to first be familiar with students' home languages and backgrounds. They must also recognize that there are a number of language varieties, even within one language, and the language varieties are typically divided into five distinct categories:

- Pidgin: A new language develops in situations where speakers of different languages need to communicate but don't share a common language.

- Creole: When the first language of the community becomes the pidgin, a Creole language is created. It is a distinct language with most of its vocabulary taken from another language.

- Regional dialect: This is not a distinct language, but a variety of a language spoken in a particular area of a country.

- Minority dialect: Sometimes members of a particular minority ethnic group have their own variety.

- Indigenized variety: This variety is spoken as a second language, mainly in ex-colonies with multilingual populations. (Language Varieties, 2005)

Language diversity is especially obvious in east Texas. Debra says she has students in her dual-language class who are native English speakers, students who are native Spanish speakers, and some students who speak *Spanglish*—a colloquial term sometimes used to refer to the mix of Spanish and English. She has some African American students who speak using Ebonics—a dialect historically spoken by African Americans. The word *ebonics* originates from the two words *ebony* and *phonics* (Lessow-Hurley, 2005). There are many forms of Ebonics, and each variety is based on the regional area where the dialect is spoken. Many African Americans are bidialectical, speaking Standard English in their place of work and Ebonics within their community. For example, Adam sometimes uses *ain't* to negate the verb in a simple sentence, such as when he was asked to stand behind a taped line in the classroom. Adam replied by stating: "I ain't gonna step on no line." Language varieties are not incorrect ways of speaking, as many people may think; they are merely different than the standard way of speaking. Language varieties have unique ways to pronounce words, and they include specialized vocabulary. Debra often explains to her students the importance of speaking Standard English in academic or work settings. She explains that there is a time and place for dialect, and there is a time and place for Standard English.

LANGUAGE LEARNING IS CULTURAL LEARNING

When learning a new language, one must also learn the culture behind the language. Culture is complex because it is much more than learning the holidays and heroes of a particular group of people (Nieto, 2002). Culture is typically defined as groups of people who share a common set of beliefs, values, and customs that are transmitted from one generation to the next. Culture is ever changing, and all groups of people have a culture. It is extremely important for teachers to connect learning to the student's background when the student is learning a new language. Debra and Maria connect their students' backgrounds to language learning in many ways. They make connections between English words and Spanish words in lessons throughout the content areas. Spanish is Debra's second language. When she began teaching, she began learning Spanish, and she also thought it was important to learn about the Mexican American culture. She read books, traveled to Mexico, and made new

Spanish-speaking friends. Maria is Mexican American and a native Spanish speaker. She naturally makes connections to students' background experiences in the classroom because she also immigrated to the United States when she was in elementary school. She understands firsthand what it is like to learn English and live in a place that is very different. Debra and Maria are exceptional teachers because they make the effort to learn about their students' lives and, by doing so, connecting culture to language learning comes easily.

LANGUAGE LEARNING IS A LONG-TERM PROCESS

Learning a new language takes a long time, and learning a language for academic purposes is an especially long-term process. When beginning a discussion on language learning, one must first examine the differences between social and academic language. Cummins (1981a, 1981b, 1984, 1986, 1996) popularized the distinction between two levels of proficiency: What are the differences between social and academic language? Cummins defines fluency in basic conversation as basic interpersonal communication skills (BICS), whereas language learners who can negotiate more complex cognitive language demands have successfully mastered cognitive academic language proficiency (CALP). When learning any new language, a learner may be knowledgeable at several possible levels. Conversational proficiency is considered fairly easy to acquire because it can be obtained within a few years; however, academic proficiency typically takes from 4 to 7 years—if the students have already received a minimum of 4 years of schooling in their primary language (Collier & Thomas, 2002). Collier and Thomas emphasize that the greatest predictor of success in learning a second language is the amount of time a student is schooled in his or her first language. They find that short-term ESL programs are ineffective, especially when students are limited in their English ability. Because academic language is necessary for academic achievement, teachers can support ELLs by specifically teaching language and generally increasing the comprehensibility of classroom language. Most important, teachers and administrators must realize that the accountability system of the U.S. law No Child Left Behind (NCLB) does not take into consideration the unique needs of ELLs.

LANGUAGE IS LEARNED THROUGH MEANINGFUL USE AND INTERACTION

Research now shows that students learn a new language best when they are encouraged to interact with others. Such meaningful interaction takes place in Debra and Maria's classes because they find ways to connect students' backgrounds to the learning that takes place in the classroom. Earlier in this chapter, we described how Debra and Maria's understanding of language issues informed a mathematics lesson. Now, we turn to reading instruction. Recently, students voted as a class to read *The House on Mango Street* by Sandra Cisneros (1994). Debra gives students a choice regarding the books they want to read and discuss for literature circles. Literature circles are student-led groups composed of four to six students, in which each group member is assigned a role to help guide the group in discussion. At the beginning of the year, Debra trains her students on the various roles. Literature circles typically take about 3 weeks to complete, and mini reading lessons are taught during the same block of time. The mini lessons that Debra teaches focus on reading strategies or literature circle procedures. She teaches these mini lessons at times when they are most relevant. For example, when she noticed that several students assigned as the "word wizards" were having difficulty using the dictionary to look up words, she taught a mini lesson on how to use the dictionary. The mini lessons usually take about 10 minutes at the beginning or end of the 45-minute reading period.

Debra very briefly discusses these roles prior to forming the circles; however, students can also refer to a chart displayed on the wall for the specific roles (see Figure 3).

Literature circles provide a way for students to share their thoughts, concerns, and understandings of a book. Using Cisneros's book, students make connections to their own lives by comparing and contrasting their lives with the main character's life. Students work together to discuss literature in a meaningful and enjoyable environment.

LANGUAGE LEARNING INVOLVES A COMMUNITY

Using a metaphor to describe the teaching of reading, Smith (1987) states that people learn from other people, not by conscious emulation but by *joining the club* of people they see themselves as being like. In the classroom, teachers like Debra develop an environment in which reading is a learning process and a community effort. What is interesting about Smith's metaphor is that students in the literacy club are learning about reading, and they are not expected to be experts. Students join the literacy club when they begin to understand that reading has meaning in their life. Teachers like Debra help students understand how important reading is to their lives. She does this by

- providing a wide variety of literature in the classroom: fiction, nonfiction, Spanish and English books
- inviting people from the Mexican American community to enhance units of study
- integrating video and technology into her lessons
- using the language experience approach (LEA) to write about events the class witnessed. The LEA involves the learner sharing a personal story with the class as the teacher writes the students' words on paper. Then the teacher and student read the written story together.
- implementing a reading partnership between classes

Reading instruction in Debra's classroom is a community effort. She shares with students her thoughts on the books she is reading, while students gain confidence to share what they like to read. Developing such a community begins during the first week of school with the reading partnership. The reading partnership is one way that Debra thinks her students begin to value reading. Each year, her fifth-grade dual-language students are paired with a second-grade dual-language class. The fifth graders read to the younger students, and both groups gain fluency in English. Debra teaches

Word Wizard

You are responsible for analyzing unfamiliar or challenging words in the selection. You will need to identify three difficult words, guess what they mean, and then actually them up in the dictionary. Please include the page numbers where the words can be found so your group members can discuss the words.

Literary Luminary

You are responsible for choosing two passages from the reading selection to share with your group. These passages may be chosen because you find them interesting or funny. You can share these passages with your group by choosing someone to read them aloud or by reading them aloud to the group.

Reporter

You are responsible for summarizing the selection that is read. You need to summarize the main events that happened in the story. After sharing the summary, you will encourage group discussion and clarify when needed.

Connector

You are in charge of sharing the connections you made as you read the selection. You can make text-to-self, text-to-world, or text-to-text connections. After sharing these connections, you give the rest of the group time to share any connections they made as they read the text.

Discussion Director

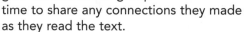

Your job is to form discussion questions. You will also be responsible for encouraging group discussion among members. Most important, you will serve as a leader for your group by making sure that everyone participates.

Figure 3. Literature Circle roles
Source: Daniels, 2001; Lacina, 2004

the fifth graders several strategies (Freeman & Freeman, 2003) that they can use when working with the younger students:

- Partner reading: The fifth graders often read to the second graders, and they are taught to use their finger to follow the words while reading.

- Echo reading: The fifth graders read with the second graders. When the second graders are not confident, they can listen to the fifth graders read. When the second graders are reading confidently, the fifth graders can fade out.

- Picture walk: The fifth graders go through the pictures in a book, discussing what is happening in the book. The two groups of students make predictions based on the text's pictures.

Although the fifth graders are serving as tutors to the second graders, both groups of students benefit. The fifth graders learn strategies to teach the second graders, and they can use these same strategies when they struggle to read a text at their own instructional level. The second graders benefit because they are paired to read and respond to literature in an enjoyable and supportive environment. Both groups of students improve their English proficiency because they have access to a wide variety of books (Freeman & Freeman, 2003), and strategies are used to ensure that books are comprehensible.

Partner reading works especially well in the dual-language program because both groups of students, native-Spanish-speaking and native-English-speaking, are learning a new language. By learning explicit strategies for reading, students who are struggling with learning either English or Spanish can find multiple ways to figure out a word's meaning. Debra and Maria find that echo reading also benefits both groups of students, because they become fluent readers in both Spanish and English. Working together to form a reading partnership allows students to work on important reading skills while allowing older students to serve as mentors to younger students.

What Are Language Learning Strategies and Why Are They Important?

Language learning strategies are techniques that learners use to acquire and retain new information in and about the target language (Oxford, 1990; Rigney, 1978). Research indicates that although language learners at all levels use strategies (Chamot & Kupper, 1989), the more proficient learners typically use a wider range of strategies. Rubin (1975) gives us general characteristics of "good" language learners. A good language learner:

- is a willing and accurate guesser
- has a strong drive to communicate
- is rarely inhibited
- is prepared to attend to form
- practices

- monitors his or her own speech and the speech of others
- attends to meaning

Using Rubin's characteristics of good language learners, teachers can create ways to teach lessons to build students' language learning strategy repertoire. Teaching language learning strategies is essential in helping students decode texts and become independent learners in their second language. Chamot and O'Malley (1994) classified language learning strategies into three separate areas: metacognitive, cognitive, and affective. Learners use metacognitive strategies to improve their ability to learn. They use cognitive strategies to improve their thinking skills. Affective strategies involve other factors, such as learning style preference, that may impact the learner's ability to learn a second language. Table 3 gives explanations and examples of the various strategies that fall under these areas.

Teachers can analyze the strengths and weaknesses of their students' language learning strategies in order to teach mini lessons, showing students how to use such strategies more effectively. There are several guidelines to consider when selecting strategies. Echevarria and Graves (2003) suggest the following steps to teaching learning strategies:

1. *Determine levels of knowledge*: Teacher should first determine what students already know; this can be done either formally or informally. For example, a student reads a few pages of a nonfiction text out loud. Based on that short reading, a teacher can gather important information, such as reading level and

Table 3. Language learning strategies

Metacognitive Strategies	Explanation	Example
Advance organizer	Planning the learning activity in advance	Miguel reviews his notes prior to class. He has created a Venn diagram on which he contrasts the political processes in two countries.
Self-management	Trying to arrange the appropriate conditions for learning	Veronica sits near the teacher and the chalkboard in order to resist classroom distractions.
Self-monitoring	Checking one's performance as one speaks	Shushien notices that her listeners are not distinguishing what she is saying when she says words that begin with a *p* or *b* and, as a result, she consciously works on pronunciation.
Self-reinforcement	Giving oneself rewards for success	Jose notices that he is doing a better job with pronunciation and, as a result, he decides to reward himself by buying a special snack

(Continued on p. 72)

Table 3 (continued). Language learning strategies.

Cognitive Strategies	Explanation	Example
Repetition	Imitating other people's speech overtly or silently	Angelica listens closely to Anne speaking and tries to imitate her U.S. accent.
Resourcing	Making use of language materials, such as dictionaries	Keyko carries an English dictionary in her purse, and when she hears a new word, she looks up the meaning in her dictionary.
Translation	Using the first language as a basis for understanding or producing the second language	Juan uses Spanish, his L1, to translate difficult science vocabulary. By referring to his Spanish/English dictionary and translating new terms, he finds that he better understands his science textbook.
Notetaking	Writing down the general idea of a paragraph or a page in a text	Maria uses sticky notes when she reads her social studies textbook. After she reads a page, she writes down the main ideas and sticks them on the page. She finds that this strategy helps her better prepare for class discussions about the text.
Key word	Using key word memory techniques, such as identifying an L2 word with an L1 word that sounds similar.	Veronica remembers what Mrs. Smith told her in math class. She can sometimes use words from Spanish to help her learn new English words. She uses this strategy to remember the meaning of the math term *median*.
Transfer	Using previous knowledge to help language learning	When Mrs. Smith introduced mean/median/mode, Kha remembered a similar lesson from his fifth-grade class in Korea, and since he already knew how to calculate the mean/median/mode, he translated the steps in his mind from Korean to English.
Social Mediation Strategy	**Explanation**	**Example**
Cooperation	Working with fellow students on language	Mrs. Smith planned a cooperative learning activity in which a small group of students worked together to solve word problems. Less fluent English speakers were paired with fluent English speakers. Each student in the group had a responsibility, and the group worked together to ensure group success in correctly answering the math problem.

Source: adapted from Cook, 2004

comprehension. Likewise, the teacher may make informal observations at the beginning of the school year and find that many students do not know how to write an outline or how to take notes. As a result, the teacher may teach a mini lesson on how to create an outline when reading a nonfiction text.

2. *Select the strategy*: It is best to teach a strategy when a large number of students have not mastered the strategy. If only a few students have difficulty with a strategy, it would be best to teach a small-group mini lesson. When selecting a strategy, teachers should keep in mind that it is best to teach a strategy that students will need to use over and over again.

3. *Keep the steps simple*: When teaching a learning strategy mini lesson, it is important to keep the steps simple. Students are then more likely to remember the strategy. Teachers can help students remember important steps by using techniques such as underlining or highlighting important points. Acronyms are helpful to students as they learn a new strategy. For example, Echevarria and Graves (2003) recommend the editing strategy of copying, overall appearance of paper, punctuation, and spelling strategy (COPS) because it is an easy acronym to remember.

4. *Follow a teaching format*: When teaching the mini lesson, it is important to follow a simple format, such as the following.

   - Opening: The teacher introduces the mini lesson by connecting the strategy to what the students already know or to a previous mini lesson. He or she discusses the importance of the strategy and why and how it will be used. The teacher needs to state the learning objective—the goal of the lesson.

   - Teacher demonstration: The teacher demonstrates and models the steps of the strategy.

   - Guided practice: The teacher and students practice together, as the teacher guides the students in learning the new strategy.

   - Independent practice: The students practice on their own.

   - Lesson closure: When ending the mini lesson, the teacher typically reviews the steps and connects the lesson to future lessons. At this time, further independent practice may follow.

When teaching mini lessons, teachers may find it necessary to repeat a lesson later in the year or, if some students still struggle with a particular strategy, to reteach in small groups. Strategy mini lessons are effective language teaching techniques for teaching and scaffolding instruction in the content areas. Such mini lessons are effective because they are explicit and are designed with the students' needs in mind.

How Do Teachers Teach Language in the Content Areas?

Debra plans language learning activities to help her students comprehend difficult material in content areas such as mathematics, reading, and language arts. Content instruction requires students to have a strong command of the English language, including English phonology, morphology, syntax, semantics, and pragmatics, as discussed earlier in the chapter. This is a complex task considering that students must also master the domains of language when they read, write, speak, and listen to English (Echevarria & Graves, 2003).

As students progress through the various grade levels, nonfiction textbooks and content-area vocabulary become more cognitively demanding. For students to be successful in mastering the domains of language in all areas, ESL teachers need to collaborate with content-area teachers to plan instruction that scaffolds language learning.

Debra and Maria scaffold language instruction regularly. Debra reinforces the difficult scientific vocabulary for fifth grade by planning lessons to explicitly teach such vocabulary. She recently helped prepare students for an upcoming science unit by using daily oral language (DOL) in a reading/language arts lesson. DOL helps students recognize and correct mistakes commonly made in writing. During the DOL lesson, Debra teaches specific science vocabulary that Maria will use in a later science lesson. Debra knows that vocabulary learning will raise students' achievement scores (Cunningham & Stanovich, 1997). During the DOL lesson, Debra often links words and sounds in English to Spanish words and sounds. She also often thinks aloud as she shows students how they can examine parts of a word, such as the root, to determine meaning. Debra knows that ESOL students who are economically disadvantaged tend to be 2 years below the norm, but when vocabulary is explicitly taught, these same students make large improvements (Chall, Jacobs, & Baldwin, 1990). Teachers can help change these startling statistics when they embrace a curriculum that promotes the teaching of word knowledge, including exposing students to a wide variety of books and explicitly teaching words and their meanings (Scott, 2004). Debra spends quite a bit of time focusing on teaching vocabulary words for content-area instruction, and she regularly makes Spanish/English connections to new vocabulary words. Cook (2004) offers the following thorough list of effective ways to teach vocabulary to ELLs (and it is evident that Debra uses many of Cook's techniques):

- Link L2 sounds to sounds of the L1 word.
- Look at the meaning of part of the word.
- Note the structure of the word's parts.
- Put the word in a topic group.
- Visualize the word in isolation.
- Link the word to a situation.
- Create a mental image of the word.
- Associate a physical sensation with the word.
- Associate the word with a key word.

When Debra teaches vocabulary to prepare students for Maria's science lesson, students are better able to tackle the difficult nonfiction science text. Working together in this way, Debra and Maria scaffold content-area instruction and teach students vocabulary strategies that they can use to become more fluent readers and writers.

How Can Teachers Collaborate to Benefit English Language Learners?
Collaboration at Texas Elementary

Collaboration is essential as all educators seek to attend to language learning needs while also teaching subject matter. Debra and Maria's collaborative effort in a dual-language program is one element of collaboration in the whole school. Debra explains that collaboration in their dual-language program exists at several levels. There are seven fifth-grade teachers and even though planning formal collaboration can sometimes be difficult, the teachers take every opportunity to communicate and collaborate informally. For example, the team often discusses grade-level plans via e-mail. At the campus level, the principal collaborates with the grade level representative, who in turn communicates back to the grade-level team. Debra states, "We found that the more collaboration we have, the more efficiently we can run our school. It is a group effort to run our school." There are different levels of collaboration between Debra and Maria, and the focus remains on how to best teach students to tackle difficult nonfiction texts.

COLLABORATION AND STATE TESTS

At the fifth-grade level, Texas recently added the content area of science to the state-mandated assessment test. This is a particularly challenging subject because reading and understanding a nonfiction text is even more difficult when a child has limited English proficiency. Debra and Maria keep detailed data on each student's English language level, according to pre- and post-IDEA test scores, and on data from the Reading Proficiency Tests in English (RPTE). At the state level, Texas fifth graders who took the science TAKS test in English passed with a 64% passing rate, whereas only 23% of the students who took the science test in Spanish passed (Texas Education Agency, 2005). Such statewide statistics closely resemble the result from Debra's class—10 of her 15 students passed the science test in English. The stakes were especially high during the 2004–2005 school year, because for the first time students had to pass both the reading and math exams to be promoted to sixth grade. Debra states that such intense pressure is the reason many teachers leave the teaching field; however, she finds that when she collaborates with her dual-language partner, meeting such standards is more achievable.

Debra and Maria find that they have little time to meet face to face because preparing students for the TAKS test often means before- and after-school tutoring. However, they find that they can collaborate easily by e-mail. The following e-mail excerpt illustrates how Debra and Maria plan.

FROM: Maria 2/23/05

I thought we might have a fun day on Friday...but we still need to do the TAKS groups. You would be proud...they [the students] worked really hard....I don't think I've ever seen a group use so many of the strategies that we've taught them. ☺

FROM: Debra 2/23/05

Bless their hearts, they have worked their little fingers to the bone. A few random thoughts....Can we plan a short movie for Friday? If we do a short movie, we could watch the endangered species tape...and you could comment on a science perspective.

Through e-mail collaboration, the two teachers also discuss student assessment results and requirements, and they find that by collaborating they can better teach test-taking strategies to their students:

FROM: Debra 2/01/05

I know this is my 100th email...sorry.... Since I don't think I can get into your reading [scores], can you print out your Compass reading that contains the TAKS mastery graph and the TAKS Tutorial Report? I have your Master Report from the meeting. No hurry

FROM: Debra 2/01/05

Tutor me please. I know you cover the scantron w/ the transp. How do you mark it with out screwing up the transp.? Or marking on the scantron? Do you just jot it down on another piece of paper as you go? Unconfuse me.

FROM: Maria 2/01/05

I use a visavis marker (blue or red works best) and mark the answers on the transparency, as I'm checking I have a list (it's attached) and write down the # that they miss, or you could just do tally marks.

E-mail provides a simple and quick means to discuss assessment and test-taking strategies. With little after-school time now available for grade-level team meetings and planning, Debra and Maria take advantage of e-mail by consistently discussing methods for teaching and assessing their students. They find that e-mail allows them to better prepare and document student progress—all while they are collaborating to meet the needs of ELLs.

COLLABORATION AND CURRICULUM

Debra and Maria also collaborate to address the district curriculum and to discuss ways that they can work together to ensure success. This year, they decide to organize their dual-language reading curriculum, to conform to a new district curriculum calendar. A district curriculum coordinator organizes district-wide planning, and she outlines each skill or concept that should be taught, according to the Texas Essential of Knowledge and Skills (TEKS). The TAKS test is based on the TEKS, so the district creates a calendar of each skill or concept that must be taught every week of the year for every content area.

Each day of the year must be aligned with a TAKS standard and, as a result, keeping up with the district curriculum can be difficult when LEP students may need further language instruction. Debra and Maria find that they must collaborate to scaffold English and Spanish instruction in reading and language arts. Debra begins the year by teaching context clues in English, whereas Maria begins with how to draw conclusions in Spanish. They meet in the middle and, according to Debra, this allows each student to receive instruction in each skill in both the first and second language (see Table 4).

Working together to meet district as well as state mandates enables Debra and Maria to scaffold both Spanish and English instruction in reading. They find that by collaborating they can better meet high standards.

Table 4. Curriculum calendar, reading

Week	Skills Taught
1	Context clues/figurative language
2	Characterization
3	Multiple-meaning words/dictionary skills
4	Main idea, facts, and details
5	Main idea, supporting facts, and details
6	Context clues: prefixes, suffixes, and roots
7	Synonyms and antonyms
8	Sequence
9	Cause and effect
10	Predicting
11	Comparison across texts
12	Plot understanding
13	Summary
14	Continued summary
15	Drawing conclusions
16	Review and spiral of all reading skills
17	Continue of review and spiral

COLLABORATING TO MENTOR STUDENTS

Each spring, Debra and Maria plan an exciting evening for their students. They prepare an orientation to the middle school, in which teachers and students from the middle school present information. Attending the district middle school is often intimidating because it is currently the largest middle school in Texas. At the orientation, Debra and Maria strongly advocate that students continue their academic study in Spanish. When students continue taking Spanish classes in middle school, the language requirement is waived at the high school. Most important, Debra and Maria highlight all of the many benefits of being bilingual, including the fact that most of their former students place out of language classes when they take the Advanced Placement test for college.

The first dual-language class is graduating this year from the high school. Jose, a former student, is the high school class president. Many of the former Texas Elementary students are academically successful, with most planning to attend either a 4-year or 2-year college. Although Texas Elementary is just one success story, the success of the dual-language program model is well documented. Texas Elementary is successful in educating ELLs because students are taught in their native language while also learning a second language. Teachers make connections between students' home cultures and languages, and content-area instruction is sheltered. Most important, teachers like Debra and Maria provide a safe, nurturing environment in which students feel comfortable taking risks.

Case Study: The Grade-Level Meeting

The third-grade teachers at an elementary school in east Texas recently met to discuss strategies that they could use to help ELLs in regular education classes improve their reading performance on the state mandated TAKS test. Two years ago, the dual-language program was dissolved, and students normally served in the program were integrated back into regular classrooms. Reading scores on the TAKS test dropped dramatically, and as a result of the programmatic changes and increased emphasis on the test, many teachers decided to move to another school district.

On the third-grade team, Tammy was the only trained ESL teacher. She recently completed the four required courses for the ESL endorsement at Austin State University, and she passed the state-mandated ESL teacher's test, the TExES. She chose to teach in east Texas because she had lived her entire life in rural east Texas and she thought that obtaining the ESL certification would help her find a job more easily. Although she is now a certified ESL teacher, she had no field experiences in ESL prior to accepting her current teaching position. The other third-grade teachers, Anne and Barbara, received no formal ESL training. Like most teachers in Texas, they simply took and passed the ESL teacher's test because no course work is mandated for state teacher certification when teachers are already certified in another subject area. Unlike Tammy, Anne and Barbara are veteran teachers. Most of their former students were monolingual. Between these two teachers, they have more than 30 years of teaching experience.

As the teachers meet, they discuss strategies that they believe will work best to help ELLs read on grade level. They begin by discussing their concerns about the five ELLs enrolled in each of their classes. Barbara mentions that Mario has only been in the United States for 1 year. She cannot understand why he is not reading on grade level even though he received English instruction each day while in second grade. Barbara thinks that he is not reading a text that is motivating enough. She suggests that a more challenging text be assigned, one that is appropriate for his grade level. She explains that the instructional reading level should be used only to provide guided reading in small groups, and Mario would be more motivated if he could read texts appropriate for his age level, even though his instructional level is much lower. Barbara says that the ELLs are bound to improve their reading rates and fluency when more challenging texts are assigned.

Anne addresses another concern and mentions that several of her students appear to speak Spanglish and frequently interject Spanish words into the text when reading the third-grade basal reader. She suggests that each third-grade teacher administer a timed reading test each week to motivate the students to read more quickly and accurately.

Tammy remains silent throughout the meeting. Although she recently completed the ESL endorsement course work and feels like she is well prepared to teach reading to ELLs, she feels insecure about stating her ideas because she has no field experience in an ESL classroom. Likewise, she realizes that Barbara and Anne are the experienced teachers, and she feels that their suggestions for improving the ELLs' reading ability must be correct because they have many more years of teaching experience. If the decision were up to Tammy, she would provide more frequent opportunities for the students to read and reread texts at their independent reading levels.

Because Tammy remains silent, Barbara and Anne decide that they all will administer the timed reading tests each week so that the ELLs will learn to read more quickly and accurately. Barbara decides to give Mario more challenging texts because he is not reading what he should be reading at the third-grade level. The teachers decide to meet again the following week to discuss the test results from the timed reading test and to discuss worksheets they could use to better prepare their students for the TAKS reading test.

QUESTIONS FOR DISCUSSION

Actors

1. How would you characterize the teachers at this grade-level meeting? (List descriptive phrases for each individual.)

2. How does Tammy view her role as an ESL teacher?

3. How are the other teachers prepared to teach ELLs?

Issues

1. What concerns does Barbara mention to the other teachers? Are her concerns justified, and do you agree with the decision that she wants to make?

2. What concerns do you have about Tammy's ideas on how to work with Mario?

3. Should Tammy remain silent? What would you do if you were in her situation?

4. Should Tammy adapt her teaching style to fit the veteran teachers' styles?

5. Where can Tammy go for support, and should she look for other ways to find out what she can do to work with struggling ELLs?

Problems or Conflicts

1. List the problems or conflicts in this case.

2. Prioritize these problems according to their impact on the students at this grade level.

Solutions

1. Determine what Tammy can do to better work with struggling readers to bring them up to grade level.

2. How can Barbara and Anne better work with Tammy?

3. Determine how these Texas teachers can collaborate more effectively.

Summary of Main Ideas
1) Defining language means considering
a)   language—students' language background: validate and acknowledge
b)   literacy—students' background in their L1 and L2—use the L1 to scaffold and build on instruction in the L2
c)   culture—take into consideration students' cultural background and ways to integrate culturally relevant readings and materials into the curriculum
2) Components of language consist of
a)   Phonology
b)   Morphology
c)   Syntax
d)   Semantics
e)   Pragmatics
3) There are numerous program models
a)   ESL pull-out
b)   ESL self-contained
c)   Newcomers programs
d)   Early exit bilingual programs
e)   Two-way bilingual programs
f)   Sheltered English programs
g)   Structured immersion programs
4) Keys to building language proficiency
a)   Engage students in a challenging theme-based curriculum
b)   Draw on students' background
c)   Organize collaborative activities
d)   Create confident students

5) Teachers collaborate effectively to improve language learning
   a) By scaffolding language instruction throughout the content areas
   b) By holding high expectations for all students
   c) By planning cooperative learning activities
   d) By making a connection between the home and school environment
   e) By validating students' first language and culture
   f) By sharing and developing materials
   g) By analyzing student results on assessments

Internet Resources

Center for Applied Linguistics (CAL). (2006). Retrieved August 21, 2006, from http://www.cal.org/
> CAL is a private, nonprofit organization in which a group of scholars and educators research and address language-related problems. CAL offers numerous articles that address language learning instruction and research. CAL also provides teacher education professional development and materials.

Crawford, J. (2006). Language policy Web site and emporium. Retrieved August 21, 2006, from http://ourworld.compuserve.com/homepages/jwcrawford/
> This site has numerous articles and resources on the politics of language and learning.

Cummins, J. (2003). Dr. Cummins' ESL and second language learning web. Retrieved August 21, 2006, from http://www.iteachilearn.com/cummins/index.htm
> Cummins' Web site offers numerous articles and resources in the area of language instruction.

The National Research Center on English Learning and Achievement. (2006). Retrieved August 21, 2006, from http://cela.albany.edu/
> This center offers products and services to improve student reading and writing achievement.

Read, Write, and Think. (2006). Retrieved August 21, 2006, from http://www.readwritethink.org/index.asp
> Read, Write, and Think is a partnership between the International Reading Association, the National Council of Teachers of English, and the MarcoPolo Education Foundation. Resources in reading and language arts instruction can be accessed and downloaded at no cost. Exemplary lessons with connections to reading/language arts national standards are posted on this Web site.

CHAPTER 5

Culture

---(**CASE STUDY**)---

Teacher Mentoring and Social Studies

Cindy began teaching in 1978 in a rural east Texas timber town. This town experienced a large influx of Mexican Americans who sought employment in the timber industry, and the schools were largely unprepared for the language learning needs of its new students. A monolingual English speaker when she first began teaching, Cindy learned to speak Spanish, and sought ongoing professional development and training to better meet the needs of her students. Early in her teaching career, Cindy learned the important connection between home and school culture. She learned that she must integrate the two in the classroom—to meet the needs of her students and to interest them in the curriculum.

Cindy is currently teaching third-grade ESL at Texas Elementary School. Her passion for teaching has not waned over the years, and this passion to meet the needs of ELLs in her classroom is evident in the following e-mail she sent her principal to initiate a collaborative effort across grade levels to better prepare third-grade students for the state mandated assessment test:

> We need a Bridge class for all ESL students between 2nd and 3rd grade especially for those who never hear English spoken at home. We need time to concentrate on nothing more than Reading, Math, Phonics, and Word Study. And we need to make sure somehow that all the third grade teachers are ESL certified—that they can reach these kids somehow. We need to look at our second grade ESL staff. We have got to have some really STRONG teachers in there. We need to have a come to Jesus (the real one, not you!) meeting and iron out what is expected for ESL K, ESL 1st, ESL 2nd, and ESL 3rd grades. I realize that we have the TEKS (Texas Essential Knowledge and Skills) on each grade level that we can look at—but we ain't getting it done!

In the e-mail, Cindy emphasizes the importance of across-grade-level meetings to discuss the TEKS and grade-level expectations. Cindy realizes that integrating reading instruction throughout the content areas must begin before third grade. Preparing students for success begins in kindergarten, and teachers at all grade levels must collaborate for such success.

This year, Cindy is mentoring Julie, a new third grade teacher. Julie passed the ESL state certification exam without completing any university ESL course work. She thought that by taking the exam and becoming ESL certified, she would have a greater chance of finding a job. And she was right. Districts desperately search for ESL and bilingual certified teachers and, if necessary, they provide district-level test preparation sessions to prepare teachers to pass the ESL state certification exam.

Cindy and Julie confer daily, mostly on an informal basis. Both teachers understand the importance of integrating language learning strategies into each content area. In Texas, because social studies content is not tested on the state mandated exam until seventh grade, many teachers do not teach social studies each week. Cindy and Julie find that if they integrate literacy instruction into social studies, they can teach social studies while preparing their students for the TAKS reading test. At the same time, both teachers find that social studies is one content area in which they can integrate and celebrate the students' culture and language in the classroom.

Cindy works with Julie throughout the year to integrate social studies and literacy instruction to meet state and national standards. Their collaborative effort results in planned units of instruction and cultural celebrations, such as a Cinco de Mayo community celebration. Collaborative efforts encourage new teachers to become more involved in the Mexican holiday and, most important, provide a way for new teachers to research and learn about their students' cultural backgrounds. Although culture is a permeating factor throughout all aspects of ELL education, it is within the social studies classroom that teachers find ways to scaffold English instruction in the content areas.

PREREADING QUESTIONS

- What is culture?
- What role does culture play in child development?
- How does culture impact education at the Pre-K to fifth-grade level?
- What does it mean to be a culturally responsive teacher?
- How can cultural instruction be integrated into the curriculum?
- How do ESL and classroom teachers work together to integrate culture into the curriculum?

What Is Culture?

There are various definitions of *culture*, and anthropological theory describes and distinguishes between individual and group-oriented concepts of culture. Integrating culture into the curriculum means moving beyond merely celebrating customs, folklore, and festivals. For the purpose of this chapter, we discuss the distributive model of culture, which implies that cultural attributes, such as values and beliefs, may vary from individual to individual, but they tend to share some common attributes. The distributive model of culture rejects the assumption that all members of a particular culture must share the same values and beliefs. Most notably, this model recognizes traits shared between the members of the larger cultural group and those members of cultural subgroups (Garcia, 1994, 2002).

At Texas Elementary the distributive model of culture enables students' cultural backgrounds to be valued during the acculturation process. In the dual-language and ESL programs at Texas Elementary, learning about culture is fun and exciting. The programs focus on ways that students can learn about each other's culture heritage without rejecting a culture because it is different from the mainstream culture. Gibson and Ogbu (1991) explain that acculturation can be either additive or subtractive, and Texas Elementary exemplifies additive acculturation because the students' cultures and backgrounds are not rejected as students are immersed into a new language and culture. Teaching culture is an integral component of effective social studies programs, according to the National Council for the Social Studies (2006). As Cindy and Julie work together to plan ways to integrate culture into their social studies curriculum, Cindy explains how she collaborated with other teachers to plan school-wide cultural celebrations in the past, as a way to culminate a social studies unit:

> In my classroom of ESL Spanish-speaking third graders, I look for ways to include their culture in the things we learn in our classroom. The obvious and easiest ways are to celebrate the Mexican holidays such as 16 de septiembre and Cinco de Mayo. We read about what has made each of those days special for the Mexican people and then always do some sort of art or music project for each day. We have been fortunate to find a lot of history for both days on the Internet and that is another way the students can find out more about their own culture. Many of them celebrate these days—especially Cinco de Mayo—but have not the faintest idea why they do. Our music teachers always help out by teaching the kids special songs and dances for each of these days. We ask the students to wear costumes; the girls wear Mexican dresses and the boys wear white shirts, jeans, bandana scarves at the neck, and hats. We bring all of the school to the front of the building where the music teachers have moved the sound equipment out into the parking lot. There we have celebrated in song and dance many times as an entire school body. We have had wonderful times making large tissue paper flowers and "noise makers" out of water bottles and paper plates. We also make small Mexican flags for the students to hold and wave in rhythm to the songs. It is a great day for the kids and we also enjoy it!

Cindy has taught at several grade levels. As a first-grade team, Cindy explains that the teachers involved the entire school community in planning a cultural celebration as a culminating event to a Texas history unit:

> When I taught first grade—every year around Texas Independence Day we had a big multicultural unit about Texas under Six Flags. We had six first grade teachers and each one was responsible for providing information about each of the six flags that Texas has been under. We culminated the unit with a great feast of food specific to each of the Six Flags of Texas. Each teacher was responsible for making enough food for 125 kids and about 20 adults to celebrate each of the six flags. That was a lot of work—but also a lot of fun. The kids learned a lot about their heritage as Texans and we had a wonderful time doing it.

Cindy finds that in-depth studies that connect social studies and the students' cultural backgrounds are a way that she can make instruction meaningful to her students. The school-wide cultural events excite the entire school about special cultural celebrations, and Cindy likes to end units of study with such celebrations. Celebrating culture keeps Cindy excited about teaching—and most important, such celebration shows students that she cares about their backgrounds. Exemplary teachers have a passion for teaching, which is often ignited by the small daily successes of students and a continued quest for self-improvement (Allington & Johnson, 2002). Cindy is exemplary because she continually seeks new strategies and teaching methods to better meet individual student needs. Teachers like Cindy impact education at the local level by valuing students' backgrounds and by holding high academic expectations.

As noted by Banks (2002), teachers use various approaches to integrate culture into the curriculum (see Figure 1). The Contributions Approach, Level 1, is the lowest level of integration and is often used by teachers at the elementary school level. This approach includes only cultural celebrations and heroes in the curriculum. Although Cindy integrates culture through the Contributions Approach, she could better challenge the curriculum by integrating issues or problems from different points of view. Figure 1 illustrates how Cindy could move to higher levels of multicultural curriculum reform. Although she teaches using the Contributions Approach, she does encourage students to use their native language in her classroom, and she views their cultural backgrounds as an asset. By doing so, she combats subtractive acculturation at a local level. Cummins (2000) explains that recent legislative initiatives severely restrict the use of students' L1. By restricting the use of the L1, educators and schools are telling students that they do not value or respect students' cultural and language backgrounds.

Teachers like Cindy, who promote academic achievement while valuing students' cultural and linguistic backgrounds need to be highlighted more often in the media as a way to resist subtractive acculturation. Policy makers often search for easy answers to win votes, and increasing school achievement with easy answers is not realistic. To meet the needs of today's students, teachers must move beyond a mere Contributions Approach to higher levels of multicultural reform. Teaching students to understand

Approaches to Multicultural Reform

Level 1
The Contributions Approach: This is how Cindy currently teaches social studies. She focuses on holidays and cultures unique to the Hispanic students in her class.

Level 2
The Additive Approach: Cindy could teach culture in social studies by studying the diverse perspectives of Hispanics within her community. She could invite various guest speakers to add to the curriculum without changing the overall curriculum structure.

Level 3
The Transformation Approach: Cindy could teach by showing her students the perspectives of diverse cultural groups. She could do this by integrating literature written by diverse authors, or she could invite guest speakers to discuss current events.

Level 4
The Social Action Approach: Cindy could extend lessons on culture by encouraging students to take action to solve societal problems or injustices. For example, based on reading about immigration, Cindy's class could write letters to President Bush, decide on ways that their community could better support new immigrants, and design a plan of action.

Figure 1. Approaches to multicultural reform

cultural viewpoints includes showing students diverse perspectives and different ways that people develop their perspectives based on their cultural, religious, and linguistic backgrounds.

What Role Does Culture Play in Child Development?

Children's beliefs and values begin at home. Family greatly influences child development, and the development of culture begins with the home culture. As children grow and develop in the home, differences between the home and school cultures become evident. For example, values, beliefs, and practices influence how to express emotions and how to communicate. Children learn from their families what is viewed as acceptable behaviors. Some families may consider it respectful for a child to keep his or her head bowed when spoken to by an adult, whereas other families may expect a child to look the adult in the eye. Such communication patterns are learned in early childhood in the home culture. Overall, the home culture radically impacts a student's beliefs and values long before that student begins kindergarten.

When do attitudes of cultural or racial differences affect children? Teachers of young children often state that young children do not recognize cultural and racial differences. However, there is a body of research that disputes such a claim. According to Banks (2002), young children are aware of racial differences, and their attitudes toward diversity mirror the adults in their life (Cross, 1991; Lasker, 1929; Stephan, 1999). Research documents that when children are given a choice, their racial preferences reflect their own race. This is particularly true of Caucasian children, whereas African American and Mexican American children tend to have varied racial preferences. Banks attributes these results to the families' cultural attitudes because parents of color in the United States tend to socialize their children to function in both their own culture and the mainstream culture. Based on research in the area of young children and culture, it is evident that multicultural education must begin in the early school years. According to Banks, there are a number of ways that teachers and families can work together to reduce prejudice and support cultural pluralism:

- Provide children with positive and realistic images of ethnic or racial groups. Instead of always purchasing toys and books that represent the mainstream cultural group, purchase toys and books that have multicultural representations of various groups of people.

- Show interest in other cultures. When a parent is interested in a particular cultural group, a child is much more likely to also show interest. The same is true for teachers. To be a multicultural teacher, one must first be a multicultural person.

- Make friends from other cultures. Learn about a new culture from someone of that culture. Showing children that you value friendships with culturally different people teaches them that you see the importance of such friendships.

Overall, families and teachers of young children must model that they value and respect diverse cultural groups in order for young children to develop a positive view of diverse cultural groups.

How Does Culture Impact Education at the Pre-K to Fifth-Grade Level?

Historically, U.S. schools have maintained a dominant culture curriculum. According to Gay (2000), teachers often teach using a middle-class, Eurocentric framework that is blind toward other cultural groups. Such teachers often believe that school is the place to teach intellectual skills and that integrating cultural diversity into the curriculum is a waste of time. Most teachers want the best for their students; however, teachers are often not educated on how to best teach students from diverse cultural and racial groups. These same teachers believe that if they treat students differently, it equates to racial discrimination (Gay, 2000). What these teachers fail to realize is that what they regard as "good" teaching and learning may be different in other cultures. U.S. school structure revolves around the European American culture, and this structure impacts how teachers teach and treat students. For example, U.S. teachers have long expected students to be attentive during a direct instruction lesson. When students are not attentive or do not keep their eyes on the teacher's face, then the teacher may view the child as inattentive. In actuality, the student may be attentive, but is taught through his or her culture to show respect to the teacher by keeping his or her head bowed. In contrast, some cultures expect teacher-directed lessons. For example, unlike the United States' student-oriented, active approach to learning, the Japanese and Korean educational systems often emphasize a more teacher-directed approach to learning. Their learning philosophy is based on Confucius' philosophy of teaching and education, which places value on rote learning and memorization of the classics. This type of classroom conflicts with the way that ESL teachers are trained to teach in the United States (Lacina, 2001). Such cultural differences between educational systems often present a conflict between students and their U.S. teachers, so it is very important for teachers to become familiar with their students' cultural backgrounds so that they can best meet their learning needs. As teachers, we need to examine ourselves as *cultural beings*, which means we need to model what it means to be a multicultural person—and to reexamine our cultural ways of knowing.

What Does it Mean to Be a Culturally Responsive Teacher?

Culturally responsive teaching means that teachers use students' prior experiences, cultural knowledge, and learning style preferences as a frame of reference when designing the curriculum (Gay, 2000). There are numerous benefits to designing a culturally responsive curriculum, including the fact that students' cultural and linguistic backgrounds are valued and that there is a connection between prior background and the school curriculum. A variety of instructional strategies are used to teach the curriculum when teachers design lessons around students' learning style preferences and, as a result, more students have the ability to be successful in school. Culturally responsive teaching teaches students to value other cultures and enables them to learn about those cultures.

How can teachers create culturally responsive classrooms? Taking a tour of Cindy's classroom illustrates how to create a culturally responsive atmosphere:

As you enter the classroom, you see brightly colored posters and a huge map on a wall. The map documents where each student in the classroom has traveled and includes pictures of people from east Texas who are currently serving in the military. Cindy's class has been writing to soldiers all over the world. Cindy explains that through this project, she can connect two subject areas: writing and geography. Next to the map is a featured poster, the Hispanic Hall of Fame, on which successful Hispanic men and women are highlighted with their accomplishments.

The shelves of Cindy's classroom are filled with rows of children's books, displaying a wide variety—mysteries, biographies, and memoirs. Most notably, there are books written by people from various ethnic and cultural groups, including books about the daily lives of people from a variety of cultural backgrounds.

On another wall, there is a large Word Wall, in which definitions of nouns, verbs, and adjectives are displayed in both Spanish and English. Student desks are clustered in groups because Cindy's teaching is student centered, and students are divided into cooperative learning groups. She circles around the room, assisting individuals and groups when they need help. As she begins to teach a social studies lesson, she starts by discussing new vocabulary and makes connections to Spanish words. When students do not quite understand English words, Cindy explains the words in Spanish. She finds ways to integrate more than just cultural celebrations into her classroom by building on students' backgrounds and connecting children's literature throughout the curriculum. Cindy shows students that she values and respects their backgrounds by attending their personal cultural celebrations after school.

This brief tour of Cindy's classroom demonstrates how positive imagery can create a culturally responsive climate. Taking a look inside a classroom provides information about a teacher's teaching philosophy. When a classroom has posters and books that represent a variety of cultural groups and more than one language that is valued, a culturally responsive teacher is likely to be found there. Cindy's classroom exemplifies a warm and caring classroom, one in which students learn about other cultural groups in an accepting environment.

How Can Cultural Instruction Be Integrated in the Curriculum?

The importance of integrating the study of culture into the curriculum is recognized at the national level. For example, culture is noted by the National Council for the Social Studies (NCSS, n.d.) as one of the ten thematic strands of social studies. The NCSS states that all teachers "should possess the knowledge, capabilities, and dispositions to organize and provide instruction at the appropriate school level for the study of Culture and Culture Diversity" (para. 1).

NCSS also suggests several ways teachers can address culture in the classroom:

- Explain ways that different groups or cultures address human concerns.

- Guide students to understand and predict how people from different cultural perspectives make decisions.

- Discuss cultural unity, and ask students to provide examples of such unity throughout the world.

- Discuss cross-cultural understanding, and facilitate student discussion of ways to implement such understanding.

- Guide learners as they construct judgments about specific cultural responses to human issues.

How Do ESL and Classroom Teachers Work Together to Integrate Culture Into the Curriculum?

In Texas, the state social studies standards are based on the NCSS standards. Like teachers in many high-stakes testing states, Cindy and Julie find that they must integrate social studies with another content area that is tested on the state exam. Otherwise, teachers often do not have the time to teach the given content area. In working with Julie to plan the third-grade social studies curriculum, Cindy emphasizes the integration of social studies/culture and reading instruction, and she shows Julie the connection between the TEKS and culture/social studies. Then Cindy shows Julie how she aligns the TEKS objectives for reading and social studies to her daily lesson plans.

TEKS

(12) Culture. The student understands ethnic and/or cultural celebrations of the United States and other nations. The student is expected to:

(A) explain the significance of selected ethnic and/or cultural celebrations in Texas, the United States and other nations such as St. Patrick's Day, Cinco de Mayo, and Kwanzaa; and

(B) compare ethnic and/or cultural celebrations in Texas, the United States and other nations. (Texas Education Agency, 2005b, p. 21)

To teach part of this standard, Cindy and Julie decide to design a unit around the theme of Cultural Celebrations around the World, in which they will compare ethnic and cultural celebrations in Texas and the United States with those in countries around the world. They begin planning by examining ways they can meet the TEKS standard using children's literature and language literacy strategies. Cindy finds that when she designs thematic units, she can more easily integrate the curriculum, and there are numerous benefits for ELLs (see Figure 2) because teachers highlight connections between more than one content area (Carrasquillo & Rodriguez, 2002, p. 108).

Cindy mentors Julie in ways to best scaffold instruction to meet the needs of ELLs. Julie also contributes to the collaborative relationship by sharing new and fresh ideas for teaching that she learned from her teacher education program, such as integrating literature circles into the curriculum and using a workshop approach in reading and writing. Cindy is eager to find new ways to meet the needs of her students. By working together, both teachers benefit, as do their students.

PRIOR BACKGROUND KNOWLEDGE

When beginning the unit, Cindy and Julie first find ways to access students' prior knowledge. They explain that integrating the students' background knowledge into each lesson is essential in social studies. Research supports that in order for students to learn a new concept, they must make connections to what they already know (Beck & McKeown, 1991; Tomkins, 2003). Research in the area of social studies suggests that students often do not have a firm grasp of the central themes of the discipline (Beck & McKeown, 1991), and because expository texts are often very difficult for ELLs to process, reading and understanding social studies textbooks can be a struggle.

Thematic Approach	Advantages for ELLs
The teacher highlights connections between and among various content areas. Objectives are made clear to learners.	The teacher introduces same concept using different content areas, mediums, and activities. Providing different learning opportunities to accomplish a particular objective increases understanding in the classroom.
Metacognitive strategies and objectives are incorporated within the unit.	Students are not as afraid to try something new or different because it is acceptable to make educated guesses. LEP students can practice different types of study skills that facilitate a more extensive variety of ways to learn one concept.
Learning opportunities are available for all students.	This promotes positive attitudes toward reading and writing.

Figure 2. Thematic approach and advantages for ELLs

Source: adapted from Carrasquillo & Rodriguez, 2002

Background knowledge and sheltered English instruction are the keys to teaching in the content areas. Teaching language learning strategies for reading expository texts provides students with the tools necessary to better understand the text. There are numerous ways that educators can access prior knowledge so that students can begin to make personal connections to difficult content area vocabulary. Graphic organizers are one way to begin planning a unit; they access students' background knowledge because students think about what they know about a particular event or concept. Students often come up with new ideas as they hear their peers brainstorming ideas. As students read and learn more information about an event, the class can record new information learned on the graphic organizer.

VOCABULARY

Vocabulary instruction is a major aspect of learning a new language (Cummins, 2000). Academic vocabulary and language structures tend to be very different from those language structures found in ELLs' homes and, for that reason, there is a gap between the home and school oral vocabulary and school vocabulary (Heath, 1983; Scott, 2004; Zentella, 1997). To close this gap, researchers suggest a comprehensive approach that includes explicit vocabulary instruction, word consciousness, and wide reading (Scott, 2004). Cindy thinks vocabulary instruction is important, especially social studies. One of the first things visitors notice when entering her classroom is a wall devoted to words. Cindy shows Julie how she keeps a word wall to teach social studies vocabulary and, during the year, Julie begins to create a word wall for her class. When the class learns new social studies vocabulary words, the words are posted on the wall. Cindy also uses concept maps to explain the definitions of words and for students to brainstorm synonyms the words. For example, for her current unit, she has posted the concept map shown in Figure 4.

Topic: Cinco de Mayo		
What I Know	**What I Want to Know**	**What I Learned**

Figure 3. What do I know about Cinco de Mayo?

Cindy finds that students refer to the wall when they integrate new words into their writing. It is an excellent reference for students when they learn English because the word wall words are used in social studies as well as reading lessons. Because Cindy's students are all native Spanish speakers, she makes a point of posting English words and their Spanish translations.

SCAFFOLDED CONTENT INSTRUCTION

Social studies instruction needs to be concerned with more than facts and terminology. Social studies is a content area that can help ELLs better understand their new country (Carrasquillo & Rodriguez, 2002). Because ELLs are often placed in content classes, it is important that all teachers be familiar with strategies for integrating language and content-area instruction (Gibbons, 2002). In content-area instruction, language can be taught through scaffolding, which is a metaphor used to describe how teachers temporarily assist students in learning a new skill. The goal of scaffolding is

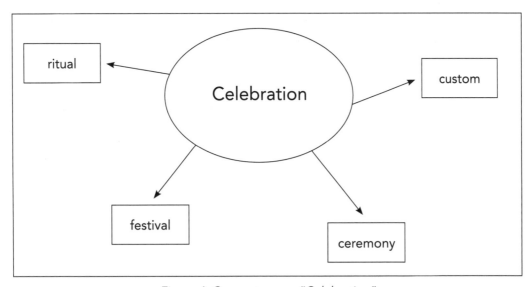

Figure 4. Concept map—"Celebration"

for students to think and work independently. Cindy shows Julie how she plans to integrate and scaffold social studies and reading instruction by integrating activities before, during, and after reading. For example, she uses visual organizers and semantic maps throughout the unit. After students read books about Cinco de Mayo and the Fourth of July, Cindy posts a Venn diagram on the board. She uses it to help guide her class in distinguishing the differences between the two celebrations.

By comparing and contrasting two holidays, Cindy meets the social studies standard for third grade, and she helps her students better understand the similarities and differences between Mexico and the United States.

TRADEBOOKS IN SOCIAL STUDIES

Textbooks are traditionally read in the social studies classroom. For ELLs, the social studies textbook is often difficult to read because topics are not discussed in depth and they read much like an encyclopedia (Tompkins, 2003; Vacca & Vacca, 2005). Tradebooks tend to be written in narrative form and can enhance the content introduced through the studies textbook. Material in tradebooks tends to be interesting and well organized, as opposed to some textbooks that simply present a list of facts (Vacca & Vacca, 2005). Most important, tradebooks allow the reader to connect to characters in the story. Using tradebooks in the classroom is an effective way to interest students in another culture because students can view a culture through the eyes of the main character. Cindy emphasizes the importance of integrating historical literature into the social studies classroom. Students in her class have a block of independent reading time each day, and they can choose which book they are most interested in reading. She finds that students better understand social studies when it is presented through a variety of methods, such literature, films, dramatizations, or even song.

COOPERATIVE LEARNING AND SOCIAL STUDIES

Cooperative learning and social studies are part of the everyday routine in Cindy's class. For ELLs, cooperative learning provides a nonthreatening environment in which

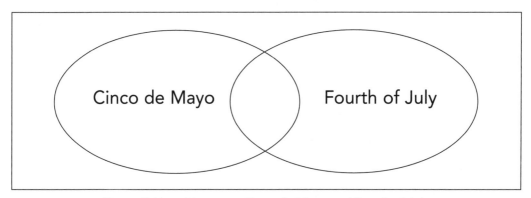

Figure 5. Venn Diagram—Cinco de Mayo and Fourth of July

to learn English and enables students to learn from one another. Most important, cooperative learning teaches children to work together to solve a problem or complete a project, a skill that is relevant to learning outside of school. Cooperative learning groups are heterogeneous and interdependent (Johnson, Johnson, & Holubec, 1990, 1991; Slavin, 1981, 1990); each student is assigned a different task. There are many different cooperative learning structures that allow students to interact and learn in a student-centered environment, several of which are summarized and integrated with NCSS (n.d.) ways to address culture in Figure 6.

Cooperative learning is an excellent way to meet NCSS standards because students are guided to understand and predict how other people think and make decisions. Cooperative learning is a helpful way to discuss other cultural groups' perspectives, and such groups allow ELLs to feel comfortable speaking while they are developing English fluency.

Cooperative Learning Structure	NCSS Ways to Address Culture	Classroom Example
Think-Pair-Shair	Discuss cultural unity—and ask students to give examples of unity throughout the world.	Students are given a problem or question, and they are to think quietly of an answer. For example, in Cindy's class, she asks students, "Why is the 4th of July not celebrated in Mexico, and is there a similar celebration for Mexicans?" Students discuss their answers with their group, and then they share with the entire class. This is a good way to assess students' understanding.
Student-Teams Achievement Division (STAD)	Guide students to understand and predict how people from different cultural perspectives make decisions.	After discussing a chapter in the third-grade social studies text about how different cultures make decisions, Cindy divides students into teams of three or four to discuss how, for example, people from different cultural backgrounds may make decisions. Each team works together to answer the questions and to discuss their rationale for their answers. Once the groups have completed the task, Cindy asks for each group spokesperson to orally summarize the group's findings.
Constructive Controversy	Guide students to understand and predict how people from different cultural perspectives make decisions.	Pairs in groups of four are assigned different sides of an issue. For example, Cindy assigns a group to discuss the British perspective of why the colonies should remain loyal to England, and the other group discusses why the settlers sought independence. Each group researches its assigned position and discusses the issue in depth. Using this cooperative learning structure allows students to better understand issues from multiple perspectives.

Figure 6. Cooperative learning structures   *(Continued on p. 96)*

Cooperative Learning Structure	NCSS Ways to Address Culture	Classroom Example
Pairs Check	Discuss cultural unity, and ask students to provide examples of such unity throughout the world.	Students work in pairs in groups of four. Within pairs students alternate roles; one solves a problem while the other coaches. For example, Cindy asks the students to find similarities between how different cultural groups came together during a time of crisis. Cindy gives each pair a list of four countries to research. After every two problems, the pair checks to see if they have the same answers as the other pair. Cindy uses this strategy when she checks for student understanding of textbook or tradebook reading. She has these groups of students answer and coach one another as they answer questions about the textbook reading.
Roundtable/ Circle of Heads	Explain ways that different groups or cultures address human concerns.	Each student in turn shares something with his or her teammates. For example, Cindy wants to move beyond mere cultural celebration in her unit. She wants her students to analyze and better understand how other people think. After viewing a film on poverty, Cindy asks cooperative learning teams how Mexicans address poverty. In their cooperative learning groups, each student writes one answer, as a paper and pencil are passed around the group. The group then discusses their responses and then the group spokesperson shares their discussion with the class.
Jigsaw	Discuss cross-cultural understanding— and have students discuss ways to implement such understanding.	Each student on the team becomes an "expert" on one topic, and for this unit, the topic is a cultural celebration. First, the team members divide into expert groups, prior to meeting with their cooperative learning group. Each expert reads and discusses a short newspaper clipping, which highlights religion's role in cultural celebrations throughout the world. When students return to their teams, each student teaches the group about their topic— and as a group, they discuss cross-cultural understanding. Then, the group spokesperson summarizes what the group learned to the rest of the class.

Figure 6 continued. Cooperative learning structures

COLLABORATION AND TEACHER MENTORING

Collaboration between third-grade teachers at Texas Elementary involves teacher mentoring. Cindy works with Julie throughout the school year to plan and develop thematic units of study. Such a collaborative effort is important, because most new teachers tend to be isolated from colleagues. One of the best ways to support and retain new teachers is to provide a new teacher support system. By pairing Julie with a veteran teacher, Texas Elementary is working to mold Julie into an exemplary teacher. There are a number of reasons that Cindy is an exemplary teacher—and the perfect mentor for Julie. Cindy is an experienced ESL teacher, and she is knowledgeable about addressing the unique needs of ELLs while at the same time meeting the needs of the regular education students in her mainstream class. Most important, Cindy shows Julie through her own personal characteristics and beliefs what it takes to be an exemplary teacher. Cindy is warm, respectful of students, and enthusiastic about teaching and learning. She respects diversity and believes that modeling and class-room talk are essential in the classroom (Allington & Johnson, 2002). She includes a variety of books in the classroom, and she connects students' cultural background to units of study. Each social studies lesson she teaches has a strong literacy component, and state and national standards guide her curriculum. Throughout the school year Cindy shows Julie, through her own example, how to integrate and teach culture in social studies. She also shows Julie how to focus on students' strengths, such as their bilingualism and cultural background. First-year teaching should not be a "survival" year. Effective mentors are teachers who model the idea of lifelong learning, and they possess an eagerness and excitement to learn new information throughout the content areas. The same is true for effective mentees. Effective mentees are eager and open to learn from their mentor teacher. Not only are they open to considering their mentor teacher's ideas for teaching and learning, but they also contribute to the relationship by sharing innovative strategies they learned from other teachers or from their teacher education program. Effective collaboration does not occur in one-sided partnerships, in which only the mentor teacher shares ideas for teaching. New teach-ers have a wealth of exciting, new strategies to share with experienced teachers. Each and every student deserves a fully competent teacher, and through such mentoring and collaborative partnerships, exemplary new teachers can be created and retained.

Case Study: Writing to Soldiers in Iraq

Cindy is passionate and patriotic. Her son is currently serving in the U.S. army in Iraq, and she learned from him how important it is for U.S. service men and women to receive letters of support, because such support boosts their morale. For that reason, Cindy decided to develop a letter-writing project with her son's unit in Iraq. It is a good way to connect writing instruction and geography, and she has found that students are more apt to want to write when they have a real purpose for doing so. Likewise, she has students map the soldiers' hometowns in the United States on the map—and then map where they travel in the Middle East.

Cindy decides to expand this project because of the success in corresponding with her son's unit. Another U.S. Army unit expressed interest in corresponding, so Cindy asks Julie if her class would also like to write letters to the soldiers. In introducing the project to Julie's class, Cindy asks the students what they know about Iraq. Here are a few of their responses:

Student 1: Iraqis are terrorists.

Student 2: Iraqi people hate Americans.

Student 3: Iraqis killed Americans on 9-11.

Cindy was shocked to find such blatant stereotypes, and she conferred with Julie after class to discuss ways that they could plan a unit on Iraq to discuss similarities and differences between the Iraqi and the U.S. perspectives and cultures. She thought that if they planned such a unit, stereotypes could be dispelled or at least questioned. Cindy thinks discussing stereotypes could go hand-in-hand with the writing project. When discussing this idea with Julie, Cindy discovers that Julie's beliefs about the Iraqi people are similar to those held by the students. Julie says, "Why would we want to teach students anything else? Our American soldiers are dying daily to fight for freedom. If it were not for terrorists in Iraq, thousands of people would be alive today. Of all people, Cindy, I would think you would be passionate for the U.S. cause. It seems unpatriotic to teach anything else."

Based on this conversation, Cindy is not sure what to do. To meet state and national cultural standards, Cindy knows that she must teach cultural understanding and cultural similarities. Julie does not share the same beliefs, and Cindy is not sure how she can make Julie understand cultural similarities. How can a teacher teach such a standard when her personal beliefs conflict with the standard? Cindy decides to confer with the school district's elementary curriculum coordinator to find out if there are any in-service training opportunities that she and Julie could attend together to better learn how to teach about Iraq. She also considers asking Julie to observe her teaching a lesson on stereotypes, an interesting and compelling lesson designed by Teaching Tolerance (Sapp, 2004). Cindy thinks if she approaches the teaching of culture as a way to meet state and national standards, Julie may better understand the importance of teaching cultural similarities. Cindy also enlists the help of a local Iraqi family; she invites the family to present information about their immigration to the United States and to describe their cultural customs and perspectives. Prior to their presentation, Cindy teaches both third-grade classes questioning skills, and they brainstorm questions to ask the family. She thinks that if students, and Julie, can hear the perspectives of a local family, then stereotypes may be dispelled, or at least questioned.

QUESTIONS FOR DISCUSSION

Actors

1. How would you characterize Cindy and Julie? (List descriptive phrases for each individual.)
2. How does Cindy view her role as an ESL teacher?
3. Why does Cindy feel responsible for working with Julie?

Issues

1. Do you think Cindy's concerns are justified?
2. What concerns do you have about Cindy's ideas on how to work with Julie and the students?

3. Should Cindy confront Julie, or should she mention Julie's obvious stereotypes to the principal because she is Julie's assigned mentor?

4. Should Julie adapt her teaching style to fit Cindy's style?

Problems and Conflicts

1. List the problems or conflicts in this case.

2. Prioritize these problems according to their impact on the students at this grade level.

Solutions

1. Determine what Cindy can do to help break down stereotypes in the classroom.

2. How can new teachers like Julie be better prepared to teach about other cultures?

3. Determine how these teachers can collaborate more effectively.

Summary of Main Ideas
1) The distributive model of culture means that
a)   group members and larger cultural group share traits
b)   values and beliefs may vary
c)   cultural background is valued during acculturation
2) Culture plays a role in child development because
a)   beliefs and values begin at home
b)   young children's beliefs mirror the beliefs of adults in their life
c)   children tend to have racial preferences when given a choice
3) Teachers and parents can support cultural pluralism by
a)   providing realistic images of ethnic and racial groups
b)   showing interest in other cultures
c)   making friends from other cultures
4) Culture instruction can be integrated into the social studies curriculum by
a)   explaining ways that different groups or cultures address human concerns
b)   guiding students to understand and predict how people from different cultural perspectives make decisions
c)   discussing cultural unity
d)   discussing cross-cultural understanding
e)   guiding learners as they construct judgments about specific cultural responses to human issues
5) Ways to teach social studies to ELLs include the following:
a)   Access prior background.
b)   Teach vocabulary.
c)   Scaffold content instruction.
d)   Integrate tradebooks into the curriculum.
e)   Use cooperative learning groups.

Internet Resources

Bardovi-Harlig, K, & Mahan-Taylor, R. (2003). Teaching pragmatics. Washington, DC: U.S. Department of State, Office of English Language Programs. Retrieved August 21, 2006, from http://exchanges.state.gov/education/engteaching/pragmatics.htm
> This Web site includes articles on how to teach pragmatics. These articles highlight 30 lessons that teachers can use.

The Cooperative Learning Center. (2006). Retrieved August 21, 2006, from http://www.co-operation.org/
> This organization provides detailed resources on cooperative learning, such as research that teaches students to be peacemakers and to work well with others.

The Early Childhood Research Institute on Culturally and Linguistically Appropriate Services (CLAS). Retrieved August 21, 2006, from http://www.clas.uiuc.edu/aboutclas.html
> This institute is a federally funded collaborative effort of the University of Illinois at Urbana-Champaign. This organization's Web site includes numerous articles on culture and early childhood.

Integrated Curriculum for Achieving Necessary Skills (I-CANS). Retrieved August 21, 2006, from http://www.literacynet.org/icans/chapter01/overview.html
> This Web site provides a succinct overview of numerous cooperative learning structures.

Jigsaw Classroom. (2006). Retrieved August 21, 2006, from http://www.jigsaw.org/index.html
> This Web site provides a thorough overview of how to integrate this cooperative learning method into the social studies classroom.

National Clearinghouse for English Language Instruction. (2006). Retrieved August 21, 2006, from http://www.ncela.gwu.edu/resabout/culture/3_diversity.html
> This Web site provides a comprehensive list of articles, videos, and book reviews on language and culture.

Saville-Troike, M. (1978). A guide to culture in the classroom. Arlington, VA: National Clearinghouse for Bilingual Education. Retrieved August 21, 2006, from http://www.ncela.gwu.edu/pubs/classics/culture/index.htm
> This book is viewable online and presents a through guide of how to integrate culture into the classroom.

Multicultural Pavilion, Teacher's Corner. (2006). Retrieved August 21, 2006, from http://www.edchange.org/multicultural/teachers.html
> This Web site provides an overview of multicultural education and offers numerous teacher resources.

Multicultural Resources for Children. Retrieved August 21, 2006, from http://falcon.jmu.edu/~ramseyil/multipub.htm
> This comprehensive Web site provides a list of links for teachers, librarian, parents, and children.

The National Center for Cultural Competence. Retrieved August 21, 2006, from http://gucchd.georgetown.edu/nccc/
> This Web site provides articles on integrating culture into the classroom.

Teaching Tolerance. Retrieved August 21, 2006, from http://www.tolerance.org/index .jsp

This Web site is devoted to fighting hate and promoting tolerance. It offers numerous teaching resources and ideas.

Assessment

(CASE STUDY)

Collaborating to Bring a New Mindfulness to the Assessment of Math

Aimee Teason is a kindergarten teacher at Trest Elementary School in Missouri. She has been a teacher for 8 years. For 7 of those years she has taught kindergarten, and she spent 1 year teaching first grade. Aimee is in her second year of teaching a sheltered English kindergarten class. In sheltered English classes, the teachers teach both language and content in order to help ELLs keep up in the content areas and continue to develop academic English. Although Aimee is a certified elementary school teacher, she does not have ESOL certification. She has, however, been taking classes to obtain her ESL endorsement. There are four kindergarten classes at Trest Elementary; two are for native speakers of English, and the other two, including Amy's, are sheltered English classes. All the teachers except Carla Portillo, who teaches the other sheltered class, are native speakers of English who speak very little Spanish or any other language.

Teachers of the same grade level at Trest Elementary meet twice a week to plan their lessons and assessments. During these meetings the kindergarten teachers discuss issues and challenges they have encountered in teaching lessons. They then give each other feedback and share ideas about how to best address problems they have in their classrooms.

Aimee is the grade-level chair and is responsible for facilitating the design of assessments and construction of rubrics with input from her colleagues. She and Carla always discuss the modifications they need to make for their sheltered classes.

The teachers make sure that their assessments are authentic and age appropriate. Furthermore, Aimee makes sure the assessments take into consideration the prior knowledge and cultures of all the students. In math, students are called on to demonstrate what they know and can do through the use of drawings, manipulatives, diagrams, and physical movement such as pointing. She scaffolds the assessments to make sure that students are able to perform the tasks using the language they already have. Aimee also makes sure that all the assessments in the sheltered classes focus on language and content. Her colleagues have found it helpful to do the same with their students who speak English as a first language as they work to develop their literacy skills.

PREREADING QUESTIONS

- What is assessment?
- What are the current issues in the assessment of English language learners?
- What kinds of criteria can be used to appropriately assess English Language Learners?
- What forms of assessment can be used for English language learners?
- How can ESL and mainstream teachers collaborate to assess English language learners in math?

What Is Assessment?

This chapter focuses mainly on assessment in the context of teaching and learning in classrooms. We approach assessment from a sociocultural perspective using Smith, Teemant, and Pinnegar's (2004) concept of sociocultural assessment, which expands upon Wiggins' (1998) idea of educative assessment. Authentic performance, ongoing feedback, and promoting student understanding are the essential elements of Wiggins' notion of educative assessment. Assessment is authentic and performance based when it asks students to perform meaningful intellectual, real-world tasks, which in turn demonstrate to teachers what students know and can do (Wiggins, 1998).

To this, Smith, et al. (2004) add the concept of equity for all students. Sociocultural perspectives of knowing, teaching, and learning form the basis of their definition of sociocultural assessment. Knowledge is viewed as understanding the language of a social group or culture and its shared meanings, ways of solving problems, and ways of thinking. Teaching in this perspective means assisting—that is, teachers scaffold and assess structured classroom activities. Learning is interactive and social, and students learn through constructing and negotiating meaning in cooperative groups. These perspectives of knowledge, teaching, and learning are crucial for teaching ELLs. Smith, et al., propose three concepts that summarize the idea of sociocultural assessment; to be sociocultural, assessment must be

- useful for stakeholders, including parents, teachers, administrators, and state and federal policy makers
- meaningful for its purposes

- equitable for all students. Feedback should be clear and based on specific criteria and should enable students to improve through a process of self-assessment. (p. 40)

Sociocultural assessment is especially important for ELLs because it focuses on learning and cultural understanding. Furthermore, it "provides the opportunity to integrate valued behaviors, cognitions and contextualized social performances into assessment activities" (Smith et al., p. 40). As with all assessments, it helps ELLs demonstrate what they can do and what they do and do not understand, and it gives them opportunities to master content and language.

IMPETUS FOR ASSESSMENT REFORM

The wave of reform in the 1990s, the introduction of standards, and new understandings of teaching and learning are three factors that brought a new focus to forms of assessment and the role of assessment as an impetus for reform (Farr & Trumbull, 1997; Lachat, 2004). While educators, administrators, and educational researchers worked on standards for content areas, they realized that effective learning, instruction, and assessment were inextricably intertwined. Consequently, as instruction was changed to reflect standards and curriculum frameworks, so were ideas about and forms of assessment. Research moved away from behaviorist views and toward more cognitive, constructivist views of learning. Recent research views learning as a constructivist process by which students participate in active knowing and thinking. As Lachat explains, "learners actively construct their understandings of the tasks and situations they encounter . . . develop as thinkers, not in isolation, but by organizing and reorganizing knowledge while they interact with others and negotiate shared understandings" (p. 19). Therefore critical thinking and problem solving in the process of building upon and discovering new knowledge are seen as paramount. Because assessment is ongoing and provides continuous feedback, students can take responsibility for their own learning and teachers can use information from these assessments to direct their instruction. The overall purpose of assessment, therefore, is to support and improve teaching and learning.

What Are the Current Issues in the Assessment of English Language Learners?

The diversity and specific characteristics of ELLs pose challenges to appropriate assessment. Current assessment issues address the complex interactions between culture, content, language, and standards.

CULTURE AND LANGUAGE

If ELLs are to do well in school, their cultures must be embraced and embedded in school contexts. Nieto (2002) defines culture as "the ever-changing values, traditions, social and political relationships, and worldview created and shared by a group of people bound together by a combination of factors" (p. 53). Cultural and linguistic factors, including race, ethnicity, social class, language, and religion, may be "key factors in explaining educational achievement" (p. 53). Because students come to school from different cultures, they most likely have different worldviews. Consequently, their modes of communication, ways of learning, demonstration of knowledge, and ways of solving problems may also be different (Lachat, 2004, p. 45). Given this understanding of culture and language, it is the role of teachers to learn about the diverse children in their classrooms and serve as bridges and cultural workers, between the school and mainstream culture and their students' home cultures. Furthermore, cultural workers defend and support their culturally and linguistically diverse learners to create conditions for their success in schools. The role of cultural worker or border crosser is imperative for teachers because "many children do poorly in school mainly because their cultural frames of reference do not match those of the mainstream culture reflected in American classrooms" (Lachat, p. 46).

Language, "the most widely used symbol system for learning and for representing knowledge (whether orally or in writing)" (Farr & Trumbull, 1997, p.120) is also crucial to the success of ELLs. Lachat (2004) illustrates how students' languages and cultures can be barriers to successful learning experiences for ELLs:

- Language use in schools does not match the cognitive and communication patterns of many ELLs' home cultures.

- The speaking patterns used for instruction are not familiar to many ELLs.

- To understand what is expected in a learning situation, these learners must have prior knowledge of the mainstream culture.

- The English facility of these students is insufficient for the language demands of many learning tasks. (p. 48)

To become effective cultural workers, teachers need to communicate with parents, their children, and communities to understand social mores, ways of teaching and learning, social interaction, and attitudes toward education (Diaz-Rico, 2004, p. 273). Teachers who are cultural workers and who collaborate with each other will link instruction and assessment to meet the needs of diverse learners.

CONTENT AND LANGUAGE

Research has increasingly demonstrated that second language instruction should be content-based. The effective integration of language and content helps strengthen learners' language development, academic skills, and content knowledge (Echevarria, Short, & Vogt, 2004; O'Malley & Valdez-Pierce, 1996; Short, 1993). By joining language and meaningful content, students are less likely to fall behind in subject-matter knowledge. Rather, they continue subject-matter learning and develop their English language skills at the same time.

To focus the instruction of ELLs on language and content, Echevarria, et al. (2004) introduced the Sheltered Instruction Observation Model (SIOP). This research-based model proposes that teachers of ELLs integrate and scaffold content and language so that language learning is contextualized. Learning language in context in the sheltered instruction classroom can also create sociocultural awareness, which is vital to the education of all learners (Short, 1993).

The SIOP model consists of three main components: preparation, instruction, and review or assessment. When preparing lessons, the model posits that lesson plans should specify both language and content objectives. A lesson plan that clearly states these objectives prepares the way for instruction that is more likely to integrate language and content successfully. Throughout their instruction, teachers of ELLs continually review and assess student comprehension of content concepts. (See the Resources section at the end of this chapter for more information on using the SIOP model.)

Whether the teaching and assessment of ELLs is conducted in sheltered classes, pull-out programs, or mainstream classrooms, ESL and classroom teachers need to collaborate to assess these children in all four skill areas: reading, writing, listening, and speaking. These skills should be integrated and contextualized in all assessments to develop and strengthen student ability to use social and academic language.

Language, oral or written, always influences assessment. With traditional paper-and-pencil tests or performance-based assessments, ELLs will most likely be required to use oral or written language. As Farr and Trumbull (1997) state, "even tasks that appear to be primarily visual (such as following a map or solving a jigsaw puzzle) are often mediated by language" (p. 120). Because language and content are interconnected in ways that make it difficult to separate the two, assessing the four skills and content can be a complex process. ELLs may understand the concepts being taught, but may not have the language to demonstrate their comprehension. In these cases teachers face the challenging task of determining "the language and content knowledge of their students and deciding if one is interfering with the demonstration of the other" (Short, 1933, p. 633).

Because language and content are inextricably intertwined, teachers should not attempt to separate the two, but rather reduce the amount of language that students might need in assessments by providing scaffolding, separate scoring of language and content, and clearly constructed rubrics (Farr & Trumbull, 1997; O'Malley & Valdez-Pierce, 1996; Tinajero & Hurley, 2001). O'Malley and Valdez-Pierce use the information in Table 1 to illustrate how the assessment of language and content can be scaffolded (p. 167).

Mathematics is one subject area in which ELLs frequently struggle with language and content. As O'Malley & Valdez-Pierce (1996) state, "virtually all students have difficulty with word problems, but ELL students can be expected to have even more difficulty because of the requirements for comprehending the verbal or written message and determining which operations are appropriate beyond having to execute the calculations correctly" (p. 191). Assessments using manipulatives, diagrams, physical movement, self-assessment, interviewing, and journal writing can "help young ESL students express their understanding of math concepts while building their English language skills" (Lee, Silverman, & Montoya, 2002, p. 30).

Table 1. Assessment with and without scaffolded prompts

Assessment Examples	Without Scaffolding	With Scaffolding
Define/describe object or concept.	Write a description of the object or concept and (if appropriate) label it.	Write a **list** of the main features of the concept, or provide labels for objects in a **picture** that is **provided**.
Provide examples of a concept and justify them.	Provide three examples and explain orally or in writing why these are good examples.	**Select** three examples from a **list provided** and explain **orally** why they were selected.
Retell or summarize text.	Write five main ideas from an article and give examples	Complete an **outline**, a **T-List**, or a **semantic map**.
Write a word problem.	Create a problem from own numbers; give equation, story, and question.	Complete a word problem **given examples and an outline** of a sample problem.
Summarize a science experiment.	Write a summary of procedures in a science experiment following scientific principles.	**Complete** a summary **given a list** of procedures in science experiments, including questions, materials, a plan, observations, and conclusions, or **demonstrate** the steps using actual materials.

Source: O'Malley & Valdez-Pierce, 1996, p. 167

In Aimee Teason's kindergarten class, the children understand the word *illustrate*. The students use drawings to demonstrate their understanding of simple addition word problems. To assess their comprehension, Aimee reads a word problem aloud and asks them to illustrate the problem using drawings as well as numbers.

What Kinds of Criteria Can Be Used to Appropriately Assess English Language Learners?

For all students, and ELLs in particular, it is vital to provide assessments that are culturally relevant. Smith, et al. (2004) state that teachers can use three concepts of sociocultural assessment as guidelines to determine if their assessments are appropriate and culturally relevant. Assessments must be useful, meaningful, and equitable.

USEFUL

Assessment is useful when it informs and drives instructional practices. Useful assessment is practical and sustains and improves student learning and performance (Smith et al., 2004). Examples include checklists of student behaviors or products, journals, reading logs, and self-evaluation questionnaires. Aimee uses informal observations and assessments of her ELLs to inform her instruction:

In her sheltered kindergarten math class, Aimee assesses how well the students have developed an understanding of counting by having them find matching sets using dot cards. As students work on this activity, Aimee asks them questions such as "How many dots are there?" "How do you know?" and "Why do they match?" She constantly gives encouragement and feedback, and she carefully makes observations in a notebook or on sticky notes about what they may or may not understand. Aimee observes the students to see if they are looking for patterns to match the cards, rather than just counting them. Several students either count the dots or do not grasp the concept of matching, so she goes around to help these students. Pedro could match all his cards, but finds it difficult to use English to explain why the dots match. Aimee helps him, saying, "They match because the numbers are the same." To reinforce student understanding of matching, she has students draw matching sets of familiar animals. Each student in her class has an assessment portfolio where she places examples of their work.

Samples of student work and Aimee's careful observation of how they complete their tasks give her clues as to how they have progressed in their understanding of mathematics and help inform her instruction. For example, the students who choose the cards and count the dots to make sure of the correct number "demonstrate their number ideas are completely tied to counting" (Van de Walle, 2004, p. 116). Students who choose cards that appear to be the same are looking at patterns and demonstrate a deeper understanding of numbers.

MEANINGFUL

Meaningful assessment provides teachers with the information they need to teach students effectively, thus it is relevant and accurate. Relevance means that the content of the assessment is noteworthy and reflects the knowledge and performance required by standards for the content areas. Tasks set by teachers should be authentic and aligned with the teacher's beliefs about learning, knowing, and goals for his or her students (Houk, 2005; Smith et al., 2004). Assessments are accurate when they have both validity and reliability. Validity means that teachers should be able to make accurate and appropriate conclusions in their study of the results or data from the assessments. For assessments to be reliable, the evidence gathered must be dependable and consistent across time. Reliability may be affected by various factors such as poor directions, student motivation, and interruptions during the test (Smith et al., 2004). Reliability can also be improved through the use of "rubrics and checklists that provide detailed guides for scoring students' performances" (Smith et al., p. 42). Videos of role plays, audiotapes of discussions, work samples, and teacher observations or anecdotal records are all examples of meaningful assessments.

EQUITABLE

Equitable assessment of ELLs is at the heart of education that is fair and just for all learners. Equitable assessment is open. It is participatory and "discloses its purposes, expectations, criteria and consequences" (Smith et al., 2004, p. 41). Equitable assessment is appropriate for the students' developmental, linguistic, and cultural needs. Teachers can determine the "appropriateness and fairness" (Lachat, 2004, p. 111) of their performance-based assessments by considering the following:

- relevant prior knowledge
- language demands and content bias
- procedural bias and scoring criteria
- opportunity to learn (p. 111)

Questions teachers can ask include the following:

- Do students have the background knowledge to make sense of the task they have been given, and to comprehend the evidence which will be used to assess their performance?
- What are the language demands of this assessment? Have I provided "alternative options for displaying understanding?"
- Have I prevented cultural and content bias in these assessments? Have I made sure that the "concepts, vocabulary, and activities important to the assessment tasks" are familiar to all my students, "regardless of their cultural backgrounds"? (Lachat, 2004, p. 112)

Teachers should also make sure that they incorporate accommodations such as extra time to eliminate procedural bias. Scoring criteria should assess students on what they know about the subject matter and what they can do. Collaboration with colleagues is crucial. Teachers need to make sure that, as scorers of the assessment, they are "sufficiently familiar with students' cultural and linguistic backgrounds to interpret student performances appropriately and to recognize and score English language learners' responses" (p. 113).

The opportunity to learn consists of making sure that teachers are qualified to teach ELLs, ensuring that all students have time to learn and prepare for assessments, supplying students with the materials and support necessary to help them be successful, and having high expectations of all students (Lachat, 2004, pp. 113–114).

Finally, equity in assessment means making accommodations to ensure that language and culture do not interfere in the demonstration of the understanding of content. A focus on what students can do, comprehensible input, meaningful questions, scaffolding, and a variety of activities using formal and informal assessments are accommodation strategies teachers can use for equitable assessment (Diaz-Rico & Weed, 2005; Echevarria et al., 2004; Houk, 2005; Lachat, 2004; Smith et al., 2004).

Teachers of ELLs may also use Farr and Trumbull's (1997) list of 13 criteria for valid sociocultural classroom assessment as a checklist for ensuring the effective assessment of ELLs. We focus here on eight of these criteria. Effective assessments, they recommend, should

- be curriculum linked and tied to known standards
- promote high-level learning for all students
- be flexible (form, administration, interpretation)
- provide for multiple ways and multiple opportunities to meet the same standards
- be cognitively complex
- call on multiple intelligences
- be used primarily to facilitate student learning and not to sort, classify, or track
- be culturally responsive and allow for variation in language, in cognitive and communicative style, and in beliefs and values (Farr & Trumbull, 1997, p. 263).

When mainstream teachers and teachers of ELLs collaborate, they can ensure that their curricula and lessons closely follow this checklist so that they provide effective sociocultural assessment of all their students.

STATE-MANDATED TESTING

As mentioned in the previous section, since the 1990s there has been a move toward classroom assessments that are authentic and performance based. Consequently, most states have moved toward forms of performance-based assessments for their large-scale tests, especially in the areas of writing, math, and reading (Lachat, 2004, p. 15). These tests have been developed and used by states to determine whether schools are achieving the goals of state curriculum frameworks. Therefore, many of these tests require students to answer multiple-choice questions, short-answer questions, and questions that call for students to demonstrate their thinking through, for example, multi-step mathematical problems. Because these tests are not educative or sociocultural according to the definitions of Wiggins (1998) and Smith, et al. (2004), we refer to them in this chapter as tests, not assessments.

With the advent of NCLB there has been a push toward high-stakes testing that holds schools accountable for achieving the goals of national and state standards (Diaz-Rico, 2004). Advocates for ELLs have grown increasingly concerned about the effect of these tests on the education of ELLs. They see these testing policies as problematic and detrimental to the educational success of ELLs (Crawford, 2004b; NABE, 2004a; TESOL, 2003. See also the Advocacy chapter in this volume).

The use of standardized testing to assess ELLs is complex and challenging, and because these students are diverse in so many ways, it is inappropriate to consider them as one group with the same needs. As Crawford (2004b) states, ELLs are diverse "in terms of socioeconomic status, linguistic and cultural background, level of English proficiency, amount of prior education, and instructional program experience" (p. 3). Other characteristics of ELLs that may influence their educational success and performance on these tests include the "length of time in the United States, mobility, and educational goals" (Lachat, 2004, p. 42).

In addition, most of these assessment tests, including math and language arts, are usually not originally designed with ELLs in mind (Crawford, 2004b; Hakuta and

Beatty, 2000). Another issue that advocates of ELLs find problematic is the NCLB requirement that ELLs be tested in math in their first year of enrollment in school. This requirement makes the assumption that students can read and understand the language necessary to solve mathematical problems. Furthermore, schools are also required to move ELLs into mainstream classes after 3 years. Research has shown that it takes ELLs anywhere from 3 to 5 years to develop oral proficiency and 4 to 7 years to develop academic proficiency in English (Collier & Thomas, 1989; Hakuta, Butler, & Witt, 2000). These tests frequently determine whether students should be placed in ELL programs, whether they should be retained, and how well they are doing in school. As Lachat (2004) states, "how schools interpret the performance of English language learners on various tests and assessments, influences . . . teacher beliefs about the abilities of these students. . . . As a result, assessment has compounded the difficulties English language learners face while trying to gain access to the high-quality education they deserve" (p. 51).

Furthermore, because these tests are designed outside the classroom, they do not serve to closely inform instruction and are often culturally and linguistically biased. Diaz-Rico and Weed (2005, p. 200) give the following example of cultural bias in standardized tests:

> Tae Sung, from Korea, looked at question number one
> **1. Her tooth came out so she put it**
> - On top of the refrigerator
> - Under the tree
> - Under her pillow
> - None of the above
>
> In Korea, a child throws the lost tooth up on the roof so that the next one will grow in straight, but none of the answers said that . . . . Borden, from the Marshall Islands, also looked a long time at the question. In his country you throw your tooth in the ocean for good luck. He raised his hand and said to his teacher, "You have to throw your tooth in the ocean." The teacher put his finger to his lips and said, "I'm sorry, I can't help you. No talking during the test please." So Borden marked *none of the above.*

This type of test frequently does not measure what ELLs know and can do (Lachat, 2004, p. 55).

These tests also tend to be decontextualized, in that they require correct responses and "contain isolated items requiring use or recognition of known answers or skills" (Wiggins, 1998, p. 22). These tests do not meet all the criteria set forth by Wiggins in his vision of educative assessment, and they are not valid, meaningful, equitable, or useful, as posited by Smith, et al. (2004).

Teachers of ELLs and mainstream teachers need to advocate in their schools and districts for accountability through the use of sociocultural assessment, especially for ELLs. Standardized tests can then be used as one form of evidence that measures the discrete skills of students, in addition to assessments that measure real understanding and development. Because most states and districts require ELLs to take state-mandated standardized tests, teachers still need to collaborate to help students pass these tests.

To prepare students for their annual state standardized tests, mainstream teachers and teachers of ELLs at Sterling Elementary collaborate to familiarize students with the format and language of standardized tests. For example, they teach these students how to fill the bubbles on their answer sheets. Joan, an ELL pull-out teacher, explains carefully to her students what will be required of them on various parts of the test. She also goes over test words such as explain, describe, and compare and contrast. Although they have no set times to meet and collaborate, Joan and the mainstream teachers find time to do so over lunch, during planning times, and even in the hallways. At the request of these teachers, Joan reinforces test-taking skills. She especially focuses on short-answer questions and student comprehension of phrases such as *explain your answer* and *show your work*. A few weeks before testing, several mainstream teachers tell her that their ELLs find word problems challenging. "All students often find word problems difficult, but because of language, ELLs tend to find them even more challenging," Joan says. Because of this, Joan works on math word problems with her students for several days until she is sure they had understood which mathematical functions they are being asked to solve.

Bethany, the ELL pull-out teacher at Trest Elementary, also collaborates with the mainstream teachers. She attends grade-level meetings when possible, goes to their classrooms to observe and never misses an opportunity to discuss with mainstream teachers how they all can work together to help ELLs. Before the state-mandated testing, Bethany works with ELLs on various types of comprehension, multiple-choice, and short-answer questions. She has students try the questions on their own, but also sometimes reads the questions to them. When working individually with students, she gives them the opportunity to change their answers after she reads the questions to them. She then informs her colleagues about students who are able to perform these tasks on their own. "I try as much as possible to scaffold, to help them do these activities on their own," she says. "Otherwise they get used to the help. I don't want to encourage them." During the state- and federally mandated testing, Bethany helps with accommodations for ELLs by reading the instructions and questions to students.

What Forms of Assessments Can Be Used for English Language Learners?

Assessments linked with instruction and content standards are more likely to be effective, appropriate, and demanding of high standards. Teachers use the TESOL (1997) standards and content-area standards when teaching and assessing ELLs. The TESOL standards were designed to help ELLs develop their English language proficiency skills as well as content-area knowledge. Lachat (2004) describes the standards as a bridge that helps teachers "understand the unique instructional and assessment considerations that must be given to English language learners if these students are to benefit from and achieve the high standards of learning that are being proposed for various subject areas" (p. 48). Connecting assessments to standards-based learning can help teachers design authentic tasks that involve problem solving and higher-order thinking.

There are several types of performance-based assessments that teachers may use to assess language proficiency and content-area knowledge, including portfolios, journals, reading logs, videos of role plays, audiotapes of discussions, work samples, and teacher observations (Huerta-Macias, 1995; O'Malley & Valdez-Pierce, 1996). It is crucial for teachers to use these assessments such that they provide systematic ways of obtaining meaningful information about students and their growth. Teachers should also include student self-assessment in all assessments (O'Malley & Valdez-Pierce, 1996, p. 12). If planned, designed, and executed properly, assessments "have the power to tell a story" (Huerta-Macias, 1995, p. 117). Table 2 describes various types of assessment and their advantages.

It is evident that sociocultural assessment has many advantages; it involves and supports students and teachers in teaching and learning. The flexibility of these assessments allows students to demonstrate understanding and ability in various ways. Because these assessments are ongoing, they help teachers monitor students' growth over a period of time and thus gain meaningful information about student learning. Teachers gather information on student learning styles, needs, strengths, and weaknesses, and can then differentiate instruction (Calkins, 1994; Houk, 2005; Huerta-Macias, 1995; Lachat, 2004; Meisels, Dorfman, & Steele, 1995; O'Malley & Valdez-Pierce, 1996; Smith et al., 2004).

How Can ESL and Mainstream Teachers Collaborate to Assess English Language Learners in Math?

At their biweekly grade-level meeting, Trest Elementary kindergarten teachers first discuss challenges they have in their classrooms. They then give advice and help each other problem solve.

The collaborative group then moves on to plan instruction, objectives, and activities for teaching students the relationships of more, less, and the same in math. Aimee, as grade-level chair, facilitates the discussion on creating objectives and assessments for the lessons for all students, including the ELLs in the two sheltered classes. From their collaboration, the teachers realize that having language objectives is important to native English speakers as well as to ELLs. Because of Aimee's input, all of the teachers also use more Total Physical Response and physical movement to teach their students.

The grade-level teachers, Aimee, Dina, Judy, and Carla, also plan activities they could use to teach students mathematical relationships. They constantly ask each other why a particular activity might be used and discuss the benefits or advantages of using various strategies and manipulatives. Some of their suggestions for teaching the concepts include using dominoes, connecting cubes, counters, and dot cards as

Table 2. Types of authentic assessment

Assessment	Description	Advantages
Oral interviews	The teacher asks students questions about personal activities, readings, and interests.	• informal and relaxed context • conducted over successive days with each student • observations recorded on an interview guide
Story or text retelling	Students retell main ideas or selected details of text experienced through listening or reading.	• students produce oral report • can be scored on content or language components • scored with rubric or rating scale • can determine reading comprehension, reading strategies, and language development
Writing samples	Students generate narrative expository, persuasive, or reference papers.	• students produce written document • can be scored on content or language components • scored with rubric or rating scale • can determine writing processes
Projects/ exhibitions	Students complete a project in a content area, working individually or in pairs.	• students make formal presentation, written report, or both • can observe oral and written products and thinking skills • scored with rubric or rating scale
Experiments/ demonstrations	Students complete an experiment or demonstrate the use of materials.	• students make oral presentation, written report, or both • can observe oral and written products and thinking skills • scored with rubric or rating scale
Constructed-response items	Students respond in writing to open-ended questions.	• students produce written report • usually scored on substantive information and thinking skills • scored with rubric or rating scale
Teacher observations	The teacher observes student attention, response to instructional materials, or interactions with other students.	• setting is classroom environment • takes little time • record observations with anecdotal notes or rating scales
Portfolios	Focused collection of student work shows progress over time.	• integrates information from a number of sources • gives overall picture of student performance and learning • strong student involvement and commitment • calls for student self-assessment

Source: O'Malley & Valdez-Pierce, 1996, p. 12

manipulatives. To connect math to literacy and the real world, Judy, who has a vast store of knowledge of children's books, suggests they read books such as *The Very Hungry Caterpillar* by Eric Carle (1987), *More, Fewer, Less* by Tana Hoban (1998), *The Doorbell Rang* by Pat Hutchins (1986), and any other books that might help reinforce these concepts. Judy also suggests they make cards with the words more, less, and same on them, and put them on the word wall. Dina agrees that this is a good idea. Except for Aimee and Carla, all the grade-level teachers have some students who can read. Carla says the sheltered English students can still try to read the words by identifying, at a minimum, the first letter sounds. Dina, who is excellent in developing rubrics, provides a checklist based on the state math standards and their objectives for the unit, which teachers might use to assess student understanding of these relationships. Aimee says she will modify the rubric to take into account the TESOL standards. The group shares ideas with each other knowing that certain aspects are left up to the direction of each teacher, individually, including how the lessons are taught, the number and type of activities that might be used, and books that they might read to help students understand the concepts being taught.

- **Content objectives:** Students will demonstrate the relationships of more, less, and the same by creating or finding sets.
- **Language objectives:** Students will use the words more, less, and the same to describe sets of numbers.
- **Show Me State Math Standard:** Students will understand numbers, ways of representing numbers, relationships among numbers, and number systems.

Aimee also adds a TESOL standard for the two sheltered classes.

- **TESOL Goal 2, Standard 1, 2, and 3:** Students will use English to interact in the classroom. Students will use English to obtain, process, construct, and provide subject matter information in spoken and written form. Students will use appropriate learning strategies to construct and apply academic knowledge.

With the understanding that depending on the level and pace of their lessons teachers may use one or all of the books, the teachers discuss how they might use the aforementioned books to introduce, scaffold, reinforce, and assess student comprehension of the math concepts. They brainstorm about how to use *More, Fewer, Less*, especially with respect to the concept of *fewer*. Thinking of her sheltered students, Carla thinks they should leave out the concept of *fewer* altogether; the teachers agree to focus on *more*, *less*, and *the same* and leave out *fewer* if they feel their students might get confused with using *less* and *fewer*.

Aimee suggests that the teachers use the books during reading to build student prior knowledge before the math unit and to introduce and review vocabulary and past learning. For example, she says *More, Fewer, Less* could be used to review lessons in shapes and colors, as the book has no text, but is full of brightly colored photographs of everyday objects and animals. As an assessment activity she suggests teachers could use the various arrangements of objects in the pictures to facilitate the pictures to the children and ask them questions like "Are there more blue shoes than red shoes?" "Where are there more?" "Where are there less?" The same sort of questioning could be done with the other two books. Reading and discussing the books, Aimee says, will encourage students to use mathematical vocabulary in their everyday conversations, which is important for all students, especially ELLs, as a strategy for improving understanding of mathematical concepts.

The kindergarten teachers agree, as they always do, that there will be ongoing assessment of student comprehension. This includes careful teacher observation, with anecdotal notes of student performance of multiple tasks individually, in pairs, and in large groups. Students will use dominoes, match dot cards, and counters to create their own sets. The teachers also assess student comprehension through their use of oral language. For example, Carla suggests that the teachers could have students select one dot card from stacks placed on their tables. They would then have to find a corresponding or same card. When they select the cards, they would show a partner their cards and describe their cards to them, using phrases like "These are the same." The same would be done with less and more. As a summative assessment, Carla also suggests that students circle sets on a worksheet to demonstrate their knowledge of the concepts. Dina suggests another task as a summative assessment; students would choose a card and then make three sets of counters that are more, less, and the same as the number of dots on the card. They could also use cookies or candy instead of counters, Judy says. She says that they could challenge their learners by also asking them to either write the words or match the word cards to the sets of counters. Aimee and Carla agree that they will most likely use fewer learning and assessment tasks for their ELLs and focus on doing them well.

Because the teachers have taught students how to recognize patterns on dot cards, Aimee reminds them to look beyond student ability to count, and look for how well students recognize patterns as they match cards and determine what is more, the same, and less. She asks them to note any challenges they might have in teaching and assessment for discussions at the next grade-level meeting. Aimee also asks her colleagues not to forget to select samples of student work to put into student portfolios. Finally, Aimee asks them to bring some of their anecdotal notes or samples of student work to the next grade-level meeting, so they might assess together what students are learning.

The teachers then move on to discuss creative extension activities they might do from the books they will read. Using or baking cookies for *The Doorbell Rang* was one suggestion. Creating caterpillars, buying caterpillars to watch them metamorphose into butterflies, and drawing pictures of their favorite everyday objects were some of the suggestions for the other two books.

The above vignette demonstrates how mainstream and ELL teachers can collaborate to teach and assess all their students. Through collaboration teachers can learn from each other how best to help students be successful learners. Students should be able to demonstrate what they have been taught, explain it, and link it to previous knowledge. They should also be able to take what they have learned and apply it to new settings. This can be done through effective, ongoing assessment in all content areas (Mather & Chiodo, 1994; Secada & Carey, 1990; Van de Walle, 2004). The vignette illustrates how, through collaboration, teachers can plan activities and support each other to implement ongoing assessments. For math assessment in particular, teachers must ask "How does the child understand it and what ideas does he/she connect it with?" (Van de Walle, p. 25)

Effective collaboration calls for and improves reflective practice. As a result of their collaboration, the kindergarten teachers at Trest Elementary have to focus and think about their teaching and assessment. They observe students, study student work, and with this data, try to see what they can learn about how well students grasp what is being taught. Calkins (1994) states that it is important for teachers to take the time to "reread our notes, to write about them, and to meet with each other—to talk, wonder, question, compare, reread, write, rethink" (p. 326). For successful collaboration, teachers must be willing to support each other's strengths and weaknesses, share ideas, and be open to learning. Through collaboration with Aimee and Carla, the grade-level teachers also learn strategies they might use to help all students learn mathematics, including making sure students are comfortable using mathematical vocabulary daily in all parts of the curriculum to communicate with themselves and their teachers (Secada & Carey, 1990; Van de Walle, 2004). Working together also ensures that content as well as cultural and linguistic bias that may have been missed by one teacher can be pointed out by a colleague.

In her book *The Art of Teaching Writing*, Calkins (1994) discusses the use of authentic assessment for writing. She calls on teachers to bring "a new mindfulness" (p. 318) to assessments. Teachers should see assessment as a meaning-making process by which over a period of time, they carefully observe students, collect and study student artifacts, develop rubrics, and tailor instruction from the information they glean (p. 325). Assessments, Calkins states, should not be evaluations; their purpose should be to help teachers get to know what their students know (p. 316). In addition to informing teaching and student learning, authentic assessments

- grow out of and reflect teacher and student values and plans
- grow out of and are woven into the very fabric of the school day

It is crucial to document student growth, Calkins suggests, but it is "not enough to teach our hearts out and hope our students are growing. Assessment is the main event; it is where the action lies" (p. 334). This view of assessment can be achieved through constant and close collaboration with other teachers.

Case Study: Teaching and Assessing Math—Subtraction Word Problems

Della Smith is a third-grade mainstream teacher at Price Elementary School. She has five ELLs in her classroom. After introducing students to subtraction, she begins to teach them subtraction word problems. As she did with addition, she teaches them key words that signal subtraction such as *take away*, *minus*, and *left*. She models one way that students can solve word problems and then writes the following problem on the board for the children to solve: "For her birthday party, Miranda had 15 party favors in all. Eight of them were green and the rest were yellow. How many of the party favors were yellow?" Before they start their work, many of the ELLs ask Della what party favors are. She explains, and they start working on the problem. When Della goes around the class to check the student work, she discovers that most of her ELLs and quite a few native English speakers added 8 and 15 to come up with 23 as their answer.

Mrs. Danne, the principal of Price Elementary, has built in grade-level planning time for all the grade levels in her school. Teachers meet twice a week to plan instruction and assessment. All three third-grade teachers at Price Elementary have ELLs. They are pulled out for 45 minutes every day to be taught by Sharon Caste, the ELL pull-out teacher. At the next grade-level meeting, Della discusses her challenges with subtraction word problems with her team, headed by Sonya Street, a veteran teacher with 10 years of experience, when Sharon comes in. Sharon decided to skip her planning time to meet with the third-grade teachers. Della explains the challenges she has been having and asks Sharon to work on math problems with the ELLs when she pulls them out. She gives Sharon some subtraction word problem worksheets and suggests that if Sharon drills them on the various word problems she might be able to help the students grasp the concepts and key words. The worksheets will also be helpful, Della adds, because she will use worksheets for her assessment. Sharon asks Della if she has used visuals in the form of pictures and if she has tried contextualizing the stories. She adds that language might be an issue and suggests that Della try using more authentic and performance-based assessments. Della says the visuals she uses are on the worksheets, but if it will help the ELLs understand how to do word problems, Sharon could go ahead and use whatever strategies she feels might work. "All of my ELLs have been here since kindergarten," Della says, "I really do not think language should be an issue. They are all pretty fluent in speaking English."

Sonya says she has had similar issues teaching math to ELLs. She states that she uses visuals and manipulatives and asks Sharon if she could come in and observe some of the ELLs in her class. She says that she is not sure whether some of the challenges they have in math are due to content, language, or both. Sharon promises to make it to her class as soon as possible. They decide to set a time to meet to discuss Sharon's observations.

Crystal Jones, a teacher with 8 years of experience, is another third-grade teacher. Crystal has several ELLs who are in their first semester in school in the United States. Because these new immigrants are in her class, Crystal is the only teacher in the third grade who has an instructional aide. This aide speaks Spanish, but Crystal has students from Vietnam, Sudan, and Ethiopia. She expresses some of the same frustrations as the other teachers and says she does not understand why her ELLs should have any problems with math. "They have all had some schooling, and after all, math is a universal language," she says. She encourages Della and the group to use more manipulatives and authentic performance-based assessments. "I find they help students quite a bit, especially ELLs," she says. Della agrees to think about it. The meeting continues and the teachers take turns discussing what they will teach, how they will teach, and how they plan to assess instruction. The teachers do not ask Sharon about strategies they might use to teach and assess the ELLs in their classes. Sharon stays silent for the rest of the meeting and takes notes on what the teachers plan to teach in each of the content areas so she can focus on some of these in her pull-out classes. The meeting ends and Sharon tells Sonya that she will try to make it to her class before Friday.

QUESTIONS FOR DISCUSSION

Actors

1. How would you characterize each of the actors in this case? (List descriptive phrases for each individual.)
2. How would you characterize the relationships among Sharon, Crystal, Della, and Sonya?
3. How does Sharon view her role as an ELL pull-out teacher?
4. What do you see as the expectations of the principal and the teachers regarding Sharon's role as an ELL pull-out teacher?

Issues

1. What are the major issues in this case?
2. Discuss Della's reaction to Sharon and Crystal's suggestions.
3. Why do you think Sharon was silent for the rest of the meeting?
4. How is the collaboration of teachers at Price Elementary similar to and different from collaboration at Trest and Sterling Elementary Schools?
5. Do you think Price Elementary has a culture of collaboration?

Problems or Conflicts

1. List some of the problems or conflicts in this case.
2. How might these problems impact the teaching and assessment of math for third-grade students, and ELLs in particular, at Price Elementary?

Solutions

1. What might Mrs. Danne do to improve teacher collaboration in her school?
2. What can the third-grade teachers and Sharon do individually and collectively to improve their collaboration?
3. What strategies can Della and her colleagues use to effectively teach and assess math to all their students?

Summary of Main Ideas

1) Sociocultural assessment is
   a) useful
   b) meaningful
   c) equitable

2) Current issues in the assessment of ELLs pertain to the areas of
    a)   culture and language
    b)   content and language
    c)   state-mandated testing

3) ELL and mainstream teachers can collaborate in assessing ELLs by
    a)   meeting as much as possible to plan instruction and assessment
    b)   reflecting, sharing ideas, and providing mutual support for instruction and assessment
    c)   collaborating to ensure the assessment of language and content
    d)   making sure assessments for ELLs are sociocultural
    e)   collaborating to ensure assessments are real-world tasks that adequately reflect what ELLs know and can do

Print Resources

Crawford, J. (2004). No Child Left Behind: Misguided approach to school account-ability for English language learners. Washington, DC: National Association for Bilingual Education, Center for Education Policy.

> This document discusses the negative impact of NCLB on English language learners.

Sharp, J. M., & Hoiberg, K. B. (2005). Learning and teaching K–8 mathematics. Boston: Pearson, Allyn & Bacon.

> This classroom-based, practitioner-oriented text is an excellent reference for pre- and in-service elementary school teachers. It includes many theoretically sound hands-on activities.

Van de Walle, J. (2004). *Elementary and middle school mathematics: Teaching developmentally* (5th ed.). Boston: Pearson.

> Ideas for some of the vignettes in this chapter were inspired by this textbook, which is a good resource for teaching mathematical understanding to children.

Internet Resources

Abedi, J., & Herman, J. L. (2004). *Issues in assessing English language learners: Opportunity to learn mathematics*. Retrieved September 15, 2006, from http://www.cse.ucla.edu/reports/r633.pdf

> This article gives examples of effective strategies for the teaching and assessment of ELLs.

Buchanan, K., & Helman, M. (1993). Reforming mathematics instruction for ESL literacy students. (Program Information Guide, No. 15). Retrieved August 21, 2006, from http://www.ncela.gwu.edu/pubs/pigs/pig15.htm

> This article has information on how mathematics teachers and teachers of ELLs can collaborate to design math curricula based on teaching and assessing language and content.

Center For Applied Linguistics (CAL). (2006). *English language learners*. Retrieved August 21, 2006, from http://www.cal.org/topics/ell/preK12.html

> This Web site has many resources on the assessment of ELLs.

Crawford, J. (2005). *Language policy Web site and emporium*. Retrieved June 10, 2005, from http://ourworld.compuserve.com/homepages/JWCRAWFORD/home.htm
This Web site has articles that look at language policy in the United States and the impact of these policies on K–12 education for ELLs.

Cummins, J. (2005). ESL and second language learning Web page. Retrieved June 19, 2005, from http://www.iteachilearn.com/cummins/
This Web site has excellent articles and links about assessing and teaching ELLs.

Lachat, M. A., & Spruce, M. (1998). *Assessment reform, equity and English language learners: An annotated bibliography*. Retrieved July 25, 2005, from http://www.alliance.brown.edu/pubs/asellbib.pdf
This is an extensive bibliography on the assessment of ELLs.

National Association of Bilingual Education (NABE). (2006). Retrieved February 9, 2006, from http://www.nabe.org
This Web site has resources for teachers of ELLs, bilingual professionals, teachers, parents, school administrators, and policy makers.

Sheltered Instruction Observation Protocol (SIOP). (2005). Retrieved September 15, 2006, from http://www.siopinstitute.net/index.html
This Web site has information on SIOP, resources that can help teachers effectively teach and assess language and content.

The Education Alliance at Brown University. Retrieved August 22, 2006, from www.lab.brown.edu/topics/assessment.shtm
This Web site has many publications, products, databases, and clearinghouses on the topics of teaching and assessing ELLs. It also has practical guidelines for creating various types of assessments and rubrics.

Teachers of English to Speakers of Other Languages, Inc. (TESOL). Retrieved February 9, 2006, from http://www.tesol.org
This Web site has resources for all the stakeholders involved in the education of ELLs.

Vanee, V. (2001). Putting ELLs to the test. Are standardized assessments setting these students up for a fall? *In Focus, 1*(1). Retrieved July 25, 2005, from http://www.infocusmagazine.org
This article can be found in the National Academies *In Focus* magazine. The Web site has many resources on the sciences, engineering, and medicine. The article by Vanee discusses the use of standardized tests for ELLs.

World-Class Instructional Design and Assessment Consortium Site (WIDA). (2006). Retrieved July 25, 2005, from http://www.wida.us
This Web site has information on the development of proficiency standards and an ELL proficiency test called ACCESS. The site also says the consortium is developing alternative academic assessments for ELLs.

CHAPTER 7

Community

(CASE STUDY)

Strengthening Community

McCoy Elementary is a K–5 school in Kansas City, Missouri. The school is situated in a low-income neighborhood and has about 310 students, 60% of whom are English language learners. These ELLs come from seven countries, and half of them have lived in the United States for less than 3 years. Eighty-nine percent of McCoy Elementary students have free or reduced lunch. McCoy is a full-service community school, with services and activities designed to strengthen community partnerships with their families, neighborhoods, and community institutions. The school provides before- and after-school care, summer programs, and educational programs for parents. McCoy holds Read-Ins, Fall Festivals, after-school family picnics, and neighborhood clean-ups. It has partnerships with more than 20 community organizations, businesses, and agencies. Of particular note is its partnership with the local agency that serves as the immigration center for the Kansas City area. This agency provides social services and translators for the immigrant families whose children attend the school. Other local and neighborhood community agencies such as the local branch of the public library, churches, and family service agencies partner with McCoy to offer services to the school, its families, and the surrounding neighborhood.

PREREADING QUESTIONS

- What are some of the frameworks for community, family, and school collaboration?
- Why is it important to develop and foster school, family, and community partnerships?

- What kinds of strategies can schools use to develop effective partnerships with families and community institutions?

- How can ESL and mainstream teachers collaborate to foster community with families and community institutions?

DEFINITIONS

For the purposes of this chapter the terms *family* and *parents* are used interchangeably and include extended families, foster parents, and any caregivers of school-aged children. In short, we use these terms to refer to people involved in any way in the educational, emotional, and physical well-being of a child. This definition parallels the closely knit extended families and large networks that form part of the social fabric of many culturally and linguistically diverse children. Community institutions include organizations and groups such as local businesses, churches, social service agencies, law enforcement, nonprofit groups, community colleges, and health agencies.

What Are Some of the Frameworks for Community, Family, and School Collaboration?

Researchers, school administrators, and teachers acknowledge the need to involve parents in the schooling and education of their children (Berger, 2002; De Carvalho, 2001; Epstein, 2000; Epstein et al., 2002; Sergiovanni, 1994, 1999; Simon & Epstein, 2001; Steglin & Wright, 1993). Teachers have identified parental involvement in their children's education as the most important factor in educating children (Epstein, 2000). Accordingly, researchers such as Sergiovanni, Boyer, and Epstein have developed theories and frameworks for effective community, family, and school collaboration.

COMMUNITIES BY KINSHIP, OF PLACE, AND OF MIND

With a vision of schools structured like families and neighborhoods, Sergiovanni (1999) defines community as "collections of people who come together because they share common commitments, ideas and values" (p. 59). Tightly knit communities, he suggests, have community by kinship, of place, and of mind, which moves individuals from a collection of *I*s to a collective *we*. These three characteristics are vital in determining if a school has formed a community. Community by kinship is the extent to which members involved in the educational process have formed and share interpersonal bonds; community of place becomes manifest when people share a common identity through the sharing of common spaces such as a school, a neighborhood, or a town; and community of mind emerges when members "share a commitment to values, norms and beliefs" (Sergiovanni, 1994, p. 6).

To form such communities in schools, Sergiovanni (1994, 1999) states that all the stakeholders need to look beyond the traditional with respect to how schools function and are perceived. Schools must move away from being formal organizations, which thrive on social contracts, to functioning as social organizations, which thrive on social covenants and moral connections (1999, p. 63). In other words, schools should not function as businesses, viewing parents and students as customers or clients, because doing so frequently leads individuals to focus on "private needs and self-interests," thinking of only themselves, often to the detriment of others (1999, p. 65). Instead, teachers and administrators, for example, need to understand that they must work with students, parents, and community institutions because they have moral obligations—*social covenants*—to see to the social and academic well-being of students. Such a view of community leads to schools where "connections are based on commitments, not trades" (1999, p. 65). Teachers and students are expected to do a good job not so that they can get rewards, but because it is important to do so. Furthermore, "discipline policies are norm-based, not just rule-based" (1999, p. 65). Sergiovanni's description of productive relationships between schools, family, and community, and his description of a community of mind, is what Wehlage (cited in Lockwood, 1996) calls *social capital*. Wehlage states that social capital "adheres in the set of relationships among people, and those relationships are productive to the extent that they are based on a common set of expectations, a set of shared values and a sense of trust among people" (Lockwood, pp. 19–20). For Wehlage and Sergiovanni, social capital should be the ultimate goal of family, school, and community collaboration.

THE BASIC SCHOOL

Another framework for building community in and with schools is based on Boyer's (1995) ideas about the Basic School. This framework has four components:

- the school as community
- a curriculum with coherence
- a climate for learning
- a commitment to character

Community is what Boyer calls the first building block of a Basic School. It is what ties the other components together. He emphasizes that it "is the glue that holds an effective school together" (p. 15). Basic Schools, Boyer recommends, should be communities of learning where teachers, administrators, students, and families have a shared vision; teachers are leaders; and parents are partners. Like Sergiovanni (1994, 1999), Boyer states that Basic Schools that have a shared vision are schools that have a clear mission, places where everyone in the building comes together to encourage learning and implement the mission of the school. The Basic School climate is "communicative, just, disciplined, and caring, with occasions for celebration" (Boyer, p. 8). Within these communities of learning, teachers need to be leaders. Boyer recommends that teachers collaborate, mentor each other, and continually pursue professional development. Creating a community of learning is not possible without parents, and Boyer states that Basic Schools must develop strong partnerships with parents from pre-school through all grade levels.

OVERLAPPING SPHERES OF INFLUENCE

The model of overlapping spheres of influence put forth by Epstein (2000) consists of the spheres of schools, families, and community, all of which influence the well-being and educational success of children. Because these three areas are vital in the successful education of all children, Simon and Epstein (2001) suggest moving away from the terms *family* or *parental involvement*, toward the broader term "school, family and community partnerships" (p. 2).

The theoretical model of overlapping spheres of influence describes and clarifies how these three contexts interact, with the child or student at the center. This model consists of external and internal models of the spheres, which overlap and influence children's lives. The external model illustrates that schools, families, and community do not always overlap; some activities are conducted separately. For example, not all family-based activities involve the community or school. However, as the model indicates, there are instances in which "families and schools, or schools, families, and communities share responsibilities for activities that support students' development and education" (Simon & Epstein, 2001, p. 3). In Epstein's model the spheres may be drawn apart or pushed together according to the number of activities that are shared among the three spheres. The number of activities shared depends entirely on the goals and efforts of families, schools, and communities and may change over time. For example, Simon and Epstein suggests that as children become older there is frequently less parental involvement; therefore the spheres of schools and families are pulled apart (p. 3).

The internal model of overlapping spheres illustrates the interpersonal relationships among the three areas. These interactions may take place at institutional or individual levels. Interactions at the institutional level occur when, for example, parents and community members are invited to school events. Interactions at the individual level, on the other hand, include a parent-teacher conference. Interactions between schools and community institutions can also be depicted in the model.

Based on her model of the overlapping spheres of influence, Epstein, et al. (2002) also provides a framework (see Figure 1) to help research, guide, develop, and organize partnerships among schools, families, and communities. The following are various types of school, family, and community involvement:

- parenting
- communicating
- volunteering
- learning at home
- decision making
- collaborating with the community

These six categories represent the types of "partnerships that support student development and academic success" (Simon & Epstein, 2001, p. 5). The categories are

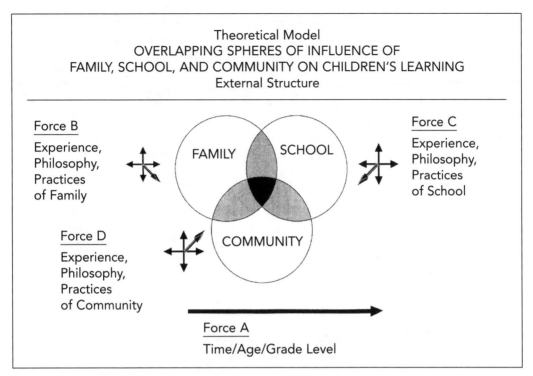

Figure 1. Theoretical model
Source: Epstein et al., 2002

equal and important in the educational and social development of children; none is more important than the other, but "all six types are essential for strong, diverse, and balanced partnership programs that enable all families to find ways to be productively involved at school and in their children's education at home and in the community" (p. 3). Table 1, a part of the Epstein et al. (2002) framework, suggests sample practices schools can use to support the specific needs of parents and students.

As schools develop practices that support their specific needs, they redefine old perceptions or definitions of types of involvement. For example, *workshop* could be broadened to mean making information available through other means than just meeting at a school at a particular time. It "may mean making information about a topic available in a variety of forms that can be viewed, heard or read anywhere, anytime" (Epstein et al., 2002, p. 15). *Volunteer* could mean anyone who supports the school's mission and goals, anywhere and at any time, "not just during the day and at the school building" (p. 15). Finally *help at home* could be redefined as not just teaching subjects learned at school, but any form of encouragement, praise, guidance, and monitoring of school work (p. 15). To have effective collaboration, families, schools, and communities must have a shared vision, a sense of place, and must develop family-like relationships that are caring, nurturing, and supportive.

Table 1. Excerpt from Epstein's framework of six types of involvement for comprehensive programs of partnerships and sample practices

Type 1 Parenting	Type 2 Communi- cating	Type 3 Volunteering	Type 4 Learning at Home	Type 5 Decision Making	Type 6 Collaborating With the Community
Help all families establish home environ- ments to support children as students	Design effective forms of school- to-home and home- to-school communica- tions about school programs and their children's progress	Recruit and organize parent help and support	Provide information and ideas to families about how to help students at home with homework and other curriculum- related activities, decisions, and planning	Include parents in school decisions, developing parent leaders and representa- tives	Identify and integrate resources from the community to strengthen school programs, family practices and student learning and development
Sample Practices					
Suggestions for home conditions that support learning at each grade- level	Conferences with every parent at least once a year, with follow-ups as needed.

Language translators assist families as needed | School and classroom volunteer program to help teachers, adminis- trators, and other parents | Information for families on skills required for students in all subjects at each grade | Active PTA/PTO or other parent organizations, advisory councils, or committees (e.g. curricu- lum, safety, personnel) for parent leadership and partici- pation | Information for students and families on community health, cultural, recreational, social support, and other programs or services |

Source: Epstein et al., 2002, p. 168

FRAMEWORK FOR COMMUNITY INSTITUTIONS

Lockwood, Stinnette, and D'Amico (1997) focus on community institutions and offer a framework that schools and communities can use to provide the necessary context for building community and increasing school, family, and community commitment and collaboration. Community institutions, they suggest, should be able to commit to offer schools shared responsibility for

- learning
- communication
- building capacity through training and volunteering

We discuss this framework further in the section on community institutions.

Why Is It Important to Develop and Foster School, Family, and Community Partnerships?

FAMILIES

Humans need community, and building community among families, schools, and community institutions is essential. As Sergiovanni (1994) explains, "The need for community is universal. A sense of belonging, of continuity, of being connected to others and to ideas and values that make our lives meaningful and significant—these needs are shared by all of us" (p. xiii).

Lack of community and fragmentation of society leads to issues of poverty, negative changes in family structure, drugs, violence, and gangs. These issues, in turn, frequently lead to behavioral and emotional problems in children, which can then affect their academic success (Anderson-Butcher & Ashton, 2004; Boyer, 1995; Sergiovanni, 1994).

There is a critical need for school, family, and community partnerships in the educational process. Henderson and Berla (1994) examined 150 studies on the role of family in the education of children. They discovered that the higher the parental involvement, the more successful children are in school. They also offer the following findings:

- The family makes vital contributions to the achievement of students, from preschool to high school.
- When parents are involved at school (in various roles) and at home, children do better in school and stay in school longer.
- When parents are involved in schools, their children go to better schools.
- Children do well in school when their parents play the roles of teacher, supporter, advocate, and decision maker.
- When partnerships between parents and schools are comprehensive and well planned, student achievement is high.
- Strong family, school, and community institution partnerships contribute to student achievement.

Evidence from research indicates that regardless of student socioeconomic status, race, ethnicity, educational background, or cultural background, parental involvement leads to higher test scores, higher grades, better attendance, increased completion of homework, better attitudes and behavior, increased retention and graduation rates, and greater enrollment in higher education (Aspiazu, Bauer, & Spillett, 1998; Henderson & Berla, 1994; Jones & Velez, 1997; NCREL, 1997).

For minority students in general and ELLs in particular, collaboration among community institutions, schools, and families is crucial for bridging cultural and linguistic differences (Houk, 2005). Minority parents frequently do not participate in school activities because they do not feel comfortable in schools (Berger, 2002; Comer, 1986). It is the responsibility of schools to remove barriers to family and community involvement in the education of students; schools must collaborate with families and communities to ensure the academic success and physical and emotional well-being of all their children. As Berger explains, "if partnerships are to be successful, all of those involved must be encouraged to make contributions of their gifts, talents, and resources to the lives of the children and families" (p. 52).

COMMUNITY INSTITUTIONS

Along with parental involvement, collaboration with community institutions such as community groups, nonprofit agencies, elected representatives, health and mental health providers, religious leaders, neighborhood groups, and businesses is important to building community and improving student academic achievement and emotional and physical well-being. Community institutions have the financial, social, and cultural resources that can be used to help children succeed in school. Lockwood, et al. (1997) point out that "communities can provide schools with a context and environment that can . . . complement and reinforce the values, culture and learning the schools provide for their students" (para. 3). A strong community can provide schools "with crucial financial support systems as well as the social and cultural values necessary for success and survival in contemporary society" (para. 3). This is important for all children, but particularly for culturally and linguistically diverse children, who need the necessary tools to negotiate and survive in new and different social and cultural contexts.

INTERAGENCY AND INTERPROFESSIONAL PARTNERSHIPS

Collaboration between community institutions and schools can support schools and families through sharing the responsibility for learning, communication, and capacity building. Anderson-Butcher and Ashton (2004) call these wrap-around services. These researchers emphasize the need for interagency and interprofessional collaboration to help schools address student needs and problems. Interagency collaboration occurs when local, private, and nonprofit social service agencies work together to provide services to schools. Interprofessional collaboration consists of delivering "family centered, community based, and culturally competent services that improve the health, safety, education and economic well-being of children and families" (Anderson-Butcher & Ashton, p. 43).

McCoy Elementary is an example of a school with interagency and interprofessional partnerships. The school has a partnership with the Kansas City Local Investment Commission (LINC), a state-funded nonprofit organization that works to organize services for the working poor. The organization's mission is to improve the lives of low-income families through citizen and family involvement. Consequently, the services it offers include funding, support staff, and training for local low-income neighborhood schools. LINC organizes site councils "charged to direct neighborhood-level efforts" (LINC, 2005, p. 7). The site councils consist of families, local businesses, and neighbors. McCoy Elementary is a LINC Caring Communities Site; it offers school-based services to McCoy students, families, and the neighborhood. The school also has a CARE team, an interdisciplinary group of professionals who meet once a week to discuss referrals made to the school social worker.

Collaboration with community institutions helps educate the whole child and improve student learning and achievement. These community institutions can offer schools enrichment programs through sponsoring cultural fairs, arts programs, clubs, bands, and athletics. Communication is vital in building and sustaining community; therefore, deKanter, Ginsburg, Pederson, Peterson, and Rich (1997) suggest these groups collaborate to build community "networks of concerned adults, including community leaders, law enforcement officers, journalists, and others to talk about and publicize issues of concern to the schools and to the community" (Appendix B, p. 45). These networks can encourage the creation of safe environments, drug-free zones, and safe havens.

Businesses can help improve student learning by collaborating with schools through training and volunteering programs to prepare students for the real world and to build capacity. Relationships with local businesses can assist students by helping them apply their knowledge to real-world situations (NCREL, 1997). Employers and nonprofit groups can also encourage their employees to volunteer in schools' mentoring programs, help students with projects, provide schools with technology and services of specialists to help them use the donated technology, and "adopt flexible policies to accommodate parent-teacher conferences and volunteering opportunities in the schools" (deKanter et al., 1997, Appendix B, p. 45). Area agencies can also offer various social services, such as counseling, medical and dental screening, and legal assistance.

All parent, school, and community relationships need to be reciprocal. School facilities should be a resource available to the community. Schools can be used for adult education programs, family literacy programs, classes for adult ELLs, community health screenings, theatrical productions, and voting. Collaborating in such a way builds social capital, thereby strengthening the community.

What Kinds of Strategies Can Schools Use to Develop Effective Partnerships With Families and Community Institutions?

Schools can build community through family, school, and community partnerships by employing the following strategies (Berger, 2002; Epstein, 2000; Houk, 2005; Simon & Epstein, 2001; Stegelin & Wright, 1999):

- Create a welcoming school climate.
- Foster strong home-school communication.
- Encourage family involvement in decision making.
- Offer school-linked or school-based services.

CREATE A WELCOMING SCHOOL CLIMATE

Schools need to be safe and inviting places for parents. Poverty, limited experience with schools, and negative experiences in schools may cause parents to fear and therefore avoid visiting schools and participating in their children's education. It is important for teachers and administrators to get to know the parents of their students, as well as their social and cultural backgrounds, because

> parents bring different attitudes into the home school relationship. . . . [I]f their past school experiences were pleasant and successful, they are likely to enjoy visiting schools again. If their experiences were filled with failures . . . the thought of school is depressing. . . . [I]f they do approach the school it is with trepidation. (Berger, 2002, p. 150)

A welcoming school environment makes it possible for parents to participate in their children's education no matter their circumstances or work schedules. Part of creating a welcoming, accessible environment includes scheduling key events such as parent-teacher conferences and school activities when it is convenient for all or the majority of parents. Schools need to be aware of the challenges families might face such as lack of childcare, unemployment, and illness, and should be ready to work with them to find the resources needed to help them.

A welcoming school environment is particularly important for parents of linguistically and culturally diverse students. These parents may not have had any schooling or may come from countries where schooling is different. They need to feel welcome and comfortable if they are to help schools educate their children. In a welcoming school environment, administrators have positive attitudes toward parents. Staff in the principal's office should make all visitors feel welcome; designating a greeter to stand at the front door and having all staff members greet family members when they see them can achieve this (Berger, 2002; Houk, 2005).

A celebration on first day of school is another activity that can contribute to a welcoming school environment. Teachers, other parents, administrators, and perhaps board members can invite families to a formal ceremony that welcomes new students and families. As Boyer (1995) recommends, "on this celebrative occasion, goals can be discussed, a tour offered, refreshments served" (p. 54). Families may also enter a covenant for learning at the beginning of each school year. This covenant is not a contract, but a pledge by parents to help their children be successful in school, for example, by helping with homework and attending parent-teacher conferences. For its part, the school can pledge to communicate regularly with parents and have clear goals for students (Boyer, p. 54; Epstein et al., 2002).

Other strategies for creating a welcoming school atmosphere include posting student work in hallways and entry areas of schools, "representing all families in a public celebratory way," and providing a parents' or family room or center where parents can meet, "sit, drink coffee or tea, post and read announcements in different languages, or meet fellow parents" (Houk, 2005, p. 63). A parents' room demonstrates to parents that they are expected to be and feel comfortable in the building. The room should be equipped and stocked by the parents. If there is no available physical space, there should at least be "an interactive bulletin board" (p. 64) for notices. School programs that involve parent implementation and participation, such as read-ins, cultural potluck dinners, and trips to the library, also serve to strengthen family, school, and community partnerships (Berger, 2002; Boyer, 1995; Houk, 2005). Both Gladstone and McCoy Elementary Schools have such activities to strengthen collaboration with families and community institutions.

FOSTER STRONG HOME-SCHOOL COMMUNICATION

Effective and meaningful home-school communication is vital if parents are to participate in the education of their children. To strengthen family, school, and community partnerships, educators need to ensure strong relationships among the spheres through strong communication strategies. These strategies should include one-way and two-way communication.

One-way communication strategies include newsletters, school handbooks, phone trees in diverse languages, school-home activity packets that focus on the curriculum and are enjoyable for families and the students, and bulletin boards. But because one-way communication only informs parents about school activities, two-way communication is a better form of communication between schools and families. Two-way communication involves face-to-face interaction, which provides more opportunies to clarify issues and ask questions. Through face-to-face interaction, educators can support and guide parents with the information needed to help with their children's homework. Two-way strategies include parent-teacher conferences, workshops, home visits, telephone tutors or homework hotlines, "volunteer participation, shared videos, shared journals and decision-making boards" (Stegelin & Wright, 1999, p. 54; see also Berger, 2002; Hiatt-Michael, 2001).

Family presence in schools strengthens the relationships between teachers and parents. For many parents, trips to school are usually undertaken because they have been summoned to school because of their children's behavioral or disciplinary problems. Parents should be invited to celebrate learning with their children frequently to "normalize the presence of families in the classroom and school" (Houk, 2005, p. 66). Teachers can share classroom activities by videotaping lessons and sending them home for parents to watch. The videos can be accompanied with a comment sheet.

Parents who do not have VCRs may watch the videos at school. The idea behind this strategy is for parents and teachers to have "points of interest for discussion" (Stegelin & Wright, 1999, p. 61) during parent teacher conferences. Shared journals can also serve as a means of communication between parents, teachers, and students. Newsletters are an effective and equitable way to communicate with parents; however, if the resources are available, educators should increase the use of technology such as the Internet, school Web sites, and e-mail.

Strong home-school communication is especially important for parents who may not speak English. Schools and districts must offer translation services at parent-teacher conferences and for newsletters and notes that are sent home. Houk (2005) explains that, "whether schools have staff that can be called on, community translators who are available, district interpreter services that can be accessed, there must be a formal, steady, and reliable process for translating information for parents" (p. 64). McCoy Elementary relies on the local immigration service center and the school district to provide translation services for ELLs and their parents.

To strengthen relationships with families, families new to the school should immediately be put in touch with a family of a similar background and a school staff member who can help them navigate the administrative process and access community resources. In addition, schools should create panels of interested parents with different linguistic and cultural backgrounds to help facilitate communication and avoid cultural conflict. These parents and others should be encouraged to discuss with educators their expectations for teaching, learning, their children's behavior, and what parental engagement should look like (Houk, 2005, p. 67). This discussion would help educators become more aware of cultural differences and help them work to solve potential problems. Culture is "not only the filter through which people see the world but also the raw dough from which each person fashions a life that is individual and satisfying" (Diaz-Rico & Weed, 2005, p. 233). Teacher acceptance of this definition of culture and dialogue with families can lead to less stereotyping and help all concerned parties understand that ethnic groups might have similar cultural patterns, but they might live these patterns in a different and individual manner (Derman-Sparks, 1989). The more effective the communication between families and children, the less stress children have to go through as they try to navigate home and school cultures (Hiatt-Michael, 2001).

The key to strong home-school communication is that both sides, particularly educators, need to be willing to listen, to share and be open about how to solve issues. When educators communicate with parents who do not speak English proficiently, they need to make the extra effort to listen and identify any miscommunication. As Berger (2002) states, "when parents or teachers listen they not only increase knowledge and understanding of the message, but they also demonstrate a caring attitude" (p. 210). Table 2 describes how parents and teachers can become effective communicators.

Table 2. Effective communication for successful partnerships

Teachers are good communicators when they:	Parents become partners in the educational process when they:
• Give their total attention to the speaker. They establish eye contact and clearly demonstrate through body language that their interest is focused on what is being said.	• View the teacher as a source of support for their child and themselves.
• Restate the parents' concern. They clarify what has been said and try to discern the speakers meaning and feeling. They avoid closed responses or answering as a critic, judge or moralist.	• Listen carefully and give total commitment to the speaker.
• Show respect for the other person. They recognize that their concerns, opinions, and questions are significant factors in mutual understanding and communication.	• Show respect for the teacher—recognize that the teacher's concerns, opinions, and questions are significant to mutual understanding and communication.
• Recognize the parents' feelings. How much can you discuss with parents? Perhaps you need to establish a better parent-teacher relationship before you can completely share your concerns for the child.	• Recognize that the teacher has a difficult challenge to meet the needs of all students. They help the teacher succeed.
• Tailor discussions to fit the parents' ability to handle the situation.	• Rephrase and check out understanding of messages during conversations or conferences.
• Do not touch off the fuse of a parent who might not be able to handle a child's difficulties. They do not accuse; they spend more time with the parent in other communication and conferences.	• Speak openly and honestly about the child.
• Emphasize that concerns are no one's fault. Teacher and parents have to work on problems together to help the child. They use concerns as forums for understanding one another.	• Use concerns as forums for understanding the school and the teacher.
• Remember that no one ever wins an argument. Calmly, quietly, and enthusiastically they discuss the good points of the child before bringing up any concerns.	• Become allies with the teacher.
• Protect the parents' egos. They don't place blame or make them believe that they are to blame for the child's deficiencies. They focus on plans for the future. On the other hand, they give parents credit for their child's achievements.	
• Focus on one issue at a time. They are specific about the child's progress and concerns.	
• Listen. They hear the feeling and meaning of the message, and rephrase and check the message to be sure that they received it correctly.	
• Become allies with parents.	

Source: Berger, 2002, p. 208

ENCOURAGE FAMILY INVOLVEMENT IN DECISION MAKING

The relationship between strong home-school communication and family involvement in decision making in schools should be a synergetic one because strong and effective communication makes parents more comfortable in schools. This in turn may lead to a stronger family presence, with parents feeling supported enough to discuss school policies and decisions that affect their children. Schools that are truly dedicated to strong family and community partnerships involve families in decision making. Houk (2005) states that, by doing so, schools incorporate families, especially ELL families, into the fabric of the schools and demonstrate their commitment to cultural democracy (p. 67). School administrators and teachers, especially principals, should provide leadership with respect to democratic decision making as part of the school culture (Davies, 2001, p. 110). Anderson-Butcher and Ashton (2004) stress that in school, family, and community collaboration, parents should, as much as possible, be viewed as experts of their situations.

Family involvement in school decision making is directly linked with advocacy. Because such involvement contributes "strongly to school reform so that all students can achieve academic success with high standards" (Davies, 2001, p. 109). Involvement in the school's decision making also helps families and community members learn and practice democratic procedures, which in turn helps develop a more civic and democratic society. This is especially important to families of ELLs because it helps them learn about systems of governance and democracy, which they may not have experienced in their native countries. However, as Houk (2005) cautions, not all families of ELLs are comfortable participating in decision making right away, so schools need to make it easier "for parents to have say in the day-to-day happenings of the school" (p. 67). Schools also need to provide opportunities for parents who might want to take on more formal leadership roles; in time, these parents may become strong advocates.

Families can be involved in decision making in various ways. On an individual level, families can work directly with teachers. For example, parents should contribute to planning and approve their children's individual education plans (Davies, 2001). They can also influence the adoption and implementation of school policies, and they can vote on bond issues and lobby local, state, and federal authorities about educational matters that may affect their children. Collectively, families can form groups to influence school decision making (Davies, 2001, p. 110). Houk (2005) recommends five strategies for involving families in decision making in schools:

- Make sure parents are represented on the school council, but do not include them merely as a token presence.

- Develop parent groups like the PTA to support and influence school decisions. This group should be inclusive across lines of race, ethnicity, gender, and social class (Davies, 2001), so that it works to ensure the academic success and well-being of all students.

- Include parents in the hiring process of new faculty and staff.

- Establish groups of parents to collaborate with teachers and staff to tackle specific issues in the school. Notions of discipline vary across cultures, and input from parents could help schools solve discipline problems.

- Listen to what parents have to say, even if the opinions and ideas are negative.

SCHOOL-LINKED AND SCHOOL-BASED SERVICES

As mentioned earlier, in order to develop strong and lasting school, family, and community partnerships, all three spheres should be equally involved in building community. One way to ensure this is for community institutions and schools to offer what Allington and Cunningham (2002) call *school-linked* or *wrap-around* services for children. These are services offered by community institutions in partnerships with schools, but they may or may not be available on school premises. When these services are available at the school, they are called *school based*. Both types of services consist of "comprehensive, individualized, and family-driven services and supports" (Anderson-Butcher & Ashton, 2004, p. 43) provided to families and children. In addition to offering students a good academic program, Boyer's (1995) Basic School model also recommends the availability of these services to ensure the physical, emotional and social well-being of students. These services include offering classes for adult ELLs through partnerships with literacy groups and giving space to service providers to offer medical and dental checkups, mental health services, youth development services, and so forth (Anderson-Butcher & Ashton, 2004; Boyer, 1995; Houk, 2005). If set up properly, these school-linked services will help avoid the duplication of social services in the community (Anderson-Butcher & Ashton, 2004). To help students achieve academically, Adelman and Taylor (1996) believe that schools cannot work any harder, "so they must work smarter. . . . [W]orking smarter involves resource coordination, integration and redeployment" (p. 312).

McCoy Elementary, a full-service community school, offers school-based services for its students, their families, and the neighborhood. The school's Panda Place Wellness Center has a nurse practitioner and provides health services and screenings to children and their families. These services include physical examinations; hearing, dental, and vision screening; and immunizations. In partnership with a local hospital, the school also has a clinical social worker.

To encourage McCoy students and families to lead healthy lives, the school has a healthy classrooms initiative called Healthy Steps. Some of the interventions the school has started after initiating the program include

- establishing a health club for fourth and fifth graders
- partnering with a local community food bank to provide families with fresh produce
- creating a health newsletter for the school and its families
- developing a health tip of the day
- collecting healthy recipes from teachers and families to go into a bilingual recipe book

Researchers suggest that parent surveys are the best way to assess parents' needs and to decide which services should be offered. In cases of parenting classes and literacy programs, Houk (2005) suggests, whenever possible, that parents provide the leadership in these situations because school staff, especially teachers, are frequently stretched too thin. Schools may also offer their site to various community groups for meetings. Strategies for providing services and education to families include the following:

- Foster mentoring services to integrate communities into the school. Such partnerships may be very helpful for new immigrant families who speak little or no English. Mentoring could consist of "parent mentors for other parents, community mentors for parents, parent mentors for students or community mentoring for students" (Houk, 2005, p. 70).

- Offer parents the opportunity to join their children in school activities during and after school hours.

Families may need translators, transportation, and light meals to participate fully in these programs, and the programs, especially those related to family education, must be offered on a continuous basis (Houk, 2005).

How Can ESL and Mainstream Teachers Collaborate to Foster Community With Families and Community Institutions?

Gladstone Elementary follows Boyer's (1995) recommendation for all-school grouping to build and strengthen community. Students, teachers, and staff are grouped into vertical families. There are four families, Red, Yellow, Blue, and Green, representing each grade level. Like McCoy, Gladstone is situated in a low-income neighborhood. It has approximately 537 students, 64% of whom are ELLs. Eighty-four percent of the students receive a free or reduced lunch. The school has a strong commitment to promoting balanced literacy. The vertical families at Gladstone have times scheduled into the school calendar during which they meet to discuss curriculum issues, plan activities to strengthen the home-school connection, and engage in professional development activities.

At the Red family meeting one afternoon, the group discusses how they can most effectively work with all their learner for the state-mandated test called the Missouri Assessment Program (MAP). The teachers review the concepts and skills the fourth-grade students need for the test, which include fractions, place value to the millions, and position in number line. They pass around a Zap the MAP tip sheet to help teachers prepare their students for the test. The teachers also decide to develop a user-friendly benchmark book with quarterly objectives in reading and the content areas for Grades K–6. Kordai Ayub and Ian Rodriguez, both teachers of ELLs, suggest that teachers start using test vocabulary immediately so that students, especially ELLs, will be familiar with the vocabulary by test time.

The teachers then move on to discuss a chapter of *Mosaic of Thought* by Ellin Keene and Susan Zimmermann (1997). They talk about metacognition and how to facilitate it with their students, which leads to a lively conversation about whether they should *turn the light on* for their students or wait for them to discover some strategies for themselves. The teachers all agree with the comment that teaching reading should be more than just teaching children to use strategies and that comprehension involves developmental processes. For the next meeting, teachers are to read chapter 4 of *Mosaic of Thought*.

The Accelerated Reader Program (AR) has recently been introduced to Gladstone. AR is a software program that helps teachers monitor and assess students' reading through a series of quizzes. In a previous meeting teachers expressed their concerns about using AR and incorporating it into the curriculum. Many of the teachers are strong proponents of balanced literacy and feel that AR diametrically opposes the goals of balanced literacy, which include a lifelong love of reading. Cynthia Kearne asked how they could teach children to love reading and be lifelong readers if their goal is to take tests to move up a level. She also expressed concern about students losing the ability to choose their just right books—a term used in balanced literacy to refer to books that are on the children's reading level. Other concerns about AR were that it provided little variety and not enough easy reading books for first graders.

The principal, Dr. Cook, is present at the meeting today to address teacher concerns. She emphasizes the fact that AR is in no way supposed to supplant balanced literacy instruction. She says Accelerated Readers are helpful because many of the children, especially ELLs, know how to decode words but lack comprehension. Dr. Cook suggests that AR be used as an assessment tool rather than a way of teaching and says it need not be used on a daily basis.

Finally the Red Family moves on to plan Red Family Night. The teachers come up with a date and several ideas about what they can do. Kay Pole suggests that they make and sell T-shirts, highlighting that the Green Family had done so to raise money for uniforms. Very few of the teachers think this is a good idea because many families may be unable to afford it. They decide against a party at a skating rink for the same reasons. Amy Lockheart suggests a read-in night and all the teachers agree that this is a good idea. Theo Sayles says a read-in night would be both a social and an academic activity. A reading night emphasizes the importance of reading, encourages lifelong reading, and perhaps encourages families to create a literary environment in their homes. Ablade Peters suggests using the cafeteria or gym and contacting the public library so that some of its librarians could come and help families sign up for library cards. Theo says that they should serve refreshments and ask parents to volunteer to do reading and storytelling. Mercy Simon suggests that they contact local bookstores to see if they will donate books that children can take home. Kordai states that it is important to emphasize to parents that they must attend if at all possible and avoid simply dropping their kids off. The purpose of these nights, she says, is for parents to be secure and comfortable enough to participate in school activities, to get to know the teachers, students, staff, and other families who are part of the Red family. The Red Family decides to continue planning for the read-in at their next family meeting.

All-school grouping in the form of vertical families is an excellent vehicle for teacher collaboration. The description of the Red Family meeting illustrates how mainstream teachers and teachers of ELLs can collaborate to create a community of learning within the school and strengthen partnerships with families. Boyer (1995) states that such groupings help "affirm the school as a community for learning" (p. 131).

The meeting also illustrates the shared vision of balanced literacy, student academic success, and the need for maintaining strong school, family, and community partnerships.

Through participation in the vertical families, teachers develop and build upon collaborative and leadership skills. At Gladstone, the teachers have a voice and they demonstrate leadership, for example, in their discussion of the advantages and disadvantages of using AR and how it might best serve the needs of their students. Leadership ability helps in "human interactions" (Berger, 2002, p. 234); teachers with leadership skills "encourage problem-solving, and critical thinking . . . and set the stage for learning" (p. 234). The vertical family structure also serves as a vehicle for professional development, in that teachers read books that help them improve their teaching and student's learning.

CONCLUSION

Research has shown that well-developed and -implemented school, family, and community partnerships can lead to enhanced performance at school and emotional and physical well-being of children. It is vital to note that it is not the strategies themselves that are important, but rather their implementation. While implementing these strategies, Barton, Drake, and Perez (2004) suggest that it is imperative for schools to move away from considering parental engagement as an object or outcome, or merely as what parents do with schools to help in their children's educational success. They suggest a shift toward considering parental understanding of the "hows and whys of their engagement, and how this engagement relates more broadly to parents' experiences and actions both inside and out of the school community" (Barton, Drake, & Perez, p. 3). They find that this is particularly crucial for families of urban and linguistically and culturally diverse children. De Carvalho (2001) cautions schools to be particularly careful in their collaboration with these children and their families, warning not to impose middle-class or cultural values that are antithetical to their ways of being. This means that partnerships be just that: equal collaboration between families and the community to ensure the social well-being and academic success of all children.

Case Study: Diversity Day

At the first faculty and staff meeting of the year, Mr. Kendon, the principal of Greene Elementary School, tells teachers and staff that he would like to strengthen student, family, and community partnerships. Sixty percent of the students at Greene are ELLs, and they represent eight countries. The majority of these ELLs speak Spanish as a first language; however, many of the other children are from countries in Africa and the Middle East.

Mr. Kendon says he would like to start with strong home-school connections and gradually grow to form tighter partnerships with families and the community. He asks teachers to brainstorm for ideas with respect to how this goal could be achieved. Connie Gonzalez, Adjeley Birch, and Bill Powell, the ELL teachers, say that the school needs to be more welcoming. They suggest that welcome signs in the students' native languages be posted at the front door and that student work be put up in the hallways. Nancy Billings, the art teacher, and Connie volunteer to head this project. Other ideas that teachers offer include continuing to send out classroom and school-wide newsletters, encouraging parents to volunteer in the school, and helping parents create conditions at home that help their children at school. Connie, who translates the school-wide newsletters into Spanish, also suggests that the school make more of an effort to employ language translators to assist families. Mr. Kendon says that the school does not have the money for it, but he will take it into consideration. Both Mr. Kendon and Megan West say they feel the school-wide newsletters should be sufficient at this time.

Gloria Werk suggests that teachers do home visits, but the majority of teachers do not think this is a good idea. "I think this would be an intrusion," Edwin Cheal says. However, he suggests that teachers work individually with parents to show them how to support their children's learning at home. This can be done during parent-teacher conferences, he says, during which time, teachers should also persuade parents to volunteer in the school during school hours. Adjeley asks how likely it is that many parents would be able to do this. Edwin and Mr. Kendon both say there is little anyone can do about it if these parents cannot be in school during school hours.

The teachers and staff decide that parents should be invited to a school read-in and potluck, and they form a committee to recruit parents. They decide to call the event Diversity Day. During this function, parents will be informed of the school's goal to strengthen the home-school connection. The teachers pick a Friday night at 6 p.m. and prepare feverishly to have a wonderful celebration. By the night of the potluck and read-in, hardly any parents have signed up to volunteer. Only 10 families attend. The majority of teachers and Mr. Kendon are very disappointed. However, Connie, Adjeley, and Bill are not at all surprised.

QUESTIONS FOR DISCUSSION

Actors

1. How would you characterize the characters in this case? (List descriptive phrases for each individual.)

2. How do Mr. Kendon and Edwin view the home-school connection?

3. Discuss Connie's, Megan's, and Gloria's views about communicating with parents.

Issues

1. Do you think Connie's concerns are justified?

2. Do you think Edwin's concerns about home visits are justified?

3. Should Adjeley have been more insistent about including all parents as volunteers?

4. Why might Friday at 6 p.m. be an inconvenient time for some of the families?

Problems or Conflicts

1. List the problems or conflicts in this case.

2. Prioritize these problems according to their impact on the family-school partnership.

Solutions

1. Determine what teachers can do to increase and improve parental involvement in the school.

2. What might be a broader way of looking at parents volunteering at Greene Elementary?

3. What do the principal and teachers at Green Elementary have to do to improve home-school communication?

Summary of Main Ideas

1) It is important to develop and foster school, family, and community collaboration because
   a) effective collaboration can lead to stronger, more tightly knit communities
   b) when parents are involved at school (in various roles) and at home, children do better in school and stay in school longer
   c) when parents are involved at school, their children go to better schools
   d) children do well in school when their parents play the roles of teacher, supporter, advocate, and decision maker
   e) when partnerships between parents and schools are comprehensive and well planned, student achievement is high

2) Schools can use the following strategies to develop effective partnerships with families and community institutions:
   a) effective one-way and two-way communication with families
   b) school-linked and school-based wrap-around services
   c) all-school groupings

3) ESL and mainstream teachers can collaborate in the following ways to foster community with families and community institutions:
   a) Teachers must establish a community of learning in which they collaborate to ensure the academic success of their students.
   b) They must be open to learning from each other and from their students' families about linguistic and cultural diversity.
   c) They must work together to make links with community institutions and social service agencies to address the educational, physical, and emotional needs of students and their families.

Print Resources

Epstein, J., Sanders, M. G., Simon, B. S., Salinas, K. C., Jansorn, N. R., & Van
Voorhis, F. L. (2002). *School, family, and community partnerships. Your handbook for
action* (2nd ed.). Thousand Oaks, CA: Corwin Press.
> This handbook has many resources on how to implement and sustain successful school, family, and
> community partnerships.

National PTA. (2000). *Building successful partnerships*. Bloomington, IN: Solution Tree.
> Based on the National Standards for Parent and Family Involvement, this book is a comprehensive
> guide for implementing successful partnerships among all the stakeholders in the educational process.

Internet Resources

Center for Social Organization of Schools at John Hopkins University. (n.d.).
Retrieved August 22, 2006, from http://www.csos.jhu.edu
> This site includes the Center for School, Family and Community Partnerships and provides information
> on strategies for developing strong school, family, and community relationships.

Communities in Schools (CIS). (2006). Retrieved August 22, 2006, from http://www
.cisnet.org
> This site includes information on how the organization connects schools with community resources to
> help young people stay in school.

deKanter, A., Ginsburg, A., Pederson, J., Peterson, T., & Rich, D. (1997). *A compact
for learning: An action handbook for family-school-community partnerships*. Retrieved
August 22, 2006, from http://www.ed.gov/pubs/Compact/
> This handbook explores ways in which schools, parents, and communities can implement successful
> partnerships.

Local Investment Commission (LINC). Retrieved August 22, 2006, from http://www
.kclinc.org/
> LINC is a citizen-driven community collaborative including neighborhood, business, and labor leaders.
> This site includes information on the organization, its initiatives, and awards it has received.

Profiles of Successful Partnerships. (n.d.) Retrieved September 15, 2006, from http://
www.ed.gov/famInvolve/appa.html
> This site has descriptions of successful school, family, and community partnerships.

CHAPTER 8

Advocacy

CASE STUDY

Advocating for Our Learners

Kay Allen, a certified ESL teacher, is the migrant advocate for Pelican Bay Elementary School in Florida. She no longer teaches in the classroom, but is responsible for the 200 migrant students at this school. She collaborates with teachers, administrators, and the community to help improve the lives of her students and facilitate their success in school. She clearly has in-depth knowledge about the community, its attitudes, and its needs. Kay talks about the children in her care:

> Migrants are this school—they get what they need here. These children have different experiences than other children but they're just kids. They want to learn and have fun. They have "eternal optimism." They're not discipline problems. They're respectful and have intact families for the most part.

> There's no discrimination between the migrant children and the others in this school. Most kids return to Mexico for the summer for vacation purposes anyway so the migrant kids don't stand out among them. Most of the migrants live in the trailer park run by the citrus conglomerate. The camp is well kept. But those families that can afford it try to buy housing in the community and stay here full time. They're "settling out" mostly because they want their children to get a good education.

Kay keeps busy reaching out to the community to obtain funds to help migrant children and their families. For example, she noticed that migrant families needed a pre-K class, so she contacted the school district and they were able to use migrant funds to open one. There are now four pre-K classes, all taught by certified teachers. She also wrote a grant to help fund a community health center. "In my job," she says, "I just pray to have the eyes and ears to see the needs in this community."

- What is advocacy?
- Why do teachers need to advocate for English language learners?
- How can teachers advocate for English language learners?
- How can teachers collaborate to effectively advocate for English language learners?

What is Advocacy?

The essence of child advocacy is "caring, a recognition of need, and a willingness to do something about that need" (Berger & Berger, 1999, p. 476). Whether advocating on a public level to maintain or change educational programs, or working on a personal level to improve the lives of students in their classrooms, teachers who care do not just teach, they help their students be successful. In order to advocate for children, advocates must start from the premise that children have rights and that these rights are enforceable (Knitzer, 1999). Advocacy should focus "on institutional failures that exacerbate problems" (Knitzer, p. 120). Because advocates take a stand to address grievances, maintain effective programs, and uphold the rights of children and their families to help improve their lives, all advocacy is political (Knitzer, 1999).

Why Do Teachers Need to Advocate for English Language Learners?

Changes in legislation, the rising rate of poverty, the growing number of students in general, and ELLs in particular, are just a few reasons teachers need to advocate for students and their families. The federal government has established laws that make it illegal for children to be discriminated against in schools because of race, ethnicity, disability, religion, and gender. In the case of ELLs in particular, the Elementary and Secondary Education Act of 1965 made it legal for schools to offer bilingual education to this group of students. U.S. Supreme Court decisions in cases such as *Meyer v. Nebraska* (1923) and *Lau v. Nichols* (1974) established that "students' languages were also civil rights" (Herrera & Murry, 1999, p. 114). The justices ruled that in order for children to have equal opportunity in the classroom, schools should provide them with an education in their own language, or offer ESL programs. However, the court left it up to the individual states to regulate how they would implement this ruling. Consequently, states sought to carry out this mandate in different ways, which included offering monolingual classes as well as various kinds of bilingual programs (Berger & Berger, 1999; Herrera & Murry, 1999).

In 2002, the Bilingual Education Act was repealed and replaced by NCLB. Title III of NCLB provides guidelines related to the education of limited-English-proficient children. Because this new law emphasizes high standards for students and accountability from schools in order to achieve these standards, organizations such as the National

Association of Bilingual Education (NABE) supported the goals of NCLB when it was first passed (Crawford, 2004b; NABE, 2004a). However, much to the dismay of proponents of bilingual education, all references to bilingual education were deleted from NCLB, and goals such as offering programs that develop students' proficiency in their own languages were removed.

As the new law was implemented, educators started to question just how beneficial Title III of NCLB really was for ELLs. First, the mandate was not adequately funded. Second, educators realized that the law did not really serve ELLs as a group because lawmakers had not taken into consideration the diversity of this group of students with respect to factors such as culture, language, previous education, and socioeconomic status. These educational stakeholders were particularly concerned about the parts of the law that require ELLs to take the same mandated tests as other students, in English, after their third year of education in the United States. The law also requires students to take math assessments in their first year of schooling in the United States. Research has shown that, depending on factors such as socioeconomic status, it may take ELLs 4 to 7 years to attain academic English language proficiency (Collier & Thomas, 1989; Hakuta et al., 2000). Crawford and organizations such as TESOL and NABE find that NCLB has set arbitrary and unrealistic targets for student achievement (Crawford, 2004b, p. 2; NABE, 2004b; TESOL, 2004).

NCLB does allow for accommodations, including the possibility of ELLs taking tests in their native language for 3 to 5 years, but this particular accommodation is not without complications. Native-language tests are not available in all languages; not all students are literate in their native languages; and direct translations of these tests are not always meaningful, reliable, and valid (Crawford, 2004b).

Stakeholders in the education of ELLs believe that, by not taking the unique features of ELLs into consideration, NCLB sets them up to fail (NABE, 2004a; TESOL, 2004). Another concern is the punitive sanctions that are meted out to schools when they fail to meet the standards required by NCLB. These standards are measured by the state-mandated tests and are used to determine the Adequate Yearly Progress (AYP) of schools. Sanctions for not attaining AYP include loss of jobs and local control. It is for these reasons that advocates for ELLs find NCLB's system of accountability for ELLs in particular to be "inappropriate, unworkable and inequitable in approach" (Crawford, 2004b, p. 2).

In order to advocate for children whom they see as disadvantaged by NCLB, civil rights and education organizations such as NABE, the Children's Defense Fund, Forum for Education and Democracy, and the National Association for Social Workers formed the Alliance for Fair and Effective Accountability (AFEA). This organization has recommended that U.S. Congress amend various parts of NCLB so that it might become more equitable for children with disabilities, poor and minority children, and ELLs (NABE, 2004a). TESOL and the AFEA have recommended that greater flexibility and more accommodations should be allowed with respect to testing ELLs and including the scores of new arrivals in AYP calculations (TESOL, 2004).

BILINGUALISM AND THE ENGLISH ONLY MOVEMENT

The previously mentioned organizations, especially NABE, have also advocated against legislative threats to bilingualism through the English-only movement and California's Proposition 227. NABE broadly defines bilingualism as "approaches in the classroom that use the native languages of English language learners (ELLs) for instruction" (NABE, 2004c, para. 2). According to this definition, all bilingual education should include some form of instruction in English language development. (For a fuller discussion on bilingualism, see chapter on language in this volume.) In June 1998, Californians approved Proposition 227, which proposed that, instead of bilingual education, all subjects be taught solely in English in California schools. This campaign was part of the English-only movement, which swept through the United States in the 1980s and 1990s (Crawford, 2000). Although advocates of bilingual education lost this battle, they continue to work to help the general public in the United States to understand the advantages of bilingual education. Proponents of bilingual education, Crawford (2004a) states, have to "publish data on program effectiveness . . . and explain second-language acquisition in an accessible way" (Crawford, 2004a, p. 124). He calls for strategic advocating for ELLs, pointing out that

> to influence decisions that are crucial to LEP students, educators must learn to participate more effectively in policy debate . . . by explaining bilingual pedagogies in a credible way—that is, in a political context that members of the public can understand and endorse. (p. 124)

RISE IN NUMBER OF IMMIGRANTS AND POVERTY

The increasing number of immigrant children in schools who do not speak English as a first language is another reason teachers need to advocate for ELLs. Adding to this is an increase in poverty in the United States as a whole. The official poverty rate increased from 12.5% in 2003 to 12.7% in 2004. This means the number of people in poverty increased by 1.1 million to 37 million in 2004. Among children, the poverty rate remained unchanged between 2003 and 2004 at 17.8% (U.S. Census Bureau, 2004). The Food Research and Action Center (FRAC) Web site states that in 2003, 36.3 million people in the United States suffered from hunger. Furthermore, 37% of immigrant families in the United States are worried about being able to afford food to feed their families (FRAC, 2005).

Statistics from the Center for Immigration Studies indicate that immigrants are more likely to be poor than citizens born in the United States. Thus it is clear that immigrant children in schools are more likely to be poor (Camarota, 2003). Payne (2004) describes poverty as a lack of access to and knowledge of available resources. These resources, she suggests, may be physical or emotional. Parents of ELLs are more likely to be poor because they have low-paying jobs and frequently speak very little English, if any. Whatever the case may be, teachers are more likely today than in the past to be faced with the challenge of educating poor immigrant children who do not speak English as a first language. The changes in legislation discussed earlier, the rising number of immigrants, and the rising levels of poverty in this group of people make it imperative for teachers to take on the role of advocating for all their students so that they have a chance at success in school.

How Can Teachers Advocate for English Language Learners?

Berger and Berger (1999) examine advocacy for all children, but their ideas can be applied specifically to ELLs. They suggest that teachers advocate for children on three levels: public, personal, and private. Private advocacy consists of advocating "for a cause in the private sector" (p. 479). This type of advocacy is less applicable to ELLs, so this section focuses on the public and personal levels.

PUBLIC ADVOCACY

Berger and Berger (1999) describe the public advocate as someone who works in a group to advocate for change in legislation, advocates for a child in court, or advocates for a cause in the public sector.

PERSONAL ADVOCACY

Personal advocacy is the kind of advocacy most teachers and parents frequently practice in schools and communities in order to improve the lives of children (Berger & Berger, 1999). To advocate for children on a personal level, Berger and Berger suggest that parents and teachers

- provide a stimulating, appropriate classroom environment so that the child can play and work productively
- advocate for a child in a classroom or for their own children
- see to it that children are in educationally and socially appropriate classes
- determine best facilities and help for a child who needs special help
- report physical and sexual abuse
- become an ombudsman and share resources with or develop resources for a parent who is neglectful because of lack of resources (p. 479)

Aimee Teason demonstrates collaborating for personal advocacy through the help she gives children in her sheltered English kindergarten class. Aimee has been an elementary school teacher for more than 8 years. She has been a sheltered kindergarten teacher at Trest Elementary for 2 years. At the beginning of the school year she noticed that Josef, one of her kindergarten students, had clearly not taken a bath for a long time. His school uniform was dirty and smelled bad. The children in class had begun to tease him and did not want to sit next to him. At their weekly grade-level meeting, Aimee consulted with her colleagues about how to address this problem. As a group they decided that Aimee should ask for help from Anna Fernandez, the school district's parent liaison. Anna contacted Josef's parents, Melisande and Josef Sr. She found that Josef Sr. had two jobs and Melisande had been very ill. Both parents spoke very little English and were recent immigrants. Josef Sr. was always working and because Melisande had been ill and very weak, she was unable to properly care for Josef and his siblings. Even though he had two jobs, Josef Sr. was barely able to make ends meet, and the family frequently only had enough money to buy food. Because the school had a room where it kept donations of clothes, Aimee and Anna were able to give Melisande two sets of uniforms for Josef and clothes for her family. Anna took her to the area's free health clinic for a medical checkup, and then to a social service agency where she was given soap, food, and other supplies. Anna also taught Melisande how to take the bus to the agency and showed her how to use the washing machines at the nearby laundromat. Aimee was pleased to see that from then on Josef came to school a clean and happy child who was able to focus on learning in her classroom.

Whereas Berger and Berger's (1999) work on advocacy focuses on all children, Herrera and Murry (1999) provide a framework specifically for ELLs, which consists of three components: currency, defensibility, and futurity. This framework extends Berger and Berger's ideas and provides a useful structure within which teachers and parents can better act on public and personal levels.

CURRENCY

Currency "suggests a concern with the extent to which educators are aware of potential threats to appropriate services for English language learners and their families" (Herrera & Murry, 1999, p. 121). This component of Herrera and Murry's framework is similar to Berger and Berger's (1999) idea of public advocacy. Teachers need to be aware of current initiatives, trends, and policies at the local, state, and national levels that may affect the teaching and learning of ELLs. These may be policies that affect students' families, such as loss of welfare benefits, or that affect programming at schools. Herrera and Murry suggest that teachers need to be able to identify these issues, study and understand them, and be ready to clarify them to their school, their school districts, and students' families.

Currency calls for teachers to actively participate and take leadership roles in working to keep abreast of the social and political trends and issues that may pose a threat to themselves, students and their families, and school programs. These issues include the increase in the number of ELLs in schools and in state-mandated tests.

Kay Allen demonstrates currency. She successfully spearheaded an initiative by the grassroots Pelican Bay Community Health Care Coalition to apply for a grant to open a community health center, and she helped find funding for pre-K classes at Pelican Bay Elementary. To do so, she had to be aware and knowledgeable of conditions in the migrant community. Teachers can remain current on issues by attending national and regional conferences, using state and federal resources (see the resource list at the end of this chapter), and joining organizations that advocate for children.

DEFENSIBILITY

Defensibility centers on reflective practice. Herrera and Murry (1999) posit that in order to be effective advocates, teachers have to engage in "defensible practice" (p. 125), which includes critical self-examination and reflection, engagement in reading and professional development, and collegiality. Defensible practice must be grounded in theory and research in order to convincingly deal with the challenges teachers may face from parents, school administrators, and local and national policies.

Hererra and Murry (1999) state that teachers must have the ability to critically examine themselves as teachers and reflect upon their practice and the theory that undergirds it. They state that if "professionals are to defend their perspectives on the needs of students and families, as well as appropriate programs to address those needs, then those perspectives and the programs which flow from them must prove the conduct of reflective thinking" (p. 124). For ELLs in particular, teachers must have a concrete understanding of the theories of second language acquisition, the complexities of language development and acquisition, and best pedagogical practices for ELLs (Houk, 2005). However, the theories that teachers espouse are frequently not actually what they practice. Critical self-examination and reflection can help teachers bring the two together. For example, in order to be effective advocates for ELLs, teachers need to demonstrate the "theory-in-use capacity to feel *with* rather than feel *for* their students" (Herrera & Murry, 1999, p. 125). It is Kay's capacity to feel with her migrant students that led her to be an important part of the grassroots effort started by the Pelican Bay Community Health Care Coalition to obtain healthcare for the migrant and immigrant families.

Professional development, staying abreast of current practices through reading, and collegiality encourage defensible best practices and are all ways that teachers can formulate and articulate rationales for advocacy. With a clearly articulated, defensible rationale, teachers are better equipped to make changes within their schools, their districts, their states, and the nation.

Whether teachers choose to advocate on a personal or public level, they need to do their homework and be prepared to answer questions and justify their solutions to the problem (Berger & Berger, 1999). Teachers have to be prepared and proactive to advocate effectively. They must communicate with all the stakeholders in the educational process, especially families. Most of all, teachers must be able to articulate "what we're doing, and why we're doing it" in order not to "leave room for others to impose their beliefs and practices on our classrooms and students" (Houk, 2005, p. 184). Kay's work with the migrant community illustrates Berger and Berger's suggestions that, in order to effectively advocate, teachers must

- know their facts
- know the policies and procedures that relate to the problem, get them in writing, and refuse to accept a verbal version
- discuss various options
- write letters

Kay and the Pelican Bay Community Health Care Coalition did their homework and obtained the information needed to prove that the Pelican Bay area was medically underserved. Thus they were able to secure grants.

FUTURITY

The key in all child advocacy efforts is keeping the needs of the children at the fore and emphasizing that the changes will help improve their lives. Futurity is the idea that teachers actively work to change and improve programs for ELLs and their families. This may involve working in and with the community and fostering collaboration with families (see the chapter on community collaboration in this volume). Houk (2005) suggests that teachers constantly ask questions such as "Would this be good enough for my child? Would I make this decision for my own children's education?" (p. 182). Teacher education is also important. Schools and colleges of education need to prepare preservice teachers to become advocates for the children they teach (Herrera & Murry, 1999).

Kay is an excellent example of futurity in action. She stepped out of the traditional role of teaching and helped form the Pelican Bay Health Care Coalition. The group first applied for a grant to obtain a grant writer; this writer then wrote a grant that designated the Pelican Bay area as a medically underserved area, which enabled the coalition to apply for a grant from the Bureau of Public Health and Migrant Health in Washington, DC. With money from this grant, the health center provides the migrant community with the services of an internist, a pediatrician, and dentists. Kay continues to serve on the board of the community health center and organize food banks.

Teachers like Kay who take on leadership roles are successful advocates because they are willing to work with colleagues, administrators, parents, and the community. Such teachers and partnerships "require a clear moral purpose, demonstrate educationally defensible goals before self-interest, and are actively committed to social justice" (Herrera & Murry, 1999, p. 128; see also Houk, 2005). Teachers who are effective advocates for ELLs are ready to face challenges from and collaborate with all the stakeholders in the education process, including families and communities, legislators, the media, and other teachers. Teachers cannot ignore the sociocultural and sociopolitical factors that affect their positions as teachers, their teaching, and the lives of the children they teach. This is why advocacy is inherently political. Advocating for ELLs is particularly important because they are frequently overtly or covertly pushed toward assimilation. Their languages and cultures are often perceived as deficits compared to the middle-class cultures of schools. Furthermore, this group of students is marginalized, generally poorer, and frequently does not have the cultural capital to be successful in school without the support of teachers, administrators, and the community.

How Can Teachers Collaborate to Effectively Advocate for English Language Learners?

On Tuesday after school, Kay takes some time in her office to reflect on her day. As is usually the case, it was quite a busy and challenging day. In the morning she met with one of the mainstream teachers, Jane Martin, to discuss Maria's progress. Maria is a child of migrant farm workers. She did not do well on the standardized test and Jane feels it is necessary to retain her in third grade for another year. Kay has monitored Maria closely throughout the school year and has spoken to Jane about her progress several times.

Jane discusses why she would like Maria to remain in third grade for another year. Kay listens and then makes her case against retaining Maria. She points out that Maria did not do well on her test but has made progress in class. To support this assertion, Kay and Jane go over Maria's grades from the formal and informal assessments Jane has given her third-grade class. These assessments indicate that although Maria is still reading below grade level, she has made tremendous progress and is reading at a second-grade level. When Maria started the third grade she was reading at a first-grade level. Kay points out these facts and Jane finally agrees, rather reluctantly, that Maria be promoted with the proviso that she attend Pelican Bay's after-school tutoring for migrant children.

Next, Kay meets with Pelican Bay's principal, Mr. Lubell, to ask that Pedro, who is going to be retained in the fourth grade, be put in a different teacher's class the following academic year. Pedro has made very little progress during the school year and Kay feels that part of the problem is that his relationship with his mainstream teacher has deteriorated to the point at which there is no communication. Kay has met with this teacher frequently since Pedro's arrival at the school two semesters ago. When he arrived, Pedro spoke very little English, and he has not made much improvement. His teacher considers him to be a "slow learner" and has asked repeatedly that he be put in special education classes; however, none of the tests that Pedro has taken indicate this to be true. Upon further questioning, the teacher admits that with the number of students she has in her class, she has no time to individualize instruction for him or do the extra work needed to help him catch up with the class. Pedro has told Kay that he feels the teacher does not like him and that she ignores him in class and speaks very loudly to him.

Mr. Lubell listens carefully and decides that Pedro will be put in another fourth-grade class. Pedro's new teacher has experience teaching several grade levels and has been very successful in working with students who arrived at Pelican Bay with very little English proficiency. Finally, Kay and Mr. Lubell go through a list of migrant students who have just been tested for giftedness, and the principal gives approval for them to be in the gifted program.

At Pelican Bay, Kay is responsible for approximately 200 migrant students. She collaborates with mainstream teachers to ensure that they are included in programs and services appropriate for their social, emotional, and educational needs. Within the school Kay provides oversight on migrant educational needs. For example, she monitors academic underachievement and retention rates, oversees the gifted students, and uses test data and observations to determine how to allocate school resources for student academic achievement.

From the description of a typical day for Kay, it is clear that her advocacy for migrant ELLs fits into the frameworks laid out by Berger and Berger (1999) and Herrera and Murry (1999). She advocates for her migrant students on personal and public levels. She demonstrates futurity, currency, and defensibility in her advocacy. She collaborates with the community, her colleagues, and administrators to advocate for the ELLs in her school and community. Like Aimee at Trest Elementary, she collaborates not only to help these children succeed in school, but also to help improve their lives and the lives of their families.

ELLs are disproportionately placed in special education programs because their lack of English is frequently seen as a deficit and a marker of low intelligence (Burnette, 1998; Markowitz, Garcia, & Eichelberger, 1997; Warger & Burnette, 2000). Although this view is changing, there are still very few ELLs in gifted programs. Through collaboration with teachers and administrators in her school, Kay sees to it that the gifted migrant children under her supervision are appropriately placed in Pelican Bay's gifted program.

Kay and Aimee clearly work for social justice. Aimee works on a more personal level, while Kay demonstrates futurity and defensibility and takes her advocacy public by applying for grants and reaching out to the community to access funding and programs for the migrant population. These teachers demonstrate that the keys to successful advocacy are collaboration, leadership, knowledge, critical reflection, and a willingness to work for social justice.

Case Study: The New Student

Angelica is a new student at Texas Elementary School. She moved from the urban Houston Elementary School to rural east Texas halfway through the school year. Although Angelica is 11 years old, she was placed in a third-grade class in Houston. The school placed her in the lower grade because she did not speak English, and the school counselor and teachers thought she was not emotionally ready for fifth grade. Texas Elementary bilingual counselor Gloria Sanchez disagrees with the placement and thinks Angelica should be placed in a classroom with her same-age peers. She thinks self-contained fifth-grade ESL class is the best place for Angelica because she should be in a classroom with students her age and where the teacher will scaffold language instruction in the content areas. Gloria does not believe that schools can legally retain students because they do not speak English, but she is not sure. If Angelica is placed with her peers, she will miss the entire fourth grade because she spent the last semester in third grade in Houston. Gloria wants to find out more about why she was placed in a lower grade in order to make the best decision for Angelica, so she calls the counselor at Houston Elementary.

Although Houston Elementary is located in an urban area, it has few ELLs. The school population is predominately African American, and because there is such a low

ELL population, there are no ESL services offered on the campus. In a recent phone conversation, Houston Elementary counselor Amy Bennett explains Angelica's placement and situation to Gloria.

> Amy: Angelica came to us not speaking any English. Our fifth-grade teachers were not prepared to teach a non-English-speaking child. In fifth grade, teachers must teach the content areas in depth—and because it is an important TAKS year, Angelica would be best served in a lower grade level. This year was the first year students were tested on science content, and Angelica would not be able to understand any of the content. Likewise, she has some emotional issues. Her mother passed away in Mexico, and she acts out in class. We thought a lower grade level would offer her a more nurturing environment to learn English.
>
> Gloria: OK, I understand that the mainstream fifth-grade teachers do not feel comfortable teaching a non-English-speaking student, but what I'm not clear about is why services could still not be provided for Angelica. Most school districts have ESL teachers who travel from campus to campus when student numbers are too low at a campus to hire a full-time ESL teacher.
>
> Amy: We decided Angelica's inability to speak English was a result of her emotional issues. So, we thought by placing her in a lower grade level, she would feel more comfortable learning English—and adjust better to our school. She was a very scared and timid child. We decided that she just did not want to speak.
>
> Gloria: Thank you for giving me input on Angelica's background. Knowing a little about her background will help me make a better placement decision.

Gloria is frustrated with Angelica being placed two grade levels below peers her age and is not sure what to do, but she does know that teachers at her school will work together to welcome Angelica. Gloria decides to hold a grade-level meeting with the fifth-grade teachers prior to the Language Proficiency Assessment Committee (LPAC). She also wants to check with the district ESL/bilingual director. Can she legally place Angelica two grade levels below her peers, or would it be best to place her in the fourth grade? Can teachers base a grade-level placement on a language issue? Gloria knows that Texas Elementary teachers advocate for students, and she feels that her school faculty would make the right decision for Angelica.

QUESTIONS FOR DISCUSSION

Actors

1. How would you characterize Gloria and Amy? (List descriptive phrases for each individual.)

2. How does Gloria view her role as school counselor?

3. Why does Gloria feel responsible for finding out about Angelica's prior schooling?

Issues

1. Do you think Gloria's concerns are justified?

2. What concerns do you have about Gloria's ideas about the level at which Angelica should be placed?

3. Is Gloria following the law as she tries to serve as an advocate for Angelica?

4. Should Gloria take on the responsibility of forming teacher meetings to discuss Angelica, or should she let the LPAC make all decisions?

Problems or Conflicts

1. List the problems or conflicts in this case.

2. Prioritize these problems according to their impact on Angelica.

Solutions

1. Determine what teachers can do to serve as advocates for Angelica.

2. How can schools best serve students who move from school to school?

3. Determine how schools can collaborate more effectively to best serve students who move to a new school.

Summary of Main Ideas

1) Advocacy is
   a) caring for others
   b) being willing to help
   c) political

2) Teachers need to work for advocacy because of
   a) changes in legislation that affect the teaching and learning of ELLs
   b) changes in programming that affect the success of ELLs
   c) the increasing numbers of immigrant children who do not speak English
   d) the increasing number of immigrant children who qualify for free or reduced lunches.

3) Teachers can advocate for ELLs
   a) on personal and/or public levels
   b) by critically examining and reflecting on their role as teachers
   c) by keeping informed about the lives of students and their needs
   d) by staying abreast and keeping informed about issues that may impact their teaching, educational programs, and the educational success of ELLs
   e) By informing themselves about the resources and support available for students and their families

4) Teachers can collaborate effectively to advocate for ELLs by
   a) moving outside the classroom and working with parents
   b) establishing links and communicating with the community
   c) reaching out to other teachers and administrators
   d) becoming leaders in their schools

Internet Resources

Crawford, J. (2006). *Language policy Web site and emporium*. Retrieved August 22, 2006, from http://ourworld.compuserve.com/homepages/JWCRAWFORD/home .htm
> This comprehensive Web site has resources and discussions about U.S. language policy and ELLs.

Cummins, J. (2003). *ESL and second language learning Web page*. Retrieved August 22, 2006, from http://www.iteachilearn.com/cummins/
> This Web site has many academic articles, curriculum materials, and online resources for bilingual education teachers as well as teachers of ELLs.

National Association for Bilingual Education (NABE). (2005). *Partnerships for advocacy*. Retrieved August 22, 2006, from http://www.nabe.org/advocacy/partnerships .html
> This part of NABE's Web site has information on how it has partnered with more than 60 education and civil rights organizations to take a stand against NCLB and high-stakes testing.

National Institute for Literacy. (2006). Retrieved August 22, 2006, from http://www .nifl.gov/lincs/discussions/discussions.html
> This page has a list of various discussion groups that teachers may join to advocate for ELLs. ESL discussion groups, as well as a group on hunger and poverty, are a few that are included in the list.

Teachers of English to Speakers of Other Languages, Inc. (TESOL). *Advocacy resources*. Retrieved June 19, 2005, from http://www.tesol.org/s_tesol/seccss.asp?CID=80& DID=1550
> This Web site has an advocacy page with resources to help teachers advocate for the profession in the U.S. and abroad.

U.S. Census Bureau. (2006). Population *and household economic topics*. Retrieved August 22, 2006, from http://www.census.gov/population/www/index.html
> This Web site has statistics on income, poverty, and health of U.S. residents in general as well as information specific to immigrants, race, and ethnicity.

U.S. Department of Education. (2004). *Language instruction for limited English proficient and immigrant students. NCLB desktop reference*. Retrieved June 18, 2005, from http://www.ed.gov/admins/lead/account/nclbreference/page_pg30.html
> This desktop reference offers information on NCLB and ELLs.

Acronyms

AFEA	Alliance for Fair and Effective Accountability
ASCRIBER	A model for the process of aligning ESL standards with content standards and district curriculum: Alignment, Standard setting, Curriculum development, Retooling, Implementation, Benchmarking, Evaluation, Revision.
AYP	Adequate Yearly Progress
BICS	Basic interpersonal communication skills
CALP	Cognitive academic language proficiency
DOL	Daily oral language
ELL	English language learner
ESE	Special education
ESOL	English for speakers of other languages
FCAT	Florida Comprehensive Assessment Test
FRAC	The Food Research and Action Center
JPA	Joint productive activity
L1	First language
LEA	Language experience approach
LEP	Limited English proficient
MAP	Missouri Assessment Program
NABE	National Association for Bilingual Education
NCLB	No Child Left Behind
NCTE	National Council of Teachers of English
NCTM	National Council for the Teaching of Mathematics

RPTE	Reading Proficiency Tests in English
SIOP	Sheltered Instruction Observation Model
SQR3	A study method: survey, question, read, recite, review.
STAD	Student-Teams Achievement Division
TAKS	Texas Assessment of Knowledge and Skills
TEKS	Texas Essential of Knowledge and Skills
TESOL	Teachers of English to Speakers of Other Languages
TPR	Total physical response

Glossary

Additive Bilingualism—When learning a new language does not interfere with the learning of the first language. Both the first and second languages contribute to language proficiency.

Affective Filter—A device that is raised or lowered depending on the motivation and self-esteem of the learner. A low filter allows the learner to interact easily with native English speakers and receive increasingly larger amounts of comprehensible input.

Backward Design—Teachers have a desired curricular goal in mind and then design backward to determine the appropriate learning experiences necessary to reach that goal.

Basic Interpersonal Communication Skills (BICS)—Language that occurs within a context-embedded social environment.

Bilingual Education—According to the National Association for Bilingual Education, bilingual education is practiced in many different forms in the United States. The various program models include transitional, developmental, or two-way bilingual education. Generally, bilingual education means that two languages are used within a classroom, by both the teacher and students (http://www.nabe.org/education/index.html). Methodology and time spent learning English varies among the programs.

Cognitive Academic Language Proficiency (CALP)—The context-reduced language of a textbook.

Comprehensible Input—Language input that is understood by the learner but is a little beyond the learner's current productive competence.

Content Standards—Statements that clearly present what students should know or be able to do in any specific content area. They include the knowledge, skills, and understandings that schools need to teach students in order for those students to reach a predetermined level of competency.

Cooperative Learning—A specific kind of group work designed to teach students to work collaboratively for the development of content learning, language learning, and social skill development.

Cultural Mediators—Teachers who research their students' culturally different ways of learning so that all students are able to achieve success in the classroom.

Daily Oral Language (DOL)—A common language exercise seen in early childhood classes. Teachers write a phrase or sentence on the chalkboard or overhead projector, and students orally discuss ways to correct the sentences errors.

Dual-Language Program—Two-way bilingual program that integrates language minority and language majority students.

Echo Reading—A fluent reader reads a sentence or paragraph, and the less fluent reader repeats the lines back to the fluent reader. Such an activity is an effective way to build reading fluency.

English as a Second Language (ESL)—A professional course of study dedicated to teaching English as a second language.

English Language Learners (ELL)—Students who acquire English as an additional language.

ESL Pull-Out Program—A type of program model that is considered the most ineffective model to teach ELLs, because students are pulled out of their classroom to receive specialized English language instruction. This type of program is generally seen at the elementary school level when there is a small population of ELLs, and the ESL pull-out teacher may travel between several different campuses.

ESOL—An acronym for English for Speakers of Other Languages or English as a Second or Other Language.

Language Experience Approach (LEA)—This approach supports students' vocabulary growth while providing meaningful reading and writing activities. Typically, a teacher asks a student or the class to share a story or event that occurred in their lives. The students dictate the story while the teacher transcribes it. Then the teacher reads the story aloud, followed by the class reading the story aloud in unison. LEA is a wonderful way to develop a classroom community while supporting students' reading and writing development.

Language Learning Strategies—Strategies that students use to improve their progress learning a second language. These strategies assist the learner in remembering and retrieving a new language.

Language Varieties—There are five types of language varieties: pidgin, creole, regional dialect, minority dialect, and indigenized variety. English varieties have a distinct vocabulary and grammatical rules.

Literature Circles—An instructional strategy by which the teacher introduces several books to a class by doing a book talk. Groups of students choose books that they would like to read and discuss as a group. Each group member has specific roles and responsibilities as the group reads the book.

Metacognition—Refers to a students' awareness of his or her own knowledge.

Modeling—Teacher modeling entails explicitly showing students how to perform processes or create products that are the result of classroom instruction.

Monitor—An internal grammatical editor that is called into play as students learn the formal structure and requirements of a language.

Morpheme—A word or part of a word that conveys a grammatical or lexical meaning (such as the -ed ending that turns present tense into past tense).

Morphology—The system dealing with the structure or form of words (want, wanted, wanting, unwanted).

Picture Walk—Helps activate students' background knowledge and helps build interest in a story. To do a picture walk, the students and teacher "read" each picture in a picture story book. They make predictions about what will happen in the story based on analysis of the pictures.

Phonemes—Speech sounds that make a difference in meaning between words (such as pin/pen).

Phonology—Rules governing the sound system of a language, including sound-symbol relationships, intonational variations, stress, pitch, and juncture.

Pragmatics—The conversational rules guiding the use of language in a social situation. These rules change as a variety of social factors change (e.g., context, age, purpose).

Realia—Includes props or other items used during role plays. Realia may include menus, costumes, or fake food.

Rubric—A scoring tool used by teachers to determine the criteria to judge or evaluate a piece of work.

Scaffolding—A teaching strategy originating from Lev Vygotsky's sociocultural theory and his concept of the zone of proximal development. Scaffolding provides individualized support to students, as teachers, parents, and knowledgeable peers provide the assistance that learners need to comprehend and achieve at higher levels.

Semantic Mapping—Sometimes called spider mapping, this graphic organizer accumulates attributes arranged like the spokes of a wheel around a central concept.

Semantics—The meaning underlying a word, phrase, or sentence.

Sheltered Instruction—An approach for teaching content to ELLs in strategic ways that make the subject-matter concepts comprehensible while promoting the students' English language development.

Sheltered Instruction Observational Protocol (SIOP)—An observational form and a model of instruction for teaching language learners' content and language.

Subtractive Bilingualism—This sometimes occurs when young children emigrate. It involves the second language interfering with learning the first language.

Summarizer—An activity at the end of a learning period to help students self-assess and organize the day's learning.

Summative Assessment—Assessment done to evaluate programs and/or district or state education performance. Summative assessment is usually accomplished by district-wide testing or standardized testing.

Syntax—The system describing how words, oral or written, combine into sentences; grammar.

TESOL—An acronym for teaching English to speakers of other languages. TESOL, Inc. (Teachers of English to Speakers of Other Languages, Inc.) is the primary professional association for English language teachers.

Thematic Instruction—Sequenced learning activities revolving around many aspects of a central topic or theme, offering students opportunities to visit the learning objectives of the unit through a variety of activities using many modes of learning.

References

Adelman, H., & Taylor, S. (1996). *Policies and practices for addressing barriers to student learning: Future status and new directions*. Los Angeles: University of California, Los Angeles Center for Mental Health in Schools, Department of Psychology.

Allington, R. L., & Cunningham, P. M. (2002). *Schools that work: Where all children read and write*. Boston: Allyn and Bacon.

Allington, R. L., & Johnson, P. H. (2002). *Reading to learn: Lessons from exemplary fourth grade classrooms*. New York: Guilford Press.

Anderson-Butcher, D., & Ashton, D. (2004). Innovative models of collaboration to serve children, youths, families and communities. *Children and Schools, 26*(1), 39–52.

Arends, R. I. (2004). *Learning to teach* (6th ed.). Boston: McGraw Hill.

Aspiazu, G. G., Bauer, S. C., & Spillett, M. D. (1998). Improving the academic performance of Hispanic youth: A community education model. *Bilingual Research Journal 22*(2), 1–20.

August, D., & Hakuta, K. (1997). *Improving schooling for language-minority children: A research agenda*. Washington, DC: National Academy Press.

August, D., & Hakuta, K. (Eds.). (1998). *Educating language-minority children*. Washington, DC: National Academy Press.

August, D., & Pease-Alvarez, L. (1996). *Attributes of effective programs and classrooms serving English language learners*. Santa Cruz, CA: National Center for Research on Cultural Diversity and Second Language Learning.

Banks, J. A. (2001). Citizenship education and diversity: Implications for teacher education. *Journal of Teacher Education, 52*(1), 5–16.

Banks, J. A. (2002). *An introduction to multicultural education*. Boston: Allyn & Bacon.

Barton, A. C., Drake, C., & Perez, J. G. (2004). The ecologies of parental engagement in urban education. *Educational Researcher, (33)*4, 3–12.

Beck, I., & McKeown, M. G. (1991). Research directions: Social studies texts are hard to understand: Mediating some of the difficulties. *Language Arts, 68*, 482–9.

Berger, E. H. (2002). *Parents as partners in education: Families and schools working together*. Upper Saddle-River, NJ: Prentice-Hall.

Berger, G. R., & Berger, E. H. (1999). Rights, responsibilities and advocacy. In E. H. Berger (Ed.), *Parents as partners in education: Families and schools working together*. New York: Prentice-Hall.

Bloom, B. S. (Ed.). (1956). *Taxonomy of educational objectives: The classification of educational goals. Handbook 1: Cognitive domain*. New York: David McKay.

Boyer, E. L. (1995). *The basic school. A community for learning*. Princeton, NJ: Carnegie Foundation.

Brice, A. E. (2002). *The Hispanic child: Speech, language, culture and education*. Boston: Allyn & Bacon.

Burnette, J. (1998, March). *Reducing the disproportionate representation of minority students in special education*. Reston, VA: ERIC Clearinghouse on Disabilities and Gifted Education. (ERIC Document Reproduction Service No. ED417501)

Calkins, L. (1994). *The art of teaching writing*. New York: Heinemann.

Camarota, S. (2003). *Immigration in a time of recession: An examination of trends since 2002*. Washington, DC: Center for Immigrant Studies. Retrieved August 22, 2006, from http:// www.cis.org/articles/2003/back1603.html

Carle, E. (1987). *The very hungry caterpillar*. New York: Philomel.

Carrasquillo, A. L., & Rodriguez, V. (2002). *Language minority students in the mainstream class* (2nd ed.). Clevedon, England: Multilingual Matters.

Chall, J., Jacobs, V., & Baldwin, L. (1990). *The reading crisis: Why poor children fall behind*. Boston: Harvard University Press.

Chamot, A. U., & Kupper, L. (1989). Learning strategies in foreign language instruction. *Foreign Language Annals 22*, 13–24.

Chamot, A. U., & O'Malley, J. M. (1994). The CALLA handbook: How to implement the cognitive academic language learning approach. Reading, MA: Addison-Wesley.

Cisneros, S. (1994). *The house on Mango Street*. New York: Alfred A. Knopf.

Collier, V., & Thomas, W. P. (1989). How quickly can immigrants become proficient in school English? *Journal of Educational Issues of Language Minority Students, 5*, 26–39.

Collier, V., & Thomas, W. P. (2002). Reforming education policies for English learners means better schools for all. *The State Education Standard, 3*(1), 30–36.

Comer, J. (1986). Parent participation in schools. *Phi Delta Kappan, 67*, 442–446.

Cook, V. (2004). *Second language acquisition topics*. Retrieved October 31, 2006, from http://homepage.ntlworld.com/vivian.c/SLA/

Craske, M. L. (1985). Improving persistence through observational learning and attribution retraining. *British Journal of Educational Psychology, 55*, 138–147.

Crawford, J. (2000). *At war with diversity: US language policy in an age of anxiety*. Clevedon, England: Multilingual Matters.

Crawford, J. (2004a) *Educating English learners: Language diversity in the classroom*. (5th Ed.). Los Angeles: Bilingual Education Services.

Crawford, J., (2004b). *No child left behind: Misguided approach to school accountability for English language learners*. Forum on Ideas to Improve the NCLB Accountability Provisions for Students with Disabilities and English Language Learners. Center for Education Policy, NABE.

Cross, W. E., Jr. (1991). *Shades of black: Diversity in African-American identity*. Philadelphia: Temple University Press.

Cummins, J. (1981a). Age on arrival and immigrant second language learning in Canada: A reassessment. *Applied Linguistics, 2*, 132–149.

Cummins, J. (1981b). The role of primary language development in promoting educational success for language minority students. In California State Department of Education (Ed.), *Schooling and language minority students: A theoretical framework*, 3–50. Evaluation, Dissemination and Assessment Center, California State University, Los Angeles.

Cummins, J. (1984). *Bilingualism and special education: Issues in assessment and pedagogy*. Clevedon, England: Multilingual Matters.

Cummins, J. (1986). Empowering minority students: A framework for intervention. *Harvard Educational Review, 56*, 18–36.

Cummins, J. (1996). *Negotiating identities: Education for empowerment in a diverse society*. Los Angeles: California Association for Bilingual Education.

Cummins, J. (2000). *Language, power, and pedagogy: Bilingual children in the crossfire*. North York, Ontario, Canada: Multilingual Matters.

Cunningham, A., & Stanovich, K. (1997). Early reading acquisition and its relation to reading experience and ability 10 years later. *Developmental Psychology, 33*(6), 934–945.

Dalton, S. S. (1998). *Pedagogy matters: Standards for effective teaching practice*. Santa Cruz, CA: National Center for Research on Education, Diversity and Excellence.

Daniels, H. (2001). *Looking into literature circles*. Portland, ME: Stenhouse.

Davies, D. (2001). Family participation in decision-making and advocacy. In D. B. Hiatt-Michael (Ed.), *Promising practices for family involvement in schools*. Greenwich, CT: Information Age.

De Carvalho, M. P. (2001). *Rethinking family-school relations. A critique of parental involvement*. Mahwah, NJ: Lawrence Erlbaum.

deKanter, A., Ginsburg, A. L., Pederson, J., Peterson, T. K., & Rich, D. (1997). A compact for learning: An action handbook for family-school-community partnerships. Retrieved June 8, 2006, from http://www.ed.gov/pubs/Compact/index.html

Derman-Sparks, L. (1989). *Anti-bias curriculum: Tools for empowering young children*. Washington, DC: National Association for the Education of Young Children.

Dewey, J. (1938). *Experience and education*. New York: Macmillan/Collier.

Diamond, J. (2004). Leveling the playing field for urban school children: An interview with assistant professor John Diamond. *Harvard Graduate School of Education News*, Retrieved October 31, 2006, from http://www.gse.harvard.edu/news/features/diamond09012004.html

Diaz-Rico, L. T. (2004). *Teaching English learners: Strategies and methods*. Boston: Allyn & Bacon.

Diaz-Rico, L. T., & Weed, K. Z. (2005). *The crosscultural language and academic development handbook: A complete K–12 reference guide* (3rd ed.). Boston: Allyn & Bacon.

Discovery Works. (2000). Systems in living things. (Florida edition). Houghton Mifflin.

Doyle, D. P., & Pimental, S. (1997). *Raising the standard: Coalition for goals 2000*. Thousand Oaks, CA: Corwin Press.

Echevarria, J., & Graves, A. (2003). *Sheltered content instruction: Teaching English-language learners with diverse abilities*. Boston: Allyn & Bacon.

Echevarria, J., Short, D., & Vogt, M. (2004). *Making content comprehensible for English language learners. The SIOP Model*. Boston: Allyn & Bacon.

Edmondson, K. M., & Novak, J. D. (1993). The interplay of scientific epistemological views, learning strategies and attributes of college students. *Journal of Research in Science Teaching, 30*, 547–559.

Epstein, J. L. (2000). *School, family and community partnerships: Preparing educators and improving schools*. Boulder, CO: Westview Press.

Epstein, J. L., Sanders, M. G., Simon, B. S., Salinas, K. C., Jansorn, N. R., & Van Voorhis, F. L. (2002). *School, family, and community partnerships. Your handbook for action* (2nd ed.). Thousand Oaks, CA: Corwin Press.

Farr, B. P., & Trumbull, E. (1997). *Assessment alternatives for diverse classrooms*. Norwood, MA: Christopher-Gordon.

Finn, C. E., Petrilli, M. J., & Vanourek, G. (1998). The state of standards. *Fordham Report, 2*(5).

Florida Department of Education. (2005). *Sunshine State Standards* (n.d.). Retrieved October 31, 2006, from http://www.firn.edu/doe/curric/prek12/frame2.htm

Food Research and Action Center. (n.d.). Retrieved August 22, 2006, from http://www.frac.org/

Freeman, Y., & Freeman, D. (2003). Struggling English language learners: Keys for academic success. *TESOL Journal 12*(3), 5–10.

Gandal, M., & Vranek, J. (2001). Standards: Here today, here tomorrow. *Educational Leadership, 59*(1), 6–13.

Garcia, E. (1994). *Understanding the needs of LEP students*. Boston: Houghton Mifflin.

Garcia, E. (2002). *Student cultural diversity: Understanding and meeting the challenge* (3rd ed.). Boston: Houghton Mifflin.

Gay, G. (2000). *Culturally responsive teaching: Theory, research, and practice*. New York: Teachers College Press.

Gibbons, P. (2002). *Scaffolding language, scaffolding learning: Teaching second language learners in the mainstream class*. Portsmouth, NH: Heinemann.

Gibson, M. A., & Ogbu, J. (Eds.). (1991). *Minority status and schooling: A comparative study of immigrant and involuntary minorities*. New York: Garland.

Griego Jones, T., & Fuller, M. L. (2003). *Teaching Hispanic children*. Boston: Allyn & Bacon.

The growing numbers of limited English proficiency students, 1991–2002. (2003, March). *Horace, 19*(2). Retrieved May 17, 2006, from http://www.essentialschools.org/cs/resources/view/ces_res/290

Hadaway, N. L., Vardell, S. M., & Young, T. A. (2002). *Literature-based instruction with English language learners K–12*. Boston: Allyn & Bacon.

Hakuta, K., & Beatty, A. (Eds.). (2000). *Testing English language learners in U.S. schools*. Washington, DC: National Academy Press.

Hakuta, K., Butler, Y. G., & Witt, D. (2000). *How long does it take for English language learners to attain proficiency?* Santa Barbara, CA: Linguistic Minority Research Institute.

Heath, S. B. (1983). *Ways with words: Language, life and work in communities and classrooms*. New York: Cambridge University Press.

Henderson, A. C., & Berla, N. (1994). *A new generation of evidence. The family is critical to school reform*. Washington, DC: Center for Law and Education.

Herrera, S., & Murry, K. G. (1999). In the aftermath of Unz. *Bilingual Research Journal, 23*(2/3), 113–132.

Hiatt-Michael, D. B. (2001). Home-school communication. In D. B. Hiatt-Michael (Ed.), *Promising practices for family involvement in schools*. Greenwich, CT: Information Age.

Hoban, T. (1998). *More, fewer, less*. New York: Greenwillow.

Houk, F. (2005). *Supporting English language learners. A guide for teachers and adminstrators*. Portsmouth, NH: Heinemann.

Huerta-Macias, A. (1995). Alternative assessment: Response to commonly asked questions [Special issue]. *TESOL Journal, 5*(1), 8–11.

Hutchins, P. (1986). *The doorbell rang*. New York: Greenwillow.

Izumi, L. T. (1999). *Developing and implementing academic standards: A template for legislation and policy reform*. San Francisco: Pacific Research Institute for Public Policy.

Jacobs, H. H. (2002). *Getting results with curriculum mapping*. Alexandria, VA: Association for Supervision and Curriculum Development.

Jacobs, V. A. (2002). Reading, writing, and understanding. *Educational Leadership, 60*(3), 58–61.

Jensen, E. (1998). *Teaching with the brain in mind*. Alexandria, VA: Association for Supervision and Curriculum Development.

Johnson, D. W., Johnson, R. T., & Holubec, E. (1990). *Circles of learning: Cooperation in the classroom*. Edina, MN: Interaction Book Company.

Johnson, D. W., Johnson, R. T., & Holubec, E. (1991). *Revised cooperation in the classroom*. Edina, MN: Interaction Book Company.

Johnson, S. M., & Kardos, S. M. (2002). Keeping new teachers in mind. *Educational Leadership, 59*(6), 12–16.

Jones, T. G. & Velez, W. (1997, March). *Effects of Latino parent involvement on academic achievement*. Paper presented at the annual meeting of the American Educational Research Association, Chicago.

Keene, E., & Zimmermann, S. (1997). *Mosaic of thought. Teaching comprehension in a reader's workshop*. Portsmouth, NH: Heinemann

Knitzer, K. (1999). Responsibility for delivery services. In J. S. Mearig (Ed.), *Working for children: Ethical issues beyond professional guidelines* (pp. 223–247). San Francisco: Jossey-Bass.

Lachat, M. A. (2004). *Standards-based instruction and assessment for English language learners*. Thousand Oaks, CA: Corwin Press.

Lacina, J. (2001, October). Cultural kickboxing in the ESL classroom: Encouraging active participation. *The Internet TESL Journal, 7*(10). Retrieved May 18, 2006, from http://iteslj.org/Techniques/Lacina-Kickboxing.html

Lacina, J. (2004). *Literature circles: 7th grade Lufkin Middle School and 2nd grade NISD Charter School.* Nacogdoches, TX: Stephen F. Austin State University Office of Public Affairs.

Ladson-Billings, G. (1994). *The dreamkeepers.* San Francisco: Jossey-Bass.

Langer, G. M., Colton, A. B., & Goff, L. S. (2003). *Collaborative analysis of student work.* Alexandria, VA: Association for Supervision and Curriculum Development.

Language varieties. (2005). Retrieved August 10, 2006, from http://www.une.edu .au/langnet/index.html

Lasker, B. (1929). *Race attitudes in children.* New York: Henry Holt.

Lau v. Nichols, 414 U.S. 563 (1974).

League of United Latin American Citizens (LULAC); ASPIRA of Florida; the Farmwokers Association of Central Florida; Florida state Conference of NAACP Branches; Hatian Refugee Center; Spanish American League Against Discrimination (SALAD); American Hispanic Educator's Association of Dade (AHEAD); Hatian Educator's Association; Carolina M.; Claudia M.; Delia M.; Lydia L.; Sammy L.; Seth L.; and Juan Carlos G. vs. the Florida Board of Education, No. 90-1913, 1990 U.S. Court of the Southern District of Florida.

Lee, F. Y, Silverman, F. L., & Montoya, P. (2002). Assessing the mathematical performance of young ESL students. *Principal Magazine, 81*(3), 29–31.

Lessow-Hurley, J. (1996). *The foundations of dual language instruction.* New York: Longman.

Lessow-Hurley, J. (2005). *The foundations of dual language instruction* (4th ed.). Boston: Pearson.

Lewis, C., Perry, R., & Hurd, J. (2004). A deeper look at lesson study. *Educational Leadership, 61*(5), 18–22.

Lindholm-Leary, K. J. (2005). *Review of research and best practices on effective features of dual language education programs.* Washington, DC: George Washington University, Center for Applied Linguistics, and National Clearinghouse for English Language Acquisition.

Little, J. W. (1990). The persistence of privacy: Autonomy and initiative in teachers' professional relations. *Teachers College Record, 91*(4), 509–536.

Local Investment Commission (LINC). (2005). *McCoy Elementary Health Classrooms Initiative.* Kansas City, MO: Author.

Lockwood, A. T. (1996). Community collaboration and social capital. An interview with Gary Wehlage. Retrieved May 19, 2006, from http://www.ncrel.org/cscd/pubs/lead21/2-1m.htm

Lockwood, A. T., Stinnette, L. J., & D'Amico, J. (1997). *Collaborating for the common good. New leaders for tomorrow's schools. 2.1*. Retrieved June 8, 2006, from http://www.ncrel.org.sccd/pubs/lead21/2-b.htm

Macias, R. F. (1998). *How has the limited English proficient student population changed in recent years*? Washington, DC: George Washington University, National Clearinghouse for Bilingual Education.

Macías, R. F. (2000). The flowering of America: Linguistic diversity in the United States. In S. L. McKay & S. C. Wong (Eds.), *New immigrants in the United States* (pp. 11–57). Cambridge: Cambridge University Press.

Markowitz, J., Garcia, S. B., & Eichelberger, J. H. (March, 1997). *Addressing the disproportionate representation of students from ethnic and racial minority groups in special education: A resource document*. Alexandria, VA: National Association of State Directors of Special Education. (ERIC Document Reproduction Service No. ED406810)

Marzano, R. J. (2003). *What works in schools: Translating research into action*. Alexandria, VA: Association for Supervision and Curriculum Development.

Marzano, R. J., Pickering, D. J., & Pollock, J. E. (2001). *Classroom instruction that works: Research-based strategies for increasing student achievement*. Alexandria, VA: Association for Supervision and Curriculum Development.

Mather, J. R. C., & Chiodo, J. J. (1994). A mathematical problem: How do we teach mathematics to LEP elementary students? *The Journal of Educational Issues of Language Minority Students, 13*, 1–12.

McCoy Elementary School (2005, March). Healthy steps. Healthy classrooms initiative. *McCoy Elementary Newsletter. 1*(2), 1–2.

Meisels, S. J., Dorfman, A., & Steele, D. (1995). Equity and excellence in group-administered and performance-based assessments. In M. Nettels and A. Nettles (Eds.), *Equity and excellence in educational testing and assessment*. Boston: Kluwer Academic.

Meyer v. Nebraska, 262 U.S. 390, 43S.Ct. 625 (1923).

Mohan, B. A. (1986). *Language and content*. Reading, MA: Addison-Wesley.

National Association of Bilingual Education (NABE). (2004a). *No Child Left Behind Act*. Retrieved August 22, 2006, from http: //www.nabe.org/advocacy/nclb/html

National Association of Bilingual Education. (2004b). *Partnerships for advocacy*. Retrieved August 22, 2006, from http://www.nabe.org/advocacy/partnerships.html

National Association for Bilingual Education. (2004c). *What is Bilingualism?* Retrieved January 21, 2006, from http://www.nabe.org/education/index.html

National Clearinghouse for Bilingual Education (NCBE). (2000). *Summary report of the survey of the states' limited English proficient students and available educational programs and services, 1997–1998*. Washington, DC: George Washington University.

National Clearinghouse for English Language Acquisition and Language Instruction Educational Programs (NCELA). (2005). *Frequently asked questions*. Retrieved June 1, 2006, from http://www.ncela.gwu.edu/expert/faq/01leps.htm

National Commission on Excellence in Education. (1983). *A nation at risk: The imperative for educational reform*. Washington, DC: U.S. Department of Education.

National Council for Accreditation of Teacher Education (NCATE). (2002). *Professional standards for the accreditation of schools, colleges and departments of education*. Washington, DC: Author.

National Council for the Social Studies (NCSS). (n.d.). About NCSS. Retrieved October 1, 2006, from http://www.socialstudies.org/about/ *and* http://www.socialstudies.org/standards/teachers/vol2/thematic

National Council for Teachers of English (NCTE). (2005). Supporting linguistically and culturally diverse learners in English education. Retrieved May 1 2006, from http://www.ncte.org/groups/cee/positions/122892.htm

National Council of Teachers of Mathematics (NCTM). (1989). *Curriculum and evaluation standards for school math*. Reston, VA: Author.

National Education Goals Panel. (1991). *The national education goals report: Building a nation of learners*. Washington, DC: U.S. Government Printing Office.

Nieto, S. (2002). *Language, culture, and teaching: Critical perspectives for a new century*. Mahwah, NJ: Lawrence Erlbaum.

North Central Regional Educational Laboratory (NCREL). (1997). Pathways to school improvement—family and community. Retrieved June 8, 2006, from http://www.ncrel.org/sdrs/areas/pa0cont.htm

O'Malley, J. M., & Valdez-Pierce, L. (1996). *Authentic assessment for English language learners*. Reading, MA: Addison-Wesley.

Oxford, R. L. (1990). *Language learning strategies*. Rowley, MA: Newbury House.

Payne, R. (2004). *A framework for understanding poverty*. Highlands, TX: Aha! Process.

Piaget, J. (1971). *Genetic epistemology*. (E. Duckworth, Trans.). New York: Norton. (Original work published 1970)

Reeves, J. (2005). Like everybody else: Equalizing educational opportunity for English language learners. *TESOL Quarterly, 38,* 43–66.

Rigney, J. W. (1978). Learning strategies: A theoretical perspective. In H. F. O'Neil, Jr. (Ed.), *Learning strategies* (pp. 164–205). New York: Academic Press.

Robinson, F. P. (1970). *Effective study*. New York: Harper & Row.

Rubin, J. (1975). What the "good language learner" can teach us. *TESOL Quarterly, 9,* 41–51.

Sapp, J. (2004). Holiday stereotyping activity. Retrieved May 1, 2006, from http://www.tolerance.org/images/teach/activities/tt_holiday_stereotype.pdf

Scherer, M. (2001). How and why standards can improve student achievement: A conversation with Robert J. Marzano. *Educational Leadership, 59*(1), 14–18.

Scott, J. A. (2004). Scaffolding vocabulary learning: Ideas for equity in urban settings. In D. Lapp, C. C. Block, E. J. Cooper, J. Flood, N. Roser, & J. V. Tinajero (Eds.), *Teaching all the children: Strategies for developing literacy in an urban setting* (pp. 275–293). New York: Guilford Press.

Secada, W. G., & Carey, D. A. (1990). *Teaching mathematics with understanding to limited English proficient students.* New York: Institute on Urban and Minority Education. (ERIC Document Reproduction Service No. ED322284)

Sergiovanni, T. J. (1994). *Building community in schools.* San Francisco: Jossey-Bass.

Sergiovanni, T. J. (1999). *The lifeworld of leadership. Creating culture, community and personal meaning in our schools.* San Francisco: Jossey-Bass.

Short, D. J. (1993). Assessing integrated language and content instruction. *TESOL Quarterly, 27*(4), 627–665.

Short, D. J. (2000). Using the ESL standards for curriculum development. In M. A. Snow (Ed.), *Implementing the ESL standards for pre-K–12 students through teacher education* (pp. 103–136). Alexandria, VA: TESOL.

Simon, B. S., & Epstein, J. L. (2001). School, family, and community partnerships. In D. B. Hiatt-Michael (Ed.), *Promising practices for family involvement in schools.* Greenwich, CT: Information Age.

Slavin, R. E. (1981). A policy choice: Cooperative or competitive learning. *Character, 3,* 1–6.

Slavin, R. E. (1990). *Cooperative learning: Theory, research, and practice.* Englewood Cliffs, NJ: Prentice Hall.

Sleeter, C. E. (2001). Preparing teachers for culturally diverse schools: Research and the overwhelming presence of whiteness. *Journal of Teacher Education, 52*(2), 94–106.

Smith, F. (1987). *Joining the literacy club.* Portsmouth, NH: Heinemann.

Smith, M. E., Teemant, A., & Pinnegar, S. (2004). Principles and practices of sociocultural assessment: Foundations for effective strategies for linguistically diverse classrooms. *Multicultural Perspectives, 6*(2), 38–46.

Stegelin, D., & Wright, K. W. (1999). *Building school and community partnerships through parent involvment.* Upper Saddle River, NJ: Merrill.

Stephan, W. G. (1999). *Reducing prejudice and stereotyping in schools*. New York: Teachers College Press.

Taylor, S. V., & Sobel, D. M. (2001). Addressing the discontinuity of students' and teachers' diversity: A preliminary study of preservice teachers' beliefs and perceived skills. *Teaching and Teacher Education, 17,* 487–503.

TESOL. (1997). *ESL standards for pre-K–12 students*. Alexandria, VA: Author.

TESOL. (2003, March). Position paper on high-stakes testing for K–12 English language learners in the United States of America. Retrieved September 18, 2006, from http://www.tesol.org/s_tesol/seccss.asp?CID=32&DID=37

TESOL. (2004). *TESOL takes position against-high stakes testing*. Press release. Retrieved June 8, 2006, from http://www.tesol.org/s_tesol/seccss.asp?CID=329&DID=1935

Texas Education Agency. (2005). *Statewide TAKS result press release*. Retrieved October 31, 2006, from http://www.tea.state.tx.us/press/prtaks52005.html

Tinajero, V. J., & Hurley, S. R. (2001). Assessing progress in second-language learning. In S. R. Hurley, & V. J. Tinajero (Eds.), *Literacy assessment of second language learners*. Reading, MA: Allyn and Bacon.

Tomlinson, C. A. (1999). *The differentiated classroom: Responding to the needs of all learners*. Alexandria, VA: Association for Supervision and Curriculum Development.

Tompkins, G. E. (2003). *Literacy for the 21st century* (3rd ed.). Upper Saddle River, NJ: Merrill.

U.S. Census Bureau. (2000). Hispanic population in the United States. Retrieved October 31, 2006, from http://www.census.gov/population/www/socdemo/hispanic.html

U.S. Census Bureau. (2004). Poverty. Retrieved June 19, 2005, from http://www.census.gov/hhes/www/poverty/poverty.html

U.S. Department of Education, National Clearinghouse for English Language Acquisition and Language Instruction Educational Programs. (2002). *2000–2001 summary report. Survey of the states' limited English proficient students and available educational programs and services*. Washington, DC: Author.

Vacca, R. T., & Vacca, J. A. (2005). *Content area reading: Literacy and learning across the curriculum* (8th ed.). New York: Pearson.

Van de Walle, J. (2004). *Elementary and middle school mathematics: Teaching developmentally* (5th ed.). Boston: Pearson.

Vygotsky, L. S. (1978). *Mind in society: The development of higher psychological processes*. (M. Cole, V. John-Steiner, S. Scribner, & E. Souberman, Eds. & Trans.). Cambridge, MA: Harvard University Press.

Waggoner, D. (1998). Ethnic-linguistic minorities in the United States. *Numbers and Needs, 8*(2), 1–4.

Warger, C., & Burnette, J. (2000, August). *Five strategies to reduce overrepresentation of culturally and linguistically diverse students in special education.* Reston, VA: ERIC Clearinghouse on Disabilities and Gifted Education. (ERIC Document Reproduction Service No. E596). Retrieved October 31, 2006, from http://ericec.org/digests /e596.html

Weiner, B. (1974). *Achievement, motivation and attribution theory.* Morristown, NJ: General Learning Press.

Wiggins, G. (1998). *Educative assessment. Designing assessments to inform and improve student performance.* San Francisco: Jossey-Bass.

Wiggins, G., & McTighe, J. (1998). *Understanding by design.* Alexandria, VA: Association for Supervision and Curriculum Development.

Zeichner, K. M. (1993). *Educating teachers for cultural diversity.* NCRTL Special Report. East Lansing: Michigan State University, National Center for Research on Teacher Learning.

Zentella, A. C. (1997). *Growing up bilingual.* Malden, MA: Blackwell.

Contributors

On title page and throughout book, author's names are alphabetical. All authors contributed equally.

Jan Lacina is an assistant professor at Texas Christian University. She has taught ESL to Grades 1–6 in Texas, USA, and has taught in a university intensive English program in Kansas, USA. Currently, Dr. Lacina teaches reading and ESL classes to preservice teachers. Her research focuses on ways that teachers integrate technology into literacy instruction. Dr. Lacina's work is published in journals such as *Voices from the Middle*, *Language Arts*, *Teacher Education Quarterly*, *The Teacher Educator*, *Journal of Computing in Teacher Education*, *The Social Studies*, and *English in Texas*. She also writes the column "Technology in the Classroom" for the journal *Childhood Education*.

Linda New Levine is an ESL/EFL consultant conducting numerous workshops with ESL, EFL, and mainstream teachers on four continents. She has been a teacher of ESL for grades K–12 and staff development facilitator for the Bedford Central School District in New York, USA. She has also taught ESL methods and materials at Teachers College, Columbia University, New York. She is the author of "The Most Beautiful Place in the World" (2000) in Samway, K.D. (Ed.), *Integrating the ESL Standards Into Classroom Practice Grades 3–5*, and the forthcoming *One Class Many Paths: Teaching Learners of English in Mainstream Classrooms (K–8)* with Mary Lou McCloskey.

Patience Adjekai Sowa is an Assistant Professor at Rockhurst University. She has taught English language learners in K–12 settings as well as in formal and informal adult education programs. As a teacher educator she teaches classes in ELL and foreign language methods, second language acquisition, and research methods. Her research interests include effective preparation of foreign language and ELL teachers, literacy and English language learning, and multicultural education. A SIOP trainer, Dr. Sowa is especially interested in working with content area teachers to effectively teach English language learners in mainstream classes.

Debra Suarez is associate professor of TESOL at the College of Notre Dame of Maryland. She teaches in the MA TESOL program and in the Ph.D. program, "Educational Leadership for Changing Populations." Her areas of specialization are teacher education and heritage language learners. In addition to editing the Collaborative Partnership series, she has contributed to *TESOL Journal, Journal of Multilingual and Multicultural Development, TESOL Quarterly,* and *Educational Horizons,* and has coedited a special issue of *Heritage Language Journal.* Suarez, a former ESL/EFL teacher, has presented at TESOL conferences and taught graduate courses in countries around the world, including Korea, Guatemala, Venezuela, Ukraine, Mexico, Peru, and Syria.

Index

Page references followed by *f* and *t* indicate figures and tables, respectively.

A

Academic ability, grouping by, 16
Academic language, 10–11, 15, 34, 39, 67, 107
Academic proficiency, 67, 112
Accelerated Reader Program (AR), 139, 140
Accommodation, 9, 11, 12, 113
Acculturation, 85, 86, 99, 152
Acronyms as learning tool, 73
Across-grade-level collaboration, 83–84
Activities, instructional, 6, 11, 15
Adaptation of instruction, 11, 14, 25, 30
Addition, 108
Additive acculturation, 85, 87*f*
Adequate Yearly Progress (AYP), 147
Adult education programs, 131, 137
Advance organizers, 15, 71*t*
Advocacy for English language learners
  case studies, 154–155
  definition and characteristics of, 146, 156
  family involvement and, 136
  forms of, 149–154, 156
  need for, 146–149
AFEA (Alliance for Fair and Effective
  Accountability), 147
Affective learning strategies, 71
All-school groupings, 142
Alternative instruction, 48*t*
Ambiguity in language, 59, 64*t*

Analytical learners, 13
Analyzing, 8, 38
Anderson-Butcher, D., 130, 136
Antonyms, 16, 77*t*
The Art of Teaching Writing (Calkins), 118
Arts, content learning in, 5
ASCRIBER (alignment, standard setting,
  curriculum development, retooling,
  implementation, benchmarking,
  evaluation, revision), 40, 41
Ashton, D., 130, 136
Assessment
  accuracy of, 109
  authentic, performance based, 104, 119
  bias in, 110, 112, 118
  in content areas, 117, 121
  curriculum *versus,* 9, 111
  defined, 104–105
  design of, 103
  flexible, 111
  instruments, 6, 7, 26, 139
  language requirements for, 3, 107, 110, 155
  multiple, 3, 26, 30
  reform, 105
  results, analyzing, 81
  scaffolding in, 104, 107, 108*t*, 113
  sociocultural, 104, 105, 109–111, 114, 120,
    121
  standards, 111, 113–114
  types of, 114, 115*t*
At risk students, expectations toward, 38
Autonomy *versus* collaboration, 42–44

B

Backward design, 4

Balanced literacy, 139, 140

Balance of standards, 38, 52

Basic interpersonal communication skills (BICS), 67

Basic School model, 125, 137

Before- and after-school care, 123

Behaviorist views of learning, 105

Beliefs, probing for, 45

Beliefs and values. *See* Values and beliefs

Benchmarks and benchmarking, 35, 37, 40

Berger, E.H., 130, 134, 149, 150

Berger, G.R., 149, 150

Bias in assessments, 110, 112, 118

Bilingual education, 24–25, 61, 146, 147, 148. *See also* Dual language programs

Bilingual Education Act, 146

Bilingualism (defined), 148

Bilingual recipe books, 137

Bilingual students, 21, 27, 33, 50, 97

Bilingual teachers, 57–59, 62, 65

Boyer, E.L., 124, 125, 132, 137, 138, 140

Breadth of learning, 37

Businesses, 124, 125, 130, 131

C

California Proposition 227, 148

Calkins, L., 118

CALP (cognitive academic language proficiency), 67

Carle, E., 116

Celebrations, cultural, 84, 85–86, 87*f*, 91, 93*f*, 94, 94*f*, 95*f*, 96*f*

Charts, 16, 20, 23, 68

Child development, culture role in, 87–88, 99

Children

  caregivers of, 124

  culturally and linguistically diverse, 124, 130, 140

  with disabilities, 147

  immigrant, 148, 149–150

  minority, legislation impact on, 147

  in poverty, 147, 148

  rights of, 146

Children's Defense Fund, 147

Choral reading, 13

Cinco de Mayo (Mexican holiday), 84, 85, 91, 93*f*, 94, 94*f*

Cisneros, S., 67, 68

Civil rights organizations, 147

Clarity, 15, 16, 30, 32, 37

Classrooms

  environment, appropriate, 149

  management of, 16, 18, 26, 30

  supports, 7, 24

Cognitive academic language proficiency (CALP), 67

Cognitive challenges, 10, 14–15, 30

Cognitive learning strategies, 50, 71, 72*t*

Collaboration *versus* autonomy, 42–44

Collaborative activities, 16, 22, 23, 80

Collaborative inquiry, 42–44, 49, 53

Collaborative learning, 15–16, 24, 30, 104

Collaborative teaching

  and assessment, 107, 113, 114, 116–118, 121

  in Basic School model, 125

  case studies

    for language learning needs, 75

    in mathematics, 114, 116–117

    in reading, 91

    in science, 22, 26, 28

    in social studies, 96–97

    in writing, 33–34, 41–42

  communication skills for, 44–45, 53

  community, fostering through, 138–140, 142

  components of, 30

  and curriculum, 76–77

  diverse learners, meeting needs through, 106

  to mentor students, 78

  origin of, 1

  partnerships, 62

  requirements for effective, 2, 81

  for standards-based instruction, 49–50, 53

  and state tests, 75–76

  support for, 45–47, 49

Collective judgments. *See* Group norms

Collegiality, 44, 151

Communication

  forms and variations in, 62–63, 106

  in school, family and community partnerships, 126, 128*t*

  skills and strategies, 44–45, 53, 67, 133

Community

  definition and components of, 124–125

  language learning, role in, 68, 70

  of learning, 125, 140, 142

First language
    school as second language learning success
        predictor, 67
    student background in, 80
    tests and testing in, 60, 147
    use, positions on, 86
    validation of, 81
Fluency (defined), 67
Force and motion, unit on, 23
Fourth of July (U.S. holiday), 94, 94*f*, 95*f*
Fractions, using, 58
Futurity, 150, 152–154

G

Gender
    anti-discrimination legislation, 146
    and communication, 62–63
Geography, writing instruction, integration
    with, 89
Gifted students, 10, 153, 154
Gladstone Elementary School, 133, 138, 140
Grade-level meetings, 78–79, 113, 114,
    116–117, 119–120
Grade-level teams, 75
Grade team leaders, 46, 49
Grammar, correcting, 47
Graphic organizers, 15, 16, 26, 46, 92
Graves, A., 71, 73
Greene Elementary School, 140–141
Group activities, 16, 22, 23, 80, 117
Group facilitators, 45–46, 49
Group norms, 43, 44, 53

H

Hands-on lessons, 3, 6
Health agencies and providers, 124, 130
Health information, 128*t*
Health services, 131, 137–138, 150, 151, 152
Help at home (in school, family and
    community partnership), 126, 127,
    128*t*, 141
Heroes, cultural, 86, 89
Herrera, S., 150, 151
Hispanic population, 61
History, teaching, 17, 86, 94
Hoban, T., 116
Holidays and celebrations. *See* Celebrations,
    cultural
Home and school culture, 83, 87, 106

Home-school communication, 128*t*, 132,
    133–134, 135*t*, 142
Home-school connection, 81, 138, 141
Home visits, 133, 141
Homework, 15, 128*t*, 133
Homonyms, 58, 59*f*
Houghton Mifflin Science program, 19
Houk, F., 134, 136, 138, 152
The House on Mango Street (Cisneros), 67, 68
Houston Elementary School, 154–155
Human concerns and culture, 90, 96*f*, 99
Hutchins, P., 116

I

Immersion, 61, 63*t*, 80
Immigrants and immigration, 87*f*, 134, 148,
    149–150, 151, 156
Independent learning, 6, 7, 23, 71
In-service courses and training, 47, 49, 98
Instructional materials, 37, 42, 50, 53, 81
Instructional strategies, 12–18, 30, 50, 53, 89
Instructional variations, 13–14, 30
Interaction role in language learning, 67–68
Interactive learning, 15–16, 24, 30, 104
International Reading Association, 65
Interviews and interviewing, 14, 107, 115*t*
Iraq, teaching about, 97–98

J

Journals and journal writing, 107, 108, 114

K

Keene, E., 139
Knowledge
    applying, 8, 117–118
    demonstration of, 106
    determining levels of, 71, 73
    experience-based, 14
    framework of, 9
    multiple exposures to, 14–15
    versus skills, 38
    transfer of, 72*t*
Knowledge, prior
    accommodating, 12
    activating, 14, 15
    activities based on, 6
    and assessments, 110
    building on, 6, 9, 10, 13, 58, 73, 91–92,
    110, 117

Rigor of standards, 38

Rigorousness of curriculum, 10, 11, 14, 29, 37, 39, 52

Role play, 7, 94, 109, 114

Roundtable/Circle of Heads (cooperative learning structure), 96f

RPTE (Reading Proficiency Tests in English), 75

Rubrics, 17, 47, 107, 109, 116, 117t, 118

S

Scaffolding
  of activities, 9–10
  of assessments, 104, 107, 108t, 113
  of content learning, 23, 30, 60, 63t, 75, 93–94, 99, 106
  knowledge as, 38
  of language instruction, 58, 60, 74, 77, 81, 84, 91, 106, 154

School-home activity packets, 133

Schools
  Adequate Yearly Progress (AYP) of, 147
  climate, welcoming, 132–133, 141
  as communities, 124–125
  handbooks of, 133
  leadership of, redefined, 36
  moral obligations of, 125
  organization of, opportunities for better, 36
  parent programs at, 133
  performance, judging, 35
  services linked to, 132, 137–138, 142
  Web sites of, 134

Science
  adaptation of instruction in, 25
  assessment, 57, 155
  content learning in, 3
  experiments, 23, 25, 108t
  instruction, case studies in, 3, 19–29
  projects, 6, 25
  similarities, illustrating in, 17
  vocabulary, 5, 74

Second language development. See Language development

Self-assessment, 17, 26, 105, 107, 114, 115t

Self-contained language learning programs, 63t, 80

Self-management, 71t

Semantic maps, 94, 108t

Semantics, 64, 64t, 74, 80

Sergiovanni, T.J., 124, 125, 129

Sheltered English learning programs
  characteristics of, 63t, 103
  for content area teaching, 92
  at kindergarten level, 103, 109, 114, 149
  models for, 106–107, 122
  overview of, 1, 80
  and reading instruction, 116

Short-term ESL programs, 67

Similarities, illustrating, 17–18, 30

Similes, teaching, 42, 47

SIOP (Sheltered Instruction Observation Model), 106–107, 122

Skills, 6, 8, 10, 11, 12, 38

Social action approach to multicultural reform, 87f

Social capital, 125, 131

Social contracts and covenants, 124, 125

Social justice, 154

Social language, 39, 67, 107

Social mediation strategies, 72t

Social mores, 106

Social organizations, 124–125

Social services, 123, 124, 128t, 131, 138, 142, 149–150

Social studies
  case studies, 83–84, 86, 87f, 90, 91, 94, 95f–96f, 96–97
  content learning in, 5
  cooperative learning and, 94–95
  culture as component of, 84, 85, 86, 87f, 90, 91, 95f–96f, 99
  language instruction integration into, 91–92
  similarities, illustrating in, 17
  tradebooks in, 94
  vocabulary, 5, 92, 99

Sociocultural awareness, 106–107

Socioeconomic status and communication, 62

Songs and music, social studies instruction through, 94

Spanglish, 66, 79

Spanish-language instruction, 58, 78

Spanish-speaking support staff, 61

Speaking
  activities, 15
  assessment of, 107

Special education
  placement in, 153, 154
  students, 3, 10, 21, 22, 27, 35

Specificity of standards, 37, 52

Spiral curriculum, 8, 10, 29

Also Available from TESOL

Bilingual Education
Donna Christian and Fred Genesee, Editors

Bridge to the Classroom: ESL Cases for Teacher Exploration
Joy Egbert and Gina Mikel Petrie

CALL Essentials
Joy Egbert

Communities of Supportive Professionals
Tim Murphey and Kazuyoshi Sato, Editors

Content-Based Instruction in Primary and Secondary School Settings
Dorit Kaufman and JoAnn Crandall, Editors

ESOL Tests and Testing
Stephen Stoynoff and Carol A. Chapelle

Gender and English Language Learners
Bonny Norton and Aneta Pavlenko, Editors

Language Teacher Research in Asia
Thomas S. C. Farrell, Editor

Literature in Language Teaching and Learning
Amos Paran, Editor

More Than a Native Speaker: An Introduction to Teaching English Abroad
revised edition
Don Snow

Perspectives on Community College ESL Series
Craig Machado, Series Editor
Volume 1: Pedagogy, Programs, Curricula, and Assessment
Marilynn Spaventa, Editor
Volume 2: Students, Mission, and Advocacy
Amy Blumenthal, Editor

PreK–12 English Language Proficiency Standards
Teachers of English to Speakers of Other Languages, Inc.

Planning and Teaching Creatively within a Required Curriculum for School-Age Learners
Penny McKay, Editor

Professional Development of International Teaching Assistants
Dorit Kaufman and Barbara Brownworth, Editors

Teaching English as a Foreign Language in Primary School
Mary Lou McCloskey, Janet Orr, and Marlene Dolitsky, Editors

Teaching English From a Global Perspective
Anne Burns, Editor

Technology-Enhanced Learning Environments
Elizabeth Hanson-Smith, Editor

For more information, contact
Teachers of English to Speakers of Other Languages, Inc.
700 South Washington Street, Suite 200
Alexandria, Virginia 22314 USA
Toll Free: 888-547-3369   Fax on Demand: 800-329-4469
Publications Order Line: 888-891-0041
or 301-638-4427 or 4428
9 am to 5 pm, EST

ORDER ONLINE at www.tesol.org/

T E S O L